THE COLLECTED CORRESPONDENCE AND PAPERS OF CHRISTOPH WILLIBALD GLUCK

CHRISTOPH WILLIBALD GLUCK 1714–1787
From a portrait by J. S. Duplessis, painted in Paris 1776
in Oesterreichische Nationalbibliothek, Portraitsammlung, Vienna

The Collected Correspondence
and Papers of

CHRISTOPH WILLIBALD GLUCK

Edited by

HEDWIG AND E. H.
MUELLER VON ASOW

Translated by Stewart Thomson

ST MARTIN'S PRESS INC.
NEW YORK

FIRST PUBLISHED IN THE U.S.A.
BY ST MARTIN'S PRESS, INC.
NEW YORK 10, NEW YORK

FIRST PUBLISHED IN GREAT BRITAIN BY
BARRIE & ROCKLIFF (BARRIE BOOKS LTD)

PRINTED IN GREAT BRITAIN BY
W. & J. MACKAY & CO LTD, CHATHAM

LIBRARY OF CONGRESS CATALOGUE NUMBER 62–522

TO OUR COLLEAGUE

H. C. ROBBINS LANDON

ILLUSTRATIONS

CONTENTS

FOREWORD

Habent sua fata libelli—TERTIANUS MAURUS

FEW books can have had such a strange history as this first complete edition of Gluck's letters. In 1913, at the suggestion of my great teacher, Professor Dr Hugo Riemann, I was invited by the Gluck Society in Leipzig to collect the *maestro*'s letters. A year later the First World War broke out and brought the work to a halt. After the war, the inflation in Germany forced the Gluck Society into liquidation.

In the mid-twenties Dr George Kinsky, Director of the Heyer Museum in Cologne, proposed that I should collaborate with him on an edition of the Gluck letters, as he had acquired from a large antiquarian bookshop in Vienna for 25,000 marks thirty-eight unpublished letters by Gluck addressed to the Head of Chancery of the Austrian Embassy in Paris, Franz Kruthoffer. He was anxious to annotate this new addition to his collection himself. Pressure of work prevented my wife and myself from completing the manuscript by the agreed time. It was therefore agreed that Dr Kinsky should bring out the letters of Kruthoffer separately, in view of the fact that in 1926 the collections in the Heyer Museum were put up for auction and all their rare autographs were scattered to the four winds. Finally, when the collection of Gluck letters was nearing completion, it was Dr Kinsky who very kindly agreed that his research should be incorporated in a complete edition. For this we shall always be deeply indebted to him. Eventually, in 1939, the manuscript was ready, but once more publication was delayed by the outbreak of war. With considerable difficulty the type was set, only to be destroyed by bombs, together with the manuscript.

It was not until 1948 that we were able to start work again, and from then until his death in 1952 Dr Kinsky gave us unstinted support. Then followed several years in which we knocked in vain at the doors of Austrian and German publishers. But, thanks to the friendly intervention of Mr H. C. Robbins Landon, to whom we owe a great debt of gratitude, the firm Barrie and Rockliff, London, decided to accept the manuscript. So after forty-eight years of preparation the first edition of Gluck's collected letters has at last appeared. In order to complete the picture, we have included

Gluck's famous forewords to his operas, documents and letters addressed to Gluck, and such few fragments as have survived of Marianne Gluck's letters, etc.

In this collection twenty letters and documents appear for the first time in print. It seems, therefore, unlikely that any further discoveries of important documents will be made, although there is always the possibility that letters may still come to light in private archives. On the other hand, letters addressed to Gluck, except for a few which happened to survive, went up in flames together with the remainder of the *maestro*'s papers.

We are particularly grateful for assistance which we received not only from Professor Dr Hugo Riemann and Director Dr Georg Kinsky, whom we have already mentioned, but also from all the archives, libraries and collections which placed their autographs at our disposal: Louis Koch Collection, Aarau; Karl Geigy-Hagenbach Collection, Basel; Internationales Musiker-Brief-Archiv, Berlin; Sächsische Landesbibliothek, Dresden; Instituto Musicale, Florence; Steiermärkisches Landesarchiv, Graz; Stadtbibliothek, Leipzig; Musée et Domaine de Mariemont, Belgium; Bayerische Staatsbibliothek, Munich; Bibliothèque Municipale, Nantes; Walter Hinrichsen Collection, New York; Bibliothèque du Conservatoire National, Paris; Bibliothèque Nationale, Paris; Sibley Musical Society, Eastman School of Music, Rochester, N.Y.; Bibliothèque François Lang, Royaumont; Memorial Library of Music, University of Stanford, California; Württembergisches Hauptstaatsarchiv, Stuttgart; Library of Congress, Washington; Thueringisches Staatsarchiv, Weimar; Geheimes Staatsarchiv, Vienna; Oesterreichische Nationalbibliothek, Vienna; Stadtbibliothek, Vienna.

The following had valuable suggestions to make, for which we are also grateful: Miss Emily Anderson, London; Miss Geraldine de Courcy, New York; Mrs Edna C. Davis, Los Angeles, California; Madame Yvonne Desportes, Paris; Madame Yvette Fedorov, Paris; Frau Marie Floersheim-Koch†, Muzzano/Lugano; Madame H. Gouin, Paris; Professor Dr Edith Heischkel-Artelt, Frankfurt-am-Main; Frau Archivdirektorin Dr Hedwig Kraus, Vienna; Madame Elisabeth Lebeau, Paris; Fräulein Marie Lipsius (La Mara)†, Leipzig; Mademoiselle Simone Wallon, Paris; Mrs Eduard H. Wannemacker, New York; Miss Ruth Watanabe, Rochester, N.Y.; Fräulein Liesbeth Weinhold, Munich; Professor Dr Hermann Abert†, Berlin; Professor René Anglade, Institut Français, Berlin; Sidney Beck, New York; Richard Bertling†, Dresden; President Dr

Theodor Ebeling, Berlin; Dr Rudolf Elvers, Berlin; Vladimir Fedorov, Paris; Rudolf Floersheim, Aarau; Richard Franko Goldman, New York; Dr Franz Glück, Museum Director, Vienna; Wirklicher Hofrat Professor Dr Joseph Gregor†, Vienna; Professor Dr Robert Haas†, Vienna; Staatsoberbibliothekar Dr Hans Halm, Munich; Richard S. Hill†, Washington; Heinrich Hinterberger, Vienna; Warren R. Howell, San Francisco, California; Professor Dr Victor Junk†, Vienna; Bibliotheksrat Professor Dr Willi Kahl, Cologne; Dr med. Dieter Kerner, Mainz; Direktor Dr Karl-Heinz Koehler, Berlin; Archivdirektor Dr Max Kratochwill, Vienna; Professor Dr Robert Lach†, Vienna; Professor Dr Andreas Liess, Vienna; Günter Mecklenburg (Fa. J. A. Stargardt), Marburg; Helmut Meyer, Berlin; Louis-Marie Michon†, Paris; Professor Dr Paul Mies, Cologne; Staatsarchivrat Dr Rolf Naumann, Stuttgart; Professor Dr Leopold Nowak, Vienna; Professor Dr Vincenz Oberhammer, Vienna; Professor Dr Nathan van Patten, Stanford, California; Dr Fritz Racek, Vienna; Professor Dr Erich Schenk, Vienna; Professor Dr Roland Tenschert, Vienna; Dr Othmar Wessely, University Lecturer, Vienna; Director Vernon Westmoreland, New York; Dr Jakob Winterler, Glarus.

Finally, we would like to thank Frau Gertrud Mertins, Secretary of the Internationales Musiker-Brief-Archiv, Mr Stewart Thomson, whose difficult task it has been to translate the letters and documents faithfully from German, French and Italian, and not least Messrs Barrie and Rockliff, who have spared no effort to make this book as attractive as possible and to meet all the editors' wishes.

Berlin, 1961

Hedwig M. von Asow
E. H. M. von Asow

THE LIFE OF GLUCK

THE LIFE OF GLUCK

Christoph Willibald Gluck came of a family whose origins are unknown. His great-grandfather, Simon Gluck, lived in Rockenzahn and died before 1672, when his son, Hans Adam Gluck (born 1649), who was a forester with Count Hartung at Dietersdorf near Windisch-Eschenbach, married Anna Maria Köttnath (born 1651), daughter of a smith, Philipp Köttnath, of Erbendorf (Upper Palatinate). Shortly afterwards he entered the service of Prince Lobkowitz at Neustadt on the Waldnab. There, on 28th October 1683, the fifth child was born: Alexander Gluck, father of the composer. He is reported to have taken part in the War of the Spanish Succession (1702–1703) as gun-bearer to Prince Eugene of Savoy. Later he entered the service of the Chief Huntsman of the Palatinate, Count Johann George von der Hauben, and around 1711–1712 he became Keeper at Erasbach, near Berching. There he married Maria Walpurga, whose family name is not known. She bore him nine children, the eldest of whom, Christoph Willibald Gluck, was born on 2nd July 1714.

The house in which he was born had been built by his father a year before at the entrance to the village of Erasbach, which consisted of only sixty houses, and where the house is still standing. Gluck's parents remained only three years at Erasbach after the birth of their eldest son, who was soon followed by a second, Christoph Anton (baptised 11th April 1716), then they moved to Reichsstadt. In 1717 Gluck's father, who during his period at Erasbach had become forester to the monasteries Seligenpforten and Plankstetten as well as of Weidenwang, entered the service of Duchess Anna Maria Francisca von Toscana as senior forester. The family spent five happy years at Reichsstadt, where more children were born and where the domestic atmosphere seems to have been a very happy one. The composer himself in his later years still had the most pleasant memories of his early youth, when he went out into the woods with his father, barefoot even in the depths of winter, and was allowed to carry his hunting and surveying gear. He received a simple yet solid upbringing; only on the subject of truthfulness was strict discipline maintained. He had his first lessons in reading, writing and arithmetic at a country school, while his natural talent for music was awakened at an early age by the love of music common amongst the country folk of

Bohemia. In the year 1722, when his grandfather was buried at Neustadt on 9th January, Gluck's father moved with his family to Kreibitz in the Kamnitz area of Bohemia to take up the position of Chief Forester to Count Philipp Joseph Kinsky. At Michaelmas 1727 he became Chief Forester to Prince Philipp Hyazinth von Lobkowitz at Eisenstadt near Komotau (Bohemia). In 1731 Christoph Willibald Gluck entered the University of Prague, where he read Logic and Mathematics, but, in his own words, also studied 'how studies were at that time conducted there'. Unfortunately no reliable information is available of his musical studies. He is said to have performed on the violin and the 'cello, as a singer, on the harpsichord and on the organ, and to have frequently toured the countryside and the outlying villages with other students. Whether he also made the acquaintance of Bohuslav Czernohorsky (1690–1740), the famous 'Pater Boemus' and teacher of Tartini, who is said to have arranged for him to play at the Teinkirche, where he himself played, we do not know for certain.

From Prague Gluck moved on to Vienna. He may have found a position as chamber musician with Prince Philipp Hyazinth Lobkowitz, in whose service his father was, but this is not certain. In Vienna he was greatly influenced by both the Opera and the Hofkapelle, the leader of which at that time was Johann Joseph Fux, the author of the world-famous textbook on counterpoint, *Gradus ad Parnassum*. But the residence of Prince Lobkowitz was also a centre of artistic activity which cannot have failed to stimulate him, the noble families of Vienna had already taken to patronizing the arts on a generous scale, and many a virtuoso and nobleman must have engaged young Gluck in conversations which stimulated the young man's thirst for knowledge and widened his horizon. It was in the Lobkowitz-Althans' house (Princess Wilhelmine Lobkowitz had married Count Gundaker von Althan following her husband's death in 1735) that Gluck met Prince Antonio Maria Melzi, who in 1736 engaged him as a member of his private orchestra in Milan. There Gluck found in Giovanni Battista Sammartini a teacher under whom he made so much progress in four years that at the age of twenty-seven he had a rousing success with his first opera, which was dedicated to Count Traun and was first performed on 26th December 1741 under the title *Artaserse*. Gluck had taken the text of his first opera from the works of Metastasio, which was not surprising, as the Abbate Pietro was regarded as the most important and most creative librettist of his time. The successful performance

NANETTE GLUCK

From a silhouette in Gesellschaft der Musikfreunde, Vienna

ANTONIO SALIERI
From an engraving by Carl Traugott Riedel, Leipzig, 1802

took place in the Regio Ducal Teatro. A far-sighted impresario from Venice, who either was present at the *première* or had heard of this young and talented composer, engaged him to compose a second opera, *Cleonice* (text from Metastasio's *Demetrio*), which was also dedicated to Count Traun and which was produced in the Teatro Grimano di San Samuele on Ascension Day, at the beginning of May the following year. That his first success in Milan came up to expectations is clear from the fact that his third work, *Demofoonte* (text from Metastasio), which again was dedicated to Count Traun, was also produced at the Court Theatre there on 26th December 1742.

During these early and successful years in Italy Gluck almost certainly lived for the most part in Milan, travelling to other cities only for purposes of composition, rehearsal and stage-production. This same period saw the first appearance of his opera, *Tigrane*, in September 1743 in the small country town of Crema not far from Milan. For this opera he had chosen a text by Franceso Silvani, which Carlo Goldoni had adapted. On 26th December of the same year, the arrival of a new Governor, Prince Johann Georg Christian von Lobkowitz, was celebrated with a performance of a pasticcio, *Arsace*, the second and third acts of which were written by Giovanni Battista Lampugnani, while the first act was a Silvani text set to music by Gluck. Then on 17th January 1744 *Sofonisba* was produced in Milan with text by Silvani, adapted by Metastasio; this work was dedicated to Prince Johann Georg Christian von Lobkowitz. The season over, Gluck travelled once more to Venice to write several arias for a production to be given in the Teatro San Angelo on 13th May 1744 of Giovanni Maccari's opera *La finta schiava*, with text by Silvani. This was followed on 21st November in the Teatro San Giovanni Crisostomo by Gluck's *Ipermestra* (text by Metastasio). Gluck's fame was spreading and on 26th December 1744 he accepted an invitation to Turin, where his *Poro* (text from Metastasio's *Alessandro nelle Indie*) had its first production. Barely five weeks after this *première* came a performance of *Ippolito* in Milan, which was also dedicated to Prince Johann Georg Christian von Lobkowitz (text by G. G. Corio), and this marked the end of Gluck's first successful stay in Italy, which he had begun as an unknown student of music and which he completed as a young *maestro*.

Gluck's reason for leaving Milan was presumably an invitation from the Director of the Italian Opera in London, Lord Middlesex. As Prince Ferdinand Phillip von Lobkowitz was also planning to travel from Milan to the English capital, he allowed Gluck, whom he had known since childhood, to accompany him. The first stage of the journey was to Frankfurt-am-Main, where the travellers made a brief halt to see the Coronation of the Emperor Franz I on 4th October 1745. Then they continued via Brussels, Antwerp, Rotterdam, Calais, Dover and Canterbury to London. When Gluck arrived, England was in the grip of the Jacobite rebellion and the theatres were closed. Finally, however, Lord Middlesex obtained permission to open a season, though on one condition: the first work must be appropriate to the political conditions, which meant that it must sing the praises of the Duke of Cumberland. The text was written by the resident poet of the Haymarket Theatre, Abbé F. Vanneschi. Under the title *La caduta dei giganti*, it was produced on 7th January 1746 (Julian Calendar) with music by Gluck. It was a pasticcio, in which most of the airs had been taken from other works by Gluck. The opera was highly successful and was performed five times with the composer conducting. Then the season continued with Galuppi's opera *Il trionfo della continenza*, also conducted by Gluck. The next innovation, on 4th March 1746 (Julian Calendar), was Gluck's pasticcio *Artamene* (text by F. Vanneschi), which was performed ten times, and was followed by Lampugnani's *Alessandro nelle Indie* and Galuppi's *Antigono*, with which the season closed. Gluck had an enthusiastic reception in London. This is clear not merely from Horace Walpole's observation that opera flourished that year more than in any other, but also from the fact that the publisher Walsh printed a number of airs from Gluck's two operas. It was in London, furthermore, that Gluck met Handel, who is alleged to have said: 'Gluck knows as much about counterpoint as my cook Waltz', a judgment that the temperamental and excitable Handel may have been guilty of in a fit of bad temper. Gluck thereupon called on Handel—so the story goes—and they became firm friends. It is certainly true that Gluck remained a great admirer of Handel for the rest of his long life. On one occasion in March 1746 the two great artists played together at a concert of the Society of Music in London. Gluck himself appeared on many occasions at public concerts in London and performed with particular brilliance on the verrillon or glass-harmonica, an instrument which he is said to have invented, consisting of twenty-six drinking-glasses tuned with spring water, and for which he wrote a special concerto with orchestra. During his London period he also composed eight trio sonatas, six of which were published by J. Simpson. Exactly how long Gluck remained in England we do not know. At Carnival time in 1746, Angelo Mingotti's opera troupe produced a pasticcio *La finta schiava* in Graz, which included amongst its composers not only Vinci and Lampugnani, but also Gluck. From Graz the opera company moved on to Prague, where there were performances in spring and summer; for a short period between times the troupe also appeared in Leipzig. From Prague they went on to Dresden, and thereafter we lose track of Mingotti, until he reappears again the following year, 1747, at the Easter Fair in Leipzig, this time with his brother, Pietro. On the 15th May a concert was held at which 'airs by a great *maestro* from Italy were sung and played to storms of applause'. This great *maestro* from Italy was doubtless Gluck. In the summer, on the occasion of the double wedding of Maria Anna of Saxony with the Prince Elector Maximilian Joseph of Bavaria and Princess Maria Antonia Walpurgis of Bavaria with Prince Friedrich Christian of Saxony on 29th June 1747, Gluck's opera *Le nozze d'Ercole e d'Ebe* was performed in the Schlosspark Theatre at Pillnitz. At Dresden Gluck left the opera company and went on to Vienna. On the way he visited the family property which his father had acquired in 1736 at Hammer, near Brux, and the graves of his mother (who died 8th October 1740) and father (who died 26th July 1743) in the cemetery at Obergeorgenthal. He took the opportunity to sell his parents' property.

In Vienna Gluck's opera *Semiramide riconosciuta* (text by Metastasio) had its *première* on 14th May, the Empress Maria Theresia's birthday, when the Burgtheater was opened.

Vienna had considerably changed since Gluck was last there. That lover of pomp and ceremony, the Emperor Karl VI, and his Master of Music, the all-powerful Fux, were both dead. Under its new leader, Georg von Reutter, the Court Orchestra had deteriorated. Nevertheless, Gluck's opera had an enthusiastic reception and was repeated several times. Even at that early stage Gluck seriously considered settling permanently in Vienna, but, as Maria Theresia's Court had substantially reduced expenditure on Italian opera, Gluck saw no chance of obtaining a position. He therefore rejoined the Pietro Mingotti troupe at Hamburg in September 1748. Whereas until now he had acted mainly as a stand-in for the conductor, Paolo Scalabrini, now that Scalabrini had taken up a post with the Danish Court, he conducted all the performances. The tour proceeded from Hamburg to Copenhagen, where Gluck arrived with several members of the company at the end of November. At that time he was infatuated by the beautiful Gaspera Beccheroni, who was not exactly the most popular member of the company and is said to have been the mistress of the British Minister, Wyche. As a result of his infatuation Gluck fell seriously ill immediately on arrival and in mid-December he had not yet fully recovered. Nevertheless, he was preparing a new work, *La Contesa dei Numi*, a serenade which was to have its first performance in honour of Queen Luise after the birth of Crown Prince Christian, which took place on 29th January 1749. But as the Queen's accouchement was later than expected and her confinement lasted longer than anticipated, Mingotti had to extend his season until after Lent in order to fit in the *première* and enable the Queen to attend all the other operas. Gluck employed these weeks of freedom in performing, as he had done in London, on the verrillon. When the Queen was fully recovered, Gluck conducted all the operas in the season, ending with his own opera, with text again by Metastasio, on 9th April 1749. We also know for certain that Gluck intended to give a concert 'di Cembalo' after Easter and that on 19th or 20th April in a room in the Charlottenburg Castle, in which the Mingotti opera troupe was housed, a further concert with the verrillon was given. From Copenhagen the company paid a brief visit to Christiania, but Gluck's next destination is not known. Presumably he travelled with the company to Holland, where he established contact with Mingotti's rival, Giovanni Battista Locatelli, and may even have travelled with him.

He appears to have gone to Prague with Locatelli, for it was there in the Carnival season of 1750 that his opera, *Ezio*, with a libretto once more by the industrious Metastasio, was first performed. In Prague, too, he must have heard the news of the death of Joseph Bergin, the wealthy Viennese banker who had opposed Gluck's engagement to his elder daughter, Marianne (born 24th July 1732), and Gluck's decision to rejoin the Mingotti company in Hamburg following a successful performance of his *Semiramide* may well have been influenced by that personal rebuff. Nothing now stood in the way of his happiness. He hurried back to Vienna and on 15th September 1750 married Marianne in the Ulrichskirche. She remained utterly devoted to him to the end of his life and took a close personal interest in all his artistic plans and achievements.

The newly-weds are alleged to have moved in with his mother-in-law. This is still a matter for speculation, for in the autumn of 1750 Gluck's *Ipermestra* was again performed in Prague by Locatelli's company and his *Ezio* in Leipzig in 1751. A further indication that

Gluck had rejoined Locatelli is the fact that his *Issipile* (text by Metastasio) had its *première* at Prague in the 1752 Carnival. It was also while he was in Prague that he was invited to Naples by the Director of the Teatro San Carlo, Don Diego Tufarelli, to compose an opera. Gluck accepted the invitation and travelled to Italy with his wife. In Naples he composed Metastasio's *La clemenze di Tito*, which had a highly successful *première* on 4th November 1752. As a result of this success, when Gluck returned to Vienna, he was engaged by Prince Joseph Friedrich von Sachsen-Hildburghausen as conductor of his not inconsiderable orchestra. The Prince organized regular concerts every Friday throughout the winter and invited famous artists, who were passing through Vienna, to play at his palace. In summer he gave operatic performances in his private theatre in Schlosshof. Whether Gluck wrote works for these concerts has not been definitely established, but we do know that a number of Gluck's comic operas were written for the theatrical performances at Schlosshof. The first opera of this kind that is still extant was produced on the occasion of a brilliant festival which the Prince arranged to welcome the Emperor Franz I and Empress Maria Theresia on a visit to Schlosshof. On 24th September 1754 Metastasio's *Le Cinesi* was performed, set to Gluck's music. This performance was undoubtedly attended by Count Durazzo, who at that time took over the direction of the Hoftheater in Vienna. It was probably at his instigation that the work was performed on 17th April 1755 as prelude to a Chinese ballet in the theatre next to the Burg and that Gluck was engaged at a yearly salary of 2,000 gulden to compose 'theatrical and chamber music' for the Court. The first work Gluck produced in his new capacity was the pastoral *La danza* (text by Metastasio), which was performed at the opening of a Court ball on 5th May 1755 in the Castle of Laxenburg near Vienna. There was a repeat performance of this small work in the Burgtheater in Vienna on Maria Theresia's birthday. In the same year and in the same theatre a joint work by Durazzo and Gluck was performed on 8th December entitled *L'innocenza giustificata*, for which airs were taken from various works of Metastasio. This performance was barely over, when Gluck had to hurry off to Rome to supervise the first production of his *Antigono*, which took place on 9th February 1756 in the Teatro di Torre Argentina. This had such an enthusiastic reception that Cardinal Legate A. Albani, an admirer of Gluck, decorated the composer with the Cross of the Golden Spur. The artist was now the proud bearer of the title 'Cavaliere'. Shortly after these performances he returned to Vienna to complete his opera *Il re pastore* (text by Metastasio) for the birthday of the Emperor Franz I.

During the next few years, which Gluck spent almost exclusively in Vienna, he composed a whole series of short and long comic operas: in 1758 *La fausse esclave* (3rd October) and *L'ile de Merlin*; in 1759 *Cythère assiégée*, *Le diable à quatre* (28th May) and *L'arbre enchanté* (3rd October); in 1760 the amusing *L'ivrogne corrigé* and in 1761 *Le cadi dupé*. During this period Gluck returned once again to Italian opera and, on the occasion of the betrothal of the Archduke Joseph with Isabella of Bourbon, he set to music Gianambrogio Migliavacca's Wedding Serenade *Tetide*, which, together with Hasse's *Alcide al bivio*, was warmly applauded on 8th October 1760 in the great ballroom of the imperial castle.

But reformist ideas were already gaining ground in the circle in which Count Durazzo and Gluck moved. Amongst the leading spirits were the ballet master Gasparo Angiolini and the poet Ranieri di Calzabigi. The first fruit of this reform was the ballet *Don Juan*, which on 17th October 1761 for the first time presented that gay rococo world with a tragic ballet. In his libretto Angiolini, with great daring, reproduced a whole complex drama in pantomime. The public, though hostile, went to see this new work of art out of curiosity and because it was fashionable, with the result that it remained on the programme for several years. But before the audiences had fully appreciated what was essentially new in this creation, Gluck had produced a new work which was to become a milestone in the history of opera and to remain one of the standard productions up to the present day. This new work, *Orfeo ed Euridice*, first performed on 5th October 1762, made a profound and powerful impression. Ranieri di Calzabigi had supplied the text. The greatness of the work was immediately apparent to all who heard it; at one stroke Calzabigi and Gluck together had effected a reform in opera, for which the finest talents of the day had striven in vain.

Gluck's next work was commissioned for the opening of the theatre in Bologna: he had to set Metastasio's *Trionfo di Clelia* to music by 14th May 1763. Gluck adopted the Italian style, but tried at the same time to give further expression to his reformist ideas. On his return he had an opportunity of presenting one of his earlier works, *Ezio*, to the Viennese public. Gluck revealed his lighter side once more in the comic opera *La rencontre imprévue* (7th January 1764), which the Viennese received with more sincere enthusiasm than they had shown the serious reformers. In 1764 the *maestro* attended the election and coronation of the Emperor in Frankfurt-am-Main (27th March and 3rd April). Then he travelled on, accompanied by Count Durazzo and Marco Coltellini, to Paris, where he made a number of valuable contacts. In the same year Durazzo had to retire from his post as Director of the Vienna Theatre, as he had apparently shown too marked a preference for Gluck as against Reutter. Gluck, on the other hand, did not abandon his Court functions, but became increasingly active as composer for the imperial family's celebrations. He was commissioned to prepare a special production for the second wedding of Joseph II and Maria Josepha of Bavaria. On this occasion the sixty-seven-year-old Metastasio wrote an original libretto for Gluck, who until now had merely reset to music texts which Metastasio had written for other composers, a practice which was quite current at that time. The result was a performance in the great Schlachtensaal of Schönbrunn Castle of the opera *Il Parnasso confuso*, which shows distinct traces of the new spirit inspired by Rousseau's call to 'return to Nature'. Four Archduchesses, Maria Elisabeth, Maria Amalia, later Duchess of Parma, Maria Josepha, who later became the wife of the King of Sicily, and Maria Carolina, later Queen of Naples, performed in this short work on 24th January 1765 before an audience that consisted only of the innermost circle of the Court. Then followed a performance on 30th January 1765 in the Burgtheater in Vienna of *Telemacco*, which, contrary to all existing rules, had only two acts. Sigismondo Capece had written the text, which was originally in three acts but was condensed into two by Marco Coltellini.

The evening after the performance of *Telemacco* in Vienna, Gluck was able to produce a new *première*: Angiolini's ballet *Semiramide*, which was presented in the Castle Theatre at Schönbrunn. The Court also commissioned Gluck to set Metastasio's *La corona* (*Der Kranz*) to music, a work which, owing to the death of Franz I, was not performed until 1737. From now on Gluck worked at a reduced tempo; his compositions were more considered, and the reflective side of his character came more and more to the forefront. A year and a half had passed since the completion of *La corona* before Gluck produced a new work. To celebrate the reappearance in public of the Grand Duchess Maria Louise of Toscana after a happy delivery, Gluck's *Prologo* was presented at the Teatro della Pergola in Florence on 22nd February 1767. Lorenzo Ottavio del Rosso wrote the libretto, which was for only one solo singer (Jupiter) and choral music. In the meantime Gluck had already conceived his second great reformist work, *Alceste*, the text of which was again by Calzabigi. The *première* was in the Burgtheater on 16th December 1767 and there were forty-nine repeat performances. Gluck's reformist ideas were now fully matured and he elaborated them in writing in the Foreword to this work addressed to the Grand Duke Leopold of Toscana (cf page 22).

In the summer of 1768 Gluck wrote a new version of his *L'innocenza giustificata*, which he had composed in 1755, and it was performed in the Burgtheater under the title *La Vestale*. From the text we learn that Gluck had become a member of the 'Accademia degli Arcadi' in Rome.

For the time being Gluck, true to his Court obligations, did not give full play to his new ideas but wrote *Le feste d'Apollo* (text by Frugoni) for the betrothal of the Archduchess Maria Amalia with Don Ferdinand of Bourbon in 1769 in Parma. The Orpheus act of this piece, which consisted of three short dramas, shows traces of Gluck the reformer. As was his custom, he himself conducted the *première* on 24th August.

Gluck's reformist works had still not gained the recognition which the *maestro* wished. The critics in North Germany were openly hostile and Frederick the Great, after hearing a few airs sung by his Italians, passed the premature judgment that Gluck 'has no songs and knows nothing of grand opera as a form of art'! There was, therefore, no prospect of holding performances in Germany; Italy had quite different ideals from those of Gluck, as a result of which there was little appreciation for the *première* of his *Paride e Elena* (text by Calzabigi) in Vienna on 3rd November 1770 or for his ballets *Il convito d'Alessandro* (Laxenburg, 21st May 1765) and *L'orfano della China* (Vienna, 1st April 1774), which were originally conceived by Angiolini. Gluck's interest became involuntarily focused on France, where artists like Corneille and Racine, Lully and Rameau had flourished, artists whose talents, like his own, naturally inclined to the drama.

Material circumstances finally led Gluck to decide to travel to Paris. Gluck had found in the Attaché to the French Embassy in Vienna, the Marquis Gaud le Blanc Bailli du Roullet, a friend who understood Gluck's reformist ideas and had the necessary connexions to prepare the way for him in Paris. And Gluck also found a well-wisher and benefactor in his former pupil, Marie Antoinette. In 1773 he was invited to Paris for a production of his *Iphigénie en Aulide*, the text of which Bailli du Roullet, basing himself on Racine, had translated with fidelity and understanding. In mid-November 1773 the German *maestro* arrived in the French capital with his wife and his niece. But it was not until 19th April 1774 that the work was presented. It had a mixed reception. Only with the second performance did Gluck carry the day. Despite the fact that the old Bouffonist party (which had been in existence since 1752, when the first Italian operas arrived) and the supporters of Lully and Rameau were not won over, Queen Marie Antoinette and all others without bias—amongst them Jean Jacques Rousseau—openly expressed their appreciation of this work of genius. From two learned members of the Academy, the Abbé Francois Arnaud and Jean Baptiste Suard, Gluck received whole-hearted support in the Press. But one work alone was not sufficient to gain him lasting success. Gluck realized this and therefore produced a new version of his *Orfeo* for grand opera. On 2nd August 1774, under the title *Orphée et Eurydice*, it scored a resounding success. Both *Iphigénie* and *Orfeo* remained on the repertoire of the Paris Opéra and earned their creator the substantial income of 40,000 livres. Furthermore, after the third opera had been performed, he was given a pension for life of 600 livres and he received the same amount from Marie Antoinette. At the same time a plan was being discussed which would enable Gluck to remain permanently in Paris. He submitted certain proposals to Count Florimond de Mercy-Argenteau but they were not accepted, so Gluck returned to Vienna in autumn 1774 by way of Zweibrucken, Mannheim and Schwetzingen with his wife and his niece, whom he had now adopted.

In Vienna on 18th October 1774 he was appointed 'Hofkompositeur' (Court Composer) by Maria Theresia with a yearly income of 2,000 gulden, a distinction which he undoubtedly owed to the success of *Iphigénie* and *Orfeo*, about which the Empress had received enthusiastic letters from her daughter, Marie Antoinette.

Gluck remained only a short time in Vienna, for by early December 1774 he was back in Paris, where he stayed until 10th(?) March 1775. There was a new production of *Iphigénie en Aulide* on 13th January in the presence of the Court, which had just emerged from a period of mourning, and Gluck received tremendous ovations. On 27th February 1775, on the occasion of a Court Festival at Versailles to welcome the Archduke Maximilian of Austria, Gluck presented a new version of *L'Arbre enchanté*, dedicated to Louis XVI. He then became involved in an unpleasant dispute with the publisher Le Marchand and in a complete revision of the one-act *Cythère assiégée* to a three-act opera-ballet. The *première*, which did not take place until 1st August 1775 and for which the Director of Opera Pierre Montan Berton had composed a closing ballet, was a failure; the operatic innovations, which Paris had been led to expect, did not materialize. On his way from Paris to Vienna and back Gluck had spent a short time at the Court of Duke Karl Friedrich of Württemberg in Karlsruhe and Rastatt, in order to meet Klopstock, whom he greatly admired. The poet and the composer became firm friends.

In Vienna Gluck adapted his *Alceste* for Paris and began work on the broad outlines of *Armide* and *Roland*. His health was already seriously undermined and from August until October he was confined to bed. In mid-February 1776, when he was well enough to travel to Paris, he had to leave his wife behind in Vienna with his niece, who was suffering from smallpox. The *première* of the French *Alceste* on 23rd April 1776 was not a success. A few days later he received the sad news of the death of his niece. Nevertheless, he made some improvements to *Alceste*, brought in the character of Hercules and, on Rousseau's advice, introduced a ballet in the second act, with the result that the work gradually won recognition. In the middle of May 1776 Gluck returned to Vienna. He now devoted all his energy to the final composition of *Roland* and *Armide*, the texts of which, by Phillippe Quinault, the Vienna Opera had commissioned him to set to music. *Roland* was never completed. Gluck burnt his first trial scores when he learned that Nicolo Piccinni had also been entrusted with the composition. Of all Gluck's adversaries, Piccinni was also destined to be a serious rival when he was summoned to Paris. Gluck complained bitterly of the injustice done to him over *Roland* and was not slow to attack his critics. He wrote a letter which was published in the Press and which led to a conflict of artistic views more acrimonious than at any time before. From then on Gluckists and Piccinnists were at daggers drawn. Courtiers, musicians, critics and the general public all took sides. Gluck's supporters were led by Arnaud and Suard, while Marmontel, La Harpe and Ginguené were the main spokesmen for the opposite camp. Gluck had arrived in Paris with his wife on 29th May 1777 and on 23rd September 1777 he presented *Armide*. Once more Gluck's success was neither immediate nor complete. It took some time for the opera to win recognition. In the meantime Piccinni had not been idle. In January 1778 his *Roland* was successfully produced, but he was not happy in the role imposed upon him of rival to Gluck, nor was he entirely convinced by the success of his work, which he had been compelled to write in a language he knew only slightly. Relations between him and Gluck were friendly and Gluck is even alleged to have helped him with his rehearsals. After the successful performance of *Roland* (27th January 1778), Gluck returned in February 1778 to Vienna, where he withdrew from public life to produce his most mature and most complete work, *Iphigénie en Tauride*, for which a rough text was written by Nicolas Francois Guillard, based on Guimond de La Touche's version of Euripides's tragedy. In the beginning of November 1778 Gluck set off for Paris with his completed score and on 18th May 1779, when the curtain in the Paris Opera House fell for the last time at the end of the *première* of *Iphigénie en Tauride*, Gluck's success was assured. Even Baron Melchior Grimm, the most outspoken of the Piccinnists, was obliged to pay tribute to this work. Gluck, the reformer, had fulfilled his mission. Following a production of *Echo et Narcisse* (text by Ludwig Theodor von Tschudi) on 21st September 1779, which had a very lukewarm reception, Gluck returned on 7th October 1779 to Vienna for the last time, where his *Iphigénie en Tauride*, with a German translation by himself and Johann Baptist von Alxinger, to which the music had been adapted, was given an enthusiastic reception on 23rd October 1781.

Gluck, who had amassed a considerable fortune, spent the closing years of his life in contemplation. One major work, which had been close to his heart for many years, he still hoped to produce: Klopstock's *Hermannsschlacht*. In conception it was already complete and he frequently played it to friends and visitors, but he lacked the strength to commit it to paper. He himself was conscious of his weakness and declined a commission by the Paris Opéra to set *Les Danaïdes* to music, but he passed it on to his pupil Salieri. The first performance was on 26th April 1784 under Salieri's name and his own. In 1785 Gluck published the last of his works, a collection of odes by Klopstock, which he had completed some time before. Finally, a short time before his death, Gluck entrusted his pupil Salieri with a *De profundis*, which was subsequently played at his funeral. Apart from a composition of the 8th Psalm, *Domine, Dominus Noster*, a *Miserere*, the Motets 'Almae sedes laeta pacis' and 'Voces cantate', this is the only religious work by Gluck which is known. On 15th November 1787 the *maestro*, who had already suffered several apoplectic attacks, died in his house on the Wiedener Hauptstrasse. On 17th November his mortal remains were buried in the Matzleinsdorf Cemetery. On 29th September 1890 his bones were reinterred in the Zentralfriedhof in Vienna.

With Gluck's death one of the outstanding creative personalities in the history of music had passed away. His greatness and nobility had dominated the whole world of music in his lifetime; in the realm of operatic theory he had made a major contribution and his *Orfeo* had exercised a revolutionary influence on contemporary musicians; if his last operas did not arouse that degree of spontaneous enthusiasm that encourages imitation, it was because they represented the final stage of a process of development in operatic history which did much to make German music known throughout the world.

THE CORRESPONDENCE AND PAPERS

THE CORRESPONDENCE AND PAPERS

[TO FRANZ JOSEPH KARL PIRKER.[1] *German*]

January 1749

My dearest Pircker,

You will receive 20 ducats from Monsieur Waich[2] in accordance with Mademoiselle Becheroni's letter, and I beg you to buy the watch with it, but let the order be carried out by Srinsbeck with the name of the King on the watch-case, and please to remember that it must be in diamonds. Deal with this wisely so that of the 20 ducats enough remains for a . . . fine chain and perhaps a golden seal. You must not tell Monsieur Waich [Wyche], however, for what the money has been used but that it was given by his wife to Mad. Beccheroni.[3] Adieu, dearest Pircker, and forgive me for thus troubling you.

From the correspondence it is clear that this letter must have been written between the 8th and 14th January 1749. That it is one of Gluck's letters is confirmed by the handwriting and by a letter from Marianne Pirker of 15th January 1749, in which she wrote: '. . . I hope you have received my last letter with the little note from Mme Becharoni and Gluck. . . .'

It is worth mentioning in this context that Gluck had already written to Pirker. One of these letters, which has not so far been found, was sent from Hamburg at the end of August 1748, for Pirker reported to his wife on 10th September 1748: '. . . The unexpected handwriting of Mr Gluck gave me uncommon joy and pleasure, and I can only wish that my presence may be agreeable to him as his is to me, then we might look forward to many happy hours. Give him my most respectful compliments with the assurance that I shall devote as much care to the originals [of the trio sonatas?] as if they were my own. . . .'

[1] FRANZ JOSEPH KARL PIRKER, violinist, had at one time toured with the Mingotti opera troupe. He was married to the singer Marianne Pirker but was at that time in England. [cf. R. Krauss: 'Marianne Pirker', *Die Musik, vol.* 8]

[2] JOHN WYCHE was English Minister in Hamburg till he was recalled to London in 1748 [cf. Mueller von Asow: *Angelo and Pietro Mingotti*, p. 88; Boyer: *Annals of Queen Anne*, 1710, vol. 8, p. 386, who, unlike M. von Asow, gives the correct spelling of the name].

[3] GASPERA BECCHERONI was Wyche's mistress till she joined Pietro Mingotti's opera troupe as a buffa singer in September 1748. She travelled with Mingotti to Copenhagen and also seems to have had relations with

Gluck, for Marianne Pirker wrote to her husband about her on 3rd December 1748: 'There is a revolt here against the Buffa, for the [Grazia] Melini [1720–1781] has been received at Court, the wife of Maestro [Paolo] Scalabrini [1713–1806], and the Court wishes that she should always appear when they [i.e. Their Royal Highnesses] come to the Opera, which indeed occurs tomorrow for the first time. It serves the sow right, why has she so ruined poor Cluch [*sic*]. If Wais [Wyche] knew this, he would . . . [illegible] the hundred marks he gives her every month. It were better he should know, but most definitely not from us. So take good care, although I would dearly like to avenge Klug [*sic*].'

[Marriage Contract. *German*]

In the name of the Holiest Trinity—God the Father, the Son and the Holy Ghost. Amen.

This day, on the date stated hereafter, the following marriage contract was drawn up, ratified by a magistrate, and irrevocably concluded between the nobly-born Herr Christoph Gluckh as bridegroom on the one hand and the noble spinster Maria Anna Bergin [1] as bride on the other; in the presence of the spinster bride's mother, of the legally appointed guardian Joseph Salliet[2] and of the witnesses summoned hereto: namely:

Firstly, and after the aforementioned Herr Christoph Gluckh had duly requested the hand of the aforesaid spinster Bergin and with the approval of her mother and her guardian had received her consent to become his consort in marriage, and after this betrothal had been confirmed by both persons orally and by a clasping of hands as also by an exchange of rings and a priestly benediction, the following worldy provisions were then made:

Secondly, the said spinster promised to endow the bridegroom from her own means with a true and lawful dowry of five hundred Rhenish gulden after the wedding day against quittance, to which the aforementioned bridegroom makes a counter-settlement of one thousand Rhenish gulden, so that the marriage portion and counter-settlement together shall be one thousand five hundred gulden.

Thirdly, the aforesaid bridegroom, as a token of his special affection for his beloved bride, has promised to pay fifty gold ducats as a gift on the morning after the wedding[3], furthermore,

Fourthly, both parties are agreed that the remainder of the bride's property of four thousand gulden, say 4000 fl., is to be safely invested *ad fructificandum* and the yearly interests accruing—apart from a hundred gulden which have been expressly reserved for the free and personal use and disposal of the bride—shall be employed for their joint economy; whereas

Fifthly, whatever is earned, acquired or inherited by the grace of God during the marriage shall be common property.

Sixthly, the bride's mother, as a token of her especial maternal love, binds herself to provide the same with an appropriate and agreeable establishment and wardrobe, concerning which,

Seventhly, all goods and chattels acquired and collected during the marriage shall pass to the surviving partner, but,

Eighthly, should the marriage not be blessed with children, then, in the event of one partner dying, the half of his or her property shall pass to the surviving

J. F. REICHARDT
Engraving by Riedel from the painting by Anton Graff

JEAN FRANÇOIS LAHARPE

ROSALIE LEVASSEUR

Engraving by N. Pruneau from a bust by Philippe Dumont

partner, the other half to be freely disposed of by either party. On the other hand,

Ninthly, should one or other of the aforesaid persons depart this world leaving one or more children, the half-share will not be inherited as in the preceding paragraph but the surviving party shall inherit the whole and entire property *usus fructus* until the children are of age and only after reaching their majority shall they receive their separate portions;

Tenthly and finally each is free to make other bequests by testament, codicil or donation.

All of which is in good faith and without deceit, and as a true testimony two identical copies of this marriage contract have been drawn up, signed and sealed by both marriage-partners and by the witnesses, but without prejudice or detriment to the latter. Made in Vienna the 3rd September 1750.

[S] Maria Anna Bergin
as bride
[S] Theres Bergin widow
as bride's mother.
[S] Franz Xav. v. Concin JUDr.[4]
as witness
[S] Joseph Salliet as
lawfully appointed tutor

[S] Christopf [sic] Gluck
as bridegroom
[S] Giov. Pietro Sorosina[5]
come testimonio
dalla parte del signore sposo.

[1] MARIA ANNA BERGIN (born 24th July 1732 in Vienna, died 12th March 1800, also in Vienna) was the daughter of a bourgeois merchant, Joseph Bergin, who died at the end of January 1738 at the age of fifty-two and was buried 1st February 1738 in St Peter's in Vienna. Her mother, Maria Theresia, née Chini, died in 1756.

[2] JOSEPH NICLAS SALLIET, a bourgeois merchant and guardian of Maria Anna Bergin, died on 19th June 1757 at Oberlaa (province of Rothneusiedel).

[3] The religious ceremony took place on 15th September 1750 in the St Ulrich Church.

[4] FRANZ XAVER VON CONCIN was a Court Advocate who died in February 1771 in Vienna at the age of sixty-two.

[5] JOHANN PETER EDLER VON SOROSINA was Court Agent in the Italian Department and died in July 1789 in Vienna at the age of ninety-two.

[CHARLES SIMON FAVART[1] TO GLUCK. *French*]

Paris, June 1763

. . . Monseigneur the Count of Durazzo[2] informs me that you are due in Paris in the course of this month. No lover of the arts can fail to know your reputation. I have not the honour to know you personally but I have always wished to have this advantage. May I flatter myself that you will respond to my plea? Yes, I venture to hope, because of the high regard in which I have always held your talents; for this reason I count upon your taking no other lodging than with me. In my house I have a furnished appartment to offer you; there you will find a good clavichord as well as other instruments, a small garden, and complete freedom; in other words you will feel at home and will only see whomsoever you think fit. Though situated in one of the busiest quarters of Paris, our house, between courtyard and garden, provides the kind of solitude in which one can work as quietly as in the country. If I am fortunate enough, monsieur, that you accept my offer, I beg you to inform me in advance of the day of your arrival. My address is Rue Monconseil, near the Comédie Italienne, opposite the main gate of the Saint-Jacques-de-l'Hopital cloister. . . .

[1] CHARLES SIMON FAVART, who was born in Paris on 13th November 1710, was one of the founders of French operetta. He composed some 150 works for the stage with, it seems, the help of his wife, Maria Justine Duronceray (born Avignon, 15th June 1727, died Paris, 22nd April 1772), who played the leading part in her husband's productions and was acclaimed for her beauty and grace. Together with Count Durazzo, he arranged for the publication of Gluck's *Orfeo*, which took place in 1764. As he knew that Gluck was engaged in adapting French operettas for the Vienna Court, he was anxious to make Gluck's acquaintance. No answer from Gluck to Favart's letter has been traced.

[2] GIACOMO COUNT DURAZZO (born 27th April 1717 in Genoa, died 15th October 1794), was Director of Court and Chamber Music from 1754 to 1764. As he appears to have shown too great a preference for Gluck over Georg Reutter, he was relieved of his post and sent to Naples as Ambassador [cf. R. Haas: *Gluck und Durazzo im Burgtheater*. Vienna, 1925].

[TO GRAND DUKE LEOPOLD OF TOSCANA.[1] *Italian*]

[before 16th December 1767]

Royal Highness!

When I began to write the music for *Alceste*, I resolved to free it from all the abuses which have crept in either through ill-advised vanity on the part of singers or through excessive complaisance on the part of composers, with the result that for some time Italian opera has been disfigured and from being the most splendid and most beautiful of all stage performances has been made the most ridiculous and the most wearisome. I sought to restrict the music to its true purpose of serving to give expression to the poetry and to strengthen the dramatic situations, without interrupting the action or hampering it with unnecessary and superfluous ornamentations. I believed that it should achieve the same effect as lively colours and a well-balanced contrast of light and shade on a very correct and well-disposed painting, so animating the figures without altering their contours. So I have tried to avoid interrupting an actor in the warmth of dialogue with a boring intermezzo or stopping him in the midst of his discourse, merely so that the flexibility of his voice might show to advantage in a long passage, or that the orchestra might give him time to collect his breath for a cadenza. I did not think I should hurry quickly through the second part of an air, which is perhaps the most passionate and most important, in order to have room to repeat the words of the first part regularly four times or to end the aria quite regardless of its meaning, in order to give the singer an opportunity of showing how he can render a passage with so-and-so many variations at will; in short, I have sought to eliminate all these abuses, against which sound common sense and reason have so long protested in vain.

I imagined that the overture should prepare the spectators for the action, which is to be presented, and give an indication of its subject; that the instrumental music should vary according to the interest and passion aroused, and that between the aria and the recitative there should not be too great a disparity, lest the flow of the period be spoiled and rendered meaningless, the movement be interrupted inopportunely, or the warmth of the action be dissipated. I believed further that I should devote my greatest effort to seeking to achieve a noble simplicity; and I have avoided parading difficulties at the expense of clarity. I have not placed any value on novelty, if it did not emerge naturally from the situation and the expression; and there is no rule I would not have felt in duty bound to break in order to achieve the desired effect.

These are my principles. Happily all my intentions fitted admirably with the libretto, in which the famous author [Calzabigi],[2] having devised a new plan for the lyrical drama, had replaced florid descriptions, superfluous comparisons, sententious and frigid moralisation with the language of the heart, with strong passion, interesting situations and an ever-varied spectacle. My maxims have been vindicated by success, and the universal approval expressed in such an enlightened city [Vienna] has convinced me that simplicity, truth and lack of affectation are the sole principles of beauty in all artistic creations. None the less, in spite of repeated demands by the most respectable persons that I should decide to publish this opera of mine in print, I have realized how much danger lies in fighting against such widespread and deep-rooted prejudices, and I have found it necessary to avail myself in advance of the powerful protection of Your Royal Highness by imploring the favour of prefixing my opera with His August Name, which so justly carries with it the approval of all enlightened Europe. The great protector of the fine arts, who rules over a nation which is famed for having freed them from universal oppression and for having set in each of them the finest examples, in a city which has always been the first to break the yoke of vulgar prejudice and pave the way to perfection, can alone undertake the reform of this noble spectacle, in which all the fine arts play such a large part. When this has been accomplished, I shall have the glory of having moved the first stone, and this public testimony of Your Highness's protection, for which I have the honour to declare myself with the most humble respect

Your Royal Highness's
Most humble, most devoted,
most dutiful servant
Christoph Gluck.

[1] Grand Duke Leopold of Toscana, who later became Emperor Leopold II (born 5th May 1747, died 1st March 1792), was a particularly gifted patron of music, whom Cherubini, amongst others, had to thank for his training [cf. E. Bellasis: *Cherubini*. 1874, p. 11; E. Hohenemser: *L. Cherubini*. 1913, p. 13]. He was the last of the House of Habsburg to wield any musical influence.

[2] The famous author was Ranieri Simone Francesco Maria Calzabigi. He was born at Leghorn on 23rd December 1714. In 1740 he was already a member of the learned Accademia strusea di Cortona and in the same year published his first poem, which is still extant. From 1743 onwards he lived in Naples, where he was employed in a Ministry. In 1745 he made his first venture into drama with *L'impero del Universo diviso con Giove*, which was set to music by Gennaro Manna. He travelled to Paris around 1750, following a trial for murder by poisoning, and there he produced Metastasio's works in 9 volumes with the publishing house of Veuve Quillau. With his younger brother Giovanni Antonio and Casanova, he started a lottery in 1757. About 1761 he was a Privy Councillor with the Netherlands Chamber of Accounts in Vienna. There he won favour with Count Kaunitz, to whom he dedicated the first edition of his works in 1774. Through Kaunitz he made the acquaintance of Gluck. Apart from the works he wrote for Gluck, there were also the comic operas *La critica teatrale*, which with Gennaro Astaritta's music was produced at the Venice Carnival of 1775, and *La finta Giardiniera*, which was produced in Naples in 1767 with music by Piccinni and in Munich in 1775 with music by Mozart (and in a special adaptation by Marco Coltellini). Relations with an actress took him to Leghorn; then he moved to Pisa and from 1780 onwards he was in Naples. There he wrote the librettos of Giovanni Paesiello's *Elfrida* and *Elvira*, which were not a success. He died in Naples in July 1795. Of considerable interest are his *Dissertazione su le poesie drammatiche del Sig. Abate Pietro Metastasio* (1755) and his *Risposta* (1790), in which he defended himself and took issue with Metastasio following an attack by Stefano Arteaga in the *Rivoluzioni* (1785) [cf. G. Lazzeri: *La vita e l'opera letteraria di Ranieri Calzabigi*. 1907; *Gluck-Jahrbuch*, 2, 3 (Einstein),

4 (Michel); J.-G. Prod'homme: 'Deux Collaborateurs italiens de Gluck'. *Rivista musicale italiana*, XXIII. 1916].

[TO WENZEL ANTON PRINCE KAUNITZ-RIETBERG.[1] *German*]

pr. 3rd January 1770

Most Serene Prince!
Most Gracious Lord!

The high protection and especial favour which your Serene Highness has heaped upon me at all times encourage me to have recourse to Your Highness, in order to be able to escape the unhappy misfortune before me.

At the suggestion of His Supreme Majesty the Emperor,[2] I joined the Society of the Teatral Imprese with Lieutenant-Colonel Afflisio,[3] confident that, by virtue of the imperial decrees, he would be able to dismiss the French Comedy, and to this end I advanced $\frac{m}{90}$ f. as my share, and entered into a bond with Baron Fries[4] and Bender,[5] the first for 3,000 annually, the other 8,000 f. together with interest to meet their demand for payment over a total of six years; as this plan has now been completely set at nought by the latest decrees of H.M. the Emperor, I am not only unable to meet my commitments but, thanks to this chicanery, may be exposed to a lawsuit, and to see the money advanced disappear little by little and become lost, for I cannot seek any redress from Afflisio, as his debts by far exceed his assets; he owes $\frac{m}{50}$ f. to H:v Bender, $\frac{m}{25}$ f. to Baron Fries, $\frac{m}{30}$ f. to me, apart from what he owes His Majesty's Court and any debts which may be hidden to date, and his whole position, with deposito, Hetz and Teatral effects may amount to some $\frac{m}{90}$ f.

Now I do admit that the aforesaid d'Afflisio may have earned the ill-favour of Your Serene Highness, but the humanity which Your Serene Highness is known to have displayed at all times gives me firm confidence that Your Highness will not permit ruin to befall me; everyone is convinced that no man exists who might ever have suffered any harm through Your Supreme Highness, but Your Highness has given the world enough evidence of your good-hearted nature.

This allows me to entertain the most confident hope that Your Serene Highness will either graciously intervene in the affairs of Afflisio or, with a gesture of generosity, find a means whereby mine may soon be set at rights, especially as a part of the money has been advanced to me, while a further portion is the property of my wife, a circumstance which has so affected her that her health has already suffered.

I ask most humbly that my plea be heard and remain with deepest respect,

Most Serene Prince,
Your Serene Highness's
Most humble and obedient
Servant Christof Gluck.

Vienna 31st December
1769

[Address:]
To Your Serene Highness the
Prince von Kaunitz (P.T.)
Most humble request from me named within.

[1] WENZEL ANTON PRINCE KAUNITZ-RIETBERG was born on 2nd February 1711. After a number of foreign political missions, which took him, amongst other places, to London in 1747, he became Minister of Foreign Affairs in Vienna in 1753 and Maria Theresia's closest adviser. He was an outstanding patron of the arts and did much to encourage talented young artists. He died in Vienna on 27th July 1794.

[2] The Emperor at that time was JOSEPH II (1765–1790) who until 1780 was only co-regent with his mother for the Austrian territories and therefore wielded no particular influence.

[3] The correct name of the Italian GIUSEPPE AFFLISIO (or AFFLIGIO) appears to have been Maratti, and he is reputed to have been born in Florence *c.* 1720. He was an adventurer and gambler who had illicitly acquired an officer's commission and boasted the rank of Lieutenant-Colonel. He took over the Impresa, which was to cost Gluck so much money, on 16th May 1767. He was involved in a well-known lawsuit with Leopold Mozart. He was eventually sentenced to a term of imprisonment for forgery. He died after 1779.

[4] JOHANN VON FRIES was born in Mühlhausen on 19th May 1719 and came of an old Swiss patrician family. He devoted himself to commerce, became Burgomaster of Zürich and was President of the Council for the thirteen cantons in Switzerland. On many occasions he performed great services to Austria, and was therefore allowed to open a branch in Vienna and was knighted by Maria Theresia on 24th November 1757. In 1762 (15th December), as a reward for the financial help he had given in the Seven Years' War, he was made a Freiherr and finally on 5th April 1783 became an Imperial Count. He died in Vœslau near Vienna on 19th June 1785. He married Anna d'Escherny and his son was Moriz Count von Fries (1777–1825), the well-known patron of the arts.

[5] BENDER, probably Johann Blasius Bender, who was born in 1713 in Gengenbach in Swabia and entered the Austrian Imperial Service in 1733. For his deeds of heroism at Berlin and Torgau in 1769 and for other services rendered, Joseph II made him a Freiherr. He died in Prague on 20th November 1798.

[To Duke Don Giovanni di Braganza.[1] *Italian*]

Vienna, 30th October 1770

Highness!

In dedicating my latest work to Your Highness, I crave not so much a protector as a judge. A spirit secure against the prejudices of habit, a sufficient knowledge of the great principles of art, a taste formed not so much on great models as on the immutable foundations of beauty and truth, these are the attributes which I seek in my Maecenas and which I find united in Your Highness. The sole reason that induced me to publish my music for *Alceste*[2] was the hope of finding imitators who, spurred on by the full support of an enlightened public, would follow the new trail and would summon the courage to eliminate the abuses which have crept into the Italian theatre and bring it as near perfection as possible. I reproach myself for having thus far attempted to do this in vain. The demi-savants and professors of taste, whose number is unhappily legion and who represent the greatest barrier to artistic progress, have come out in opposition to a method which, if it should gain a footing, would destroy at once all their pretensions as critics and as creators. They believed they could pass judgment on *Alceste* after chaotic, badly directed and even more badly executed rehearsals; the attempt was made to gauge in a room the effect produced in a theatre, with the same ingenuity as was once employed in a city in Greece to judge statues, which were intended to stand on lofty colums, from a few feet away. One delicate ear found an air too harsh or a transition too forceful and badly prepared, without pausing to consider that full force of expression and maximum contrast were called for. One pedantic harmonist took advantage of a judicious oversight or a fault in the score to denounce the one and the other as unpardonable sins against the mysteries of harmony; and then voices were raised in unison against this allegedly barbarous and extravagant music.

It is true that other scores have been judged by the same criterion, and judgment on them is given with no less assurance; but Your Highness can easily see the reason for this. The more one seeks truth and perfection, the more necessary is it to be precise and exact. The qualities which distinguish Raphael[3] from a dozen other painters are imperceptible, and, any alteration of contour, which might be permissible in caricature, would wholly disfigure the portrait of a beautiful woman. Little or nothing, apart from a slight alteration in the mode of expression, would be needed to turn my aria in *Orfeo*, 'Che faro senze Euridice?', into a puppet-dance.[4] One note more or less sustained, failure to increase the tempo or make the voice louder, one appoggiatura out of place, a frill, a passage or roulade, can ruin a whole scene in such an opera. And when it is a question of executing music written according to the principles I have laid down, the presence of the composer is, so to speak, as necessary as the presence of the sun to the works of nature. He is the absolute life and soul, and without him everything remains in confusion and darkness. But one must be prepared for these obstacles as long as one lives in the same world with people who feel they have the authority to judge the fine arts just because they are privileged to possess a pair of eyes and a pair of ears, no matter which. It is unhappily an all too common mistake amongst men, this mania for talking of things they least understand, and I have lately seen one of the greatest philosophers of the century take to writing on music and pronounce like an oracle:

'Dreams of the blind and tricks of romance'.[5]

Your Highness will already have read the text of *Paris* and will have noted that it does not present the composer's imagination with those strong passions, those great images and those tragic situations, which move the audience in *Alceste* and give so much opportunity for artistic effects; for which reason one must not expect the same force and energy in the music, just as in a painting with full light one does not expect the same effects of chiaroscuro, the same sharp contrasts as the painter can employ with a subject which enables him to choose a subdued light. Here we are dealing not with a wife who is in danger of losing her husband and, in order to save him, has the courage to venture forth into the black shadows of the night and call upon infernal spirits in some fearful forest glade, who even in her last death-agony trembles for the fate of her sons and cannot tear herself away from a husband whom she adores. We are dealing with a young lover who finds himself for a time at odds with the strange humours of a noble and proud woman and finally, with all the art of a tireless passion, triumphs over her. I have been obliged to seek some variety of colour, which I found in the diverse characters of the two nations, the Phrygian and the Spartan, and I was able to contrast the roughness and wildness of the one with the tenderness and softness of the other. I believed that, as songs in an opera are merely another form of declamation, I must reproduce in Helen the native harshness of her race, and I thought that, to preserve this character in the music, it would not be held against me if from time to time I descended to the trivial. When one is in search of truth, one must vary one's style according to the subject in hand, and the greatest beauties of melody and harmony become defective and imperfect if they are not in their proper place. I do not hope for more success from my *Paris* than from *Alceste*, inasmuch as it is my aim to produce a desired reformation in composers of music, and in this I foresee greater and greater obstacles, but, as for me, I will not allow myself to be deterred from making new efforts towards this worthy end, and, should I receive the approval of Your Highness, I shall continue to repeat happily:

Tolle Syparium sufficit mihi unus Plato pro cuncto populo.[6]

I have the honour to be, with
deepest respect,
Your Highness's
Most humble, most devoted and
most obedient servant
Chevalier Christof Gluck.

[1] DUKE DON GIOVANNI DI BRAGANZA was keenly devoted to the arts. The English music historian Charles Burney writes of him in his *Diary of a musical journey* (1773, vol. II, p. 89): '. . . an excellent judge of music, and who condescended to converse with me a considerable time on the subject. This prince is a great traveller, having visited England, France, and Italy, before his arrival in Germany. He is very lively, and occasioned much mirth by his pleasantries, which were all seasoned with good humour.'

[2] Gluck's *Alceste* had been published by Trattnern in Vienna in 1769.

[3] RAPHAEL was born on 18th March 1483 in Urbino, the son of the painter Giovanni Santi and of Magia Ciarla. About 1500 he became a pupil of Perugino in Perugia. In 1504 he came to Florence and in 1509 the period of his Roman masterpieces began. In 1515 Pope Leo X made him Prefect of Antiquities. He died in Rome on 6th April 1520 and was buried in the Pantheon beside his betrothed, Marietta, a niece of Cardinal Bibbiena [cf. Venturi: *Raffaello*. 1920].

[4] How right Gluck was with his remark that a change of expression would turn the aria 'Che faro senze Euridice?' into a puppet-dance is clear from the use made of the aria in Tommaso Traetta's opera buffa *Il cavaliere errante* (Venice, 1778), in which Guido, who has gone mad and imagines himself to be Orpheus, completely debases the piece. The text was filled with comic touches by Bertati; alterations in Gluck's instrumentation and the omission of the second incidental passage increase the impression of monotony, which is already perceptible in the original, to the point of boredom [cf. *Denkmäler der Tonkunst in Oesterreich*, Vol. 44a, pp. 175ff.].

[5] The quotation 'Sogni di ciechi, e fole di romanzi' is taken from Stefano Arteaga's *Le rivoluzioni del teatro musicale italiano dalla sua origine fino al presento* (Bologna, 1783).

[6] 'Tolle Syparium . . .' is an allusion to the anecdote concerning Plato and Antimachus, which Cicero tells in his *Brutus* (chapter 51) and Plutarch refers to in his *Lysander* (chapter 18). The classical 'Plato enim mihi unus instar est omnium' has been rendered in neo-classical Latin, and the expression 'tollere siparium' (not 'syparium' as Gluck spells it) also dates the author who confuses 'siparium' (drop-scene) with 'aulaeum' (final curtain).

[To the *Mercure de France. French*]

February 1773

M.

I would lay myself open to just reproach, and I would reproach myself most severely, if, after having read the letter written from here to one of the directors of the Royal Academy of Music, which you published in the *Mercure* of October last and the subject of which is the opera *Iphigénie*—if, I say, after having expressed to the author of this letter my appreciation of the praises he was pleased to heap upon me, I did not hasten to point out that his friendship and too strong a prejudice in my favour have undoubtedly carried him away, and that I am very far from flattering myself that I deserve the praise he accords me. I would reproach myself even more, if I consented to accept the credit for having invented the new form of Italian opera, the success of which has fully justified the experiment; it is to M. de Calzabigi that the chief merit belongs; and if my music has met with some approbation, I feel bound to admit that it is to him I am indebted for this, since it is he who made it possible for me to develop the resources of my art. This author, full of genius and talent, has in his poems *Orphée*, *Alceste* and *Paris* pursued a course which is virtually unknown to the Italians. These works are full of happy situations, of those elements of terror and pathos which give a composer the opportunity to express great passion and to create forceful and moving music. Whatever talent the composer may have, he will never create more than mediocre music, if the poet does not arouse in him that enthusiasm without which all artistic productions are weak and spiritless; to imitate nature is the acknowledged aim which they must all set themselves. This is the aim which I seek to attain: always as simple and natural as possible, my music merely strives to achieve the fullest expression and to reinforce the poetic declamation. That is the reason why I do not employ the trills, passages or cadenzas in which the Italians revel. Their language, which lends itself to these so easily, therefore has no advantage for me in this respect, though it has doubtless many others; but, born in Germany, any study I may have made of the Italian language, as also of the French language, is not, I believe, sufficient to enable me to appreciate the delicate nuances which may render one preferable to the other, and I think that all foreigners should abstain from judging their respective merits; but what I think is permissible for me to say is that the language which will always appeal to me most is that in which the poet provides me with the most varied opportunities to express the emotions; this is the advantage I believe I have found in the text of the opera *Iphigénie*, in which the poetry seemed to me to have all the vigour required to inspire good music. Although I have never been in the position of offering my works to any theatre, I cannot hold it against the writer of the letter to one of the Directors that he proposed my *Iphigénie* to your Academy of Music. I confess that I would have been pleased to produce it in Paris, because, by its effect and with the help of the famous M. Rousseau[1] of Geneva whom I intended to consult, we might together, in seeking a noble, moving and natural melody with a declamation in keeping with the prosody of each language and the character of each people, have succeeded in finding the medium I have in mind for producing a type of music suited to all nations and in eliminating the absurd distinctions between national forms of music. The study I have made of this great man's works on music, amongst others the letter in which he analyses the monologue of Lully's[2] *Armide*, prove the depth of his knowledge and his sureness of taste and have filled me with admiration. I was left with the profound conviction that if he had chosen to devote himself to the application of this art, he would have been able to achieve the prodigious effects which the ancients attributed to music. I am delighted to have this opportunity of paying him publicly this tribute which I believe he deserves.

I beg you, Monsieur, to have the goodness to publish this letter in your next *Mercure*.

I have the honour to be, etc.
Chevalier Gluck.

Gluck's letter aroused the following comment in the *Mémoires secrètes* published by Bacheaumont: 'A letter has appeared in the *Mercure* from the famous Gluck, the German musician, who offered to send the Directors of the Opéra, or rather to bring them, the *Iphigénie* [*en Aulide*] of Racine [arranged by the Bailli du Roullet] set to music. These gentlemen, who have little interest in foreign music and fear that it may discredit their own, did not take up the proposal. Happily the Sr. Gluck thought fit to arrive, and, as he has the honour to be known to Madame la Dauphine [Marie Antoinette], it is to be hoped that he will enjoy enough protection to have his opera produced. This princess has given him permission to call on her at any time.'

[1] JEAN JACQUES ROUSSEAU, the famous French philosopher and writer, was born in Geneva on 28th June 1712. Although he had not studied music, he had taken an active interest in the subject from his youth. Later he composed and wrote on music. In the quarrel between the buffonists and the anti-buffonists he sided with the Italians and, together with Baron Melchior Grimm, was one of their earliest and most faithful champions. With his dramatic opera *Le devin du village* (1752) he paved the way for the French operetta, and his lyrical play *Pygmalion* (produced in Lyons in 1770 with music by Horace Goignet) was the forerunner, though this was not his intention, of the spoken melodrama. Rousseau, who belonged to the circle of the Encyclopaedists, also published a *Dictionnaire de Musique* (1767) and wrote an unpublished work on the theory of harmony. He died at Ermenonville near Paris on 2nd July 1773 [cf. A. Jansen: *J. J. Rousseau als Musiker*, 1884; A. Pougin: *J. J. Rousseau musicien*, 1901; J. Tiersot: *J. J. Rousseau*, 1912; E. Faquet: *Rousseau artiste*, 1913]. His 'Lettre sur la musique française', which Gluck mentions, also appeared in his *Œuvres complètes*, 1795, Vol. XIII, p. 243.

[2] JEAN BAPTISTE LULLY was born in Florence on 29th November 1632. He went to Paris in 1646 as a kitchen-boy, then became a music page. After joining the 24 'violons du Roi' of Louis XIV, he won the King's favour and was made leader of the group. Lully then created an élite orchestra of sixteen petits violons. In 1653 he became Court Composer. He was a skilled dancer, a good actor and a lively conductor. He died in Paris on 22nd March 1687. As a composer, Lully made a considerable mark on his period and his influence extended far beyond France. His numerous operas, in which he was ably supported by the poet Quinault, dominated the French National Opéra, which he founded, up to the time of Gluck [cf. H. Prunières: *Lully*, 1910: L. de la Laurencie: *Lully*, 1911].

The above letter is probably not an exact reproduction of Gluck's original letter but a copy of the text as edited by the Bailli du Roullet [cf. p. 67]. The initial pretext for Gluck's letter was another letter from Vienna which had appeared in the *Mercure de France* in October 1772 and which ran as follows:

[LETTER I]

Vienna in Austria
1st August 1772

The esteem due to you, Monsieur, both for your undoubtedly most distinguished talents and for the openness of your character, with which I am especially familiar, has made me resolve to write to you, in order to inform you that the famous M. Glouch [sic], so well-known throughout Europe, has made a French opera which he would like to see produced on the Paris stage. This great man, after having made more than forty Italian operas which have had the greatest success in all the theatres where this language is employed, became convinced, after making a close study of ancient and modern works and reflecting deeply on his art, that the Italians had wandered away from the true path in their theatrical compositions; that the French form was the true musical drama; that, if until now it had not achieved perfection, the fault lay not so much with the truly admirable French musicians as with the poets, who, knowing nothing of the range of which music is capable, had in their compositions preferred *esprit* to sentiment, gallantry to passion, polished and colourful verses to a moving style or situation. Following these reflections and having communicated his ideas to a man of much intelligence, talent and taste, he obtained from him two Italian poems which he set to music. He himself had these two operas produced on the stage in Parma, Milan, Naples, etc. There they had an incredible success and in Italy produced a revolution in this particular form of art. Last winter the City of Boulogne [Bologna] produced one of those operas in M. Glouch's absence.[1] His success in that city attracted more than twenty thousand spectators who were anxious to see the performances; Boulogne has earned from this production more than eighty thousand ducats, about 900,000 French livres. On his return here M. Glouch, enlightened by his own experience, formed the impression that the Italian language, more suited by the frequent repetition of vowels to what the Italians call passages, had not the clarity and forcefulness of the French language; that the very quality we have just conceded to the former had the effect of destroying true dramatic music, in which any 'passage' was out of place or at least weakened the expression. Having made these observations, M. Glouch was indignant at rash assertions by those of our famous writers who have dared to calumniate the French language by maintaining that it did not lend itself to great musical creation. On this subject no one is more competent to judge than M. Glouch; he has a complete command of both languages, and, although he speaks French with difficulty, he has a thorough knowledge of it; he has made a special study of it and knows all its finer shades of meaning, particularly in prosody on which he has made some profound observations. For some time past he has been trying out his knowledge of both languages in different forms and has been successful in a social *milieu* in which they are equally familiar, although French is commonly preferred, a *milieu*, moreover, all the more capable of judging talents of this kind as the ears and taste of the audience are continually regaled by them. Since making these observations, M. Glouch wanted to be able to support his view in favour of the French language by practical experience, and by chance the tragic opera *Iphigénie en Aulide* came his way. He believed that he had found in this work what he was seeking. The author or, more precisely, the adaptor of this poem [N. F. Guillard] seems to me to have followed Racine with the most scrupulous care. It is, in fact, his *Iphigénie* which has been made into an opera. To achieve this, it was necessary to restrict the action and to leave out the part of Euriphile. Calcas has been introduced in the first act in place of the confidant Arcas; in this way the unfolding of the situation has been changed, the subject has been simplified, and the action, being more concentrated, moves more rapidly to its climax. These changes did not, however, mean any slackening of interest, which seemed to be as sustained as in Racine's tragedy. The dénouement of this great man's work, as he devised it, could not be retained in the opera; but cutting the Euriphile episode, a much more lively dénouement has been substituted, which must be very effective and which was suggested to the author as much by the Greek tragedies as by Racine himself in the Preface to his *Iphigénie*. The entire work has been broken up into three acts, a division which seems to me more appropriate to a form of art that requires very rapid action. In each act a brilliant *divertissement* has been introduced which does not interfere with the plot but, on the contrary, is so attuned to it as to form part of it, stimulate it and round it off. Great care has been taken to maintain a contrast between situations and characters, thus producing the variety necessary to hold the audience's attention and interest throughout the entire production. Without having recourse to machinery and without incurring any great expense, ways and means have been found of presenting a spectacle which is noble and sumptuous to the eye. I do not believe a new opera has ever been produced on the stage demanding less expenditure and yet affording such a magnificent spectacle. The author of this poem, the entire presentation of which, including the *divertissements*, lasts at most two and a half hours, has made it his duty to use the thoughts and even the verses of Racine, wherever the medium of the opera, which is so different, allowed it. These verses have been incorporated with so much artistry that one is aware of virtually no disparity with the general style of the work. The choice of *Iphigénie en Aulide* seemed to me a particularly happy one as the author, by following Racine as closely as possible, was assured of the effect of his work and by this assurance was amply compensated for any loss of *amour-propre* he may have suffered.

The name of M. Glouch alone would release me from any obligation, Monsieur, to speak to you of the music of this opera, if the pleasure it gave me in several performances allowed me to keep silent. It has seemed to me that this great man had exhausted all the resources of art in this composition. Simple, natural songs, always imbued with the most true and sensitive expression and with the most flattering melody; an infinite variety of ideas and of nuances; a most impressive use of harmony to express terror, pathos and tenderness alike; a fast-moving recitative which is also noble and expressive; finally, perfect examples of French recitative at its most declamatory, a great variety of dance-airs of a new kind and most agreeably fresh, choruses, duets, trios and quartets all equally expressive and moving, with scrupulous attention to the prosody; in short, everything in this work seems very suited to our taste and nothing seemed to me to be strange to French ears. It is a work of great talent; M. Glouch is both a poet and a musician, whose genius is always apparent, yet he is at the same time a man of taste; there is nothing common or careless in his work.

As you know, Monsieur, I am no partisan and in the quarrels which have broken out over the various forms of music I have remained completely neutral; I flatter myself, therefore, that you will not feel sceptical about my eulogy of the music of the opera *Iphigénie*. I am convinced that you will feel impelled to approve; I know that no one desires the advancement of your art more than you; you have already contributed to it by your productions and the applause which I have seen you accord to those who distinguished themselves. So, both as a man of talent and as a good citizen, you will be pleased to see that a foreigner as famous as M. Glouch is working in our language and vindicating it in the eyes of Europe as a whole against the slanderous imputations of our own authors.

M. Glouch only wishes to know if the Directors of the Academy of Music have sufficient confidence in his gifts to decide to present his opera. He is prepared to travel to France but wishes first to be assured that his opera will be presented and approximately how long it will take for this to come about. If you have made no firm arrangements for the winter, for Lent or for the resumption after Easter, I believe you could not do better than to assign him one of these periods. M. Glouch is much in demand in Naples for next May; he has been reluctant to accept any engagement in that quarter, and he is determined to sacrifice any advantages which may be offered to him, if he can be assured that his opera will be accepted by your Academy, to which I beg you to pass this letter and to ask for a decision which will determine that of M. Glouch. I would be most flattered if I could share with you, Monsieur, the merit of informing our nation how much it may expect in the improvement of its language, embellished by the art which you profess. With these sentiments I remain, Monsieur, with true esteem,

Your very humble and very obedient
servant.

PS. Should the Directors mistrust the judgment I have formed of this opera, I would be pleased to send it to you at the earliest opportunity.

I omitted to tell you, Monsieur, that M. Glouch, who is naturally most disinterested, will require no more for his work than has already been decided upon for the authors of new operas.

[1] Gluck's *Orfeo ed Euridice* had its *première* in the Teatro Communale in Bologna in May 1771.

Following this letter, Chabanon had published a 'Lettre sur les propriétés musicales de la langue française' in the *Mercure de France* in January 1773:

[LETTER II]

I read, Monsieur, in the second October *Mercure* that M. Glouch, famous for the Italian operas which he has set to music, has just cast an adoptive glance at our language and applied his talent to a French poem.

M. Glouch's enterprise is in so far remarkable as it contradicts the very strong views held by M. Rousseau. (I predict that the tragic medium will not even be attempted.) Following the author of *Ernelinde* [L. Poinsinet de Sivry], this foreign artist has just lifted the ban imposed on our language; but it is not enough that he considers it will do justice to his art, he also gives it preference over all other languages. This astonishing view, particularly on the part of a foreigner who is not blinded by national prejudice, gave me the idea of discussing the reasons which might justify it and those which have been cited in support of the opposing view. Before entering into this discussion, permit me a few general reflections.

It has been said that all men are dissatisfied with their lot, each people with its language, and that we modern peoples envy the Romans their language, while the Romans envied the Greeks. Everyone bemoans his fate.

I have frequently heard it stated that one language is superior to another, but such affirmations which are, at bottom, merely the judgments of a group, are, for that reason, superficial. They are invariably based on surface observations rather than on a close study, and more on appearance than on reasoned proof. I would like languages to be judged like men, by their works. If the language which is richest in fine works of every kind is not the most beautiful, I do not know what reason it can have to envy another which is preferred to it. But if one follows the criterion which I suggest, would the language of Virgil appear inferior to that of Homer, of Hesiod or of Theocritus which the Latin poet imitated? Let the parallel be extended, by all means, to Cicero, Demosthenes, Sallust, Thucidides, etc., and the scales will remain evenly balanced; but what counterweight can one offer to Tacitus?

I wish that those who judge a language by its material content would decide what in their view is its essential character; for if such a character exists, expressed in the technique of the language and inherent in its nature, then it is clear that every writer must conform to it and be guided by it. I imagine one would reproach a writer who, employing a language which by nature is concise, attempted to be diffuse. It would be like a frog swelling up in too tight a skin. . . .

But is there any language whose character and properties can be so defined as to exclude quite different properties and quite another character? Cicero is diffuse, Tacitus concise. Which of the two knew the character of his language best? Both, with equal success, infused into it the character of their genius.

What is one to say of our French idiom? Though apparently obscure by virtue of the profusion and ambiguity of its relative pronouns, it has become noted for its extreme clarity. This is a quality which no one denies it; it is the idiom of the philosophers and, in consequence, that of reason. How is one to explain this contradiction between a radical defect of the language and the outstanding quality it has acquired? The answer is that writers have applied all their efforts to the weak side of this language; from its original defect they have produced one of its instruments of perfection. A language is what writers make of it.

The fact that our language is subject to contradictions and unfavourable suspicions is no new phenomenon. The wise Patru[1] in his time feared that it could not lend itself to the graceful simplicity of the fable. He confided his doubts and his fears to La Fontaine, who, in his own writings, soon cured him of both. This same Patru, ever timid and distrustful, expressed similar doubts to Boileau, whose writing was in a didactic style. Boileau replied with his poetic art. The author of the *Henriade* destroyed a stronger and more general prejudice, which declared our language and our taste to be anti-epic. The success of two Georgic poems has also widened the sphere of our poetry by introducing a genre to which it was not thought to be susceptible. Thus each effort by a skilful writer sacrifices, so to speak, to the language a prejudice against it, and the language, like a river as it moves away from its source, gradually extends its surface. Between it and the modern song there is still a slender barrier, but this will soon be surmounted.

There are three views on the musical properties of the French language, which are held by different sections of the public.

1) Our language is musical, but Lully has composed the only music for which it is suited.

2) Our language lends itself to the technique of the modern song, but this technique is not in keeping with the dignity of opera.

3) All good music is beyond our reach and we will never be able to sing.

When we have discussed these three views, it will only remain to put forward our own, which will serve as a reply to that of M. Glouch.

I do not know, Monsieur, if one should shrink from declaring that Lully did not create the kind of music which he is generally believed to have invented; he merely imported it from Italy, where this type of music was then in current use. Those who might be amazed by this suggestion have only to recall the music of Corelli; from this composer's French style we learn what Italian music was at one time: to become French it had only to become old, for the Italians had changed their musical idiom when we were still clinging to it.

Vienne 18 Mars 1780

je ne sçaurois differir d'avantage, Monsieur, à vous marquer le plaisir suprême que je resente en lisant vos ouvrages, et j'ai bien des obligations à Monsieur le Comte de Brancas de m'avoir fait connoître un desplus grandes Genies de la France, si j'aurois eu connoissance pendant mon sejour à Paris de Votre comedie des Philosophes et de votre Dunciade, ô que j'aurois pû en faire un bon usage contre les invectives des Marmontels et ses Confreres, si jamais je reviens à Paris, vos ouvrages me serviront d'Egide contre ses Insectes du Parnasse; Monsieur Janson qui vous presente cette lettre, est aussi enchanté que moi même de votre Genie, et desire tres fort à faire votre connoissance, il n'a pas voulu quitter ce päis sens en être le porteur, il mette cette occasion au nombre digne de celles des plus agreables de sa vie, je vous prie de ne jamais douter de l'estime qui vous m'avez inspirez, je suis avec une parfaite consideration

Monsieur

votre tres humble et tres Obeissant serviteur Gluck

LETTER FROM GLUCK TO CHARLES PALISSOT DE MONTENOY, FROM VIENNA, 18 MARCH 1780

From Collection Karl Geigy-Hagenbach, Basle

G. B. MARTINI
Engraving by Carlo Faucci

What does it matter, after all, whether this music was adopted or created by us? Is it the only music that becomes us? That is the real point at issue.

The public itself provides the solution. Lully's music must have lost much of its appeal, as so little of it is left when the works of Quinault are produced on the stage. A curious change in the fortunes of these two authors; formerly Quinault was tolerated because of his musician, or at least so it was thought. Today it is the works of Quinault which, emerging from obscurity, carry with them a few fragments of the old music, which, but for these works, would be doomed to perish. (What has been preserved from the works of Lully for the most part are his recitatives, but recitative is not, properly speaking, music. For the rest, we gladly agree that there are amongst Lully's compositions pieces of music which are striking in their simplicity, such as the beginning of the prologue of *Amadie*. We do not believe we are doing this artist an injustice by comparing him with Corelli.)

However many revolutions the French Theatre may pass through, the works of our great masters will always maintain their superiority. If at a given moment they appear to lose ground to works of lesser quality, which have the charm of novelty, then it is the result of a certain libertinism in our taste of which we disapprove even while we are gratifying it; and in this respect the public behaves like husbands who, on occasion, are unfaithful to their gentle and virtuous wives; at the bottom of their hearts they can distinguish perfectly between the object of their whims and the object of a more true and lasting affection. We can deduce from this that, if Lully's works lose ground as they grow older, the fault lies in themselves.

Let us pass on to the second view, which will not admit that what is laudable in Italian comedy may also be laudable in opera. It may seem surprising, Monsieur, that for music one should create the kind of distinction between two quarters of Paris that would hardly apply to two opposing climates. . . . But I was forgetting that we are dealing with different spectacles and that it is the dignity of the opera that is in question. We must beware of being led astray by an ill-conceived idea of nobility; do not let us treat the opera like those children of good family who grow up to be blockheads and fools because they have been given an exaggerated sense of their superior station in life.

I only ask for replies to the following questions.

Can one describe the position of a virtuous son, who has been disinherited and turned out of his paternal home and who is prepared to reappear before his father, as a noble position? Do the lines put into Sylvain's mouth lack nobility?

> Je puis braver les coups du sort,
> Mais non pas les regards d'un père.
>
> . . . .
>
> . . . .
>
> Pour un fils sensible et rebelle,
> Un père est un Dieu menaçant.

Do these lines detract from a hero's dignity, and can one set them to nobler, truer or more moving music than that of M. Grettri [Grétry]?

A slight oddity which I have noticed, Monsieur; modern music is treated as something familiar and even low, but comic opera, which was intended from the outset to be so and has remained so for so long, has only begun to rise above this level since it embraced modern music. Far from excluding the quality of nobility, modern music transmits it to anything that approaches it. What clearer indication could there be of its potentialities and even of its needs?

It only remains to discuss the third view. This is the most formidable; not that I believe it to be the most correct, but the merit and fame of its originator [M. Rousseau] give it almost as much weight as if it were correct. If our language recovers from the blows of such an adversary, if M. Rousseau's view, defended with all his eloquence, has not acquired the force of law, then it is fated never to gain credence.

There is no need for me to say at the outset that, in attacking some of M. Rousseau's propositions, I do so with no lack of respect for his great qualities. If I had the honour to know him personally, I would submit this letter to him before publishing it and enable him to judge his own case.

Letter on music. 'Our language', says M. Rousseau, consisting of 'mixed sounds and of mute, subdued or nasal syllables, possessing few resonant vowels and many consonants, is the direct opposite of "music".'

I would like to chat with M. Rousseau in order to find out exactly what he means by mixed sounds; I have not a sufficiently clear idea of the meaning of these words to be able to reply. Undoubtedly our language has many mute syllables. They help to infuse grace and variety into our pronunciation; I even believe that they are fairly closely related to certain forms of vocal music, something which I shall endeavour to prove a little further on. Here I will content myself with the suggestion that M. Rousseau, who finds the Italian language so soft because there is a constant elision of one vowel against another, should find ours even softer, because there is continual elision—and it is both more pleasing and more natural—between a mute syllable and a resonant vowel. Let us take an example, and indeed one that M. Rousseau has chosen:

Teneri saegni, è placide è tranquille
Repulse, è cari vezzi, è liete paci.

If you pronounce all these vowels without elision, you move from one hiatus to another and make the pronunciation jerky. And if you elide? You mutilate, you disfigure the words by removing one of the essential syllables; and furthermore the repetition of the E sounds is tiring to the ear.

Compare this with an elision of mute syllables:

Oui, je viens dans son temple adorer l'Eternel!

The words 'temple' and 'adorer' retain their correct pronunciation intact; and the mute syllable, by a soft elision, is quietly lost in the vowel that follows.

M. Rousseau then maintains that the lack of resonance in the vowel makes it necessary 'to give resonance to the notes, and that a subdued language makes for shrill music'.

It seems to me that quite another conclusion should be drawn from this.

The lack of resonance in the vowels is a warning against introducing it into the music. This is the conclusion M. Rousseau himself draws elsewhere in his letter when he deduces from the character of a language the character of the music best suited to it.

'The tempo of our music must be slow and wearisome. Should one attempt to quieten the tempo, its speed would resemble that of a hard, angular body rumbling over a cobbled street.'

I have searched in our language for elements that would compel our music to be slow. I find that it is a language with a wealth of short syllables. Why does a light and rapid pronunciation necessarily produce slow, lazy vocal music? Must one always proceed contrariwise from a language to its music? Why then are these inverse conclusions applied only to us?

'I assume', M. Rousseau continues, 'that the same language would be weak in prosody, without stress, without clarity, without precision; that the relationship between the long and short syllables, as regards both duration and number, would not be a simple one, likely to produce a pleasant and regular rhythm, that it would have long syllables which were more or less long, short syllables more or less short, syllables neither short nor long, etc.'

M. Rousseau in this passage merely puts forward as a supposition all that he in fact holds against the French language. What may astonish you is that the case he presents for the prosecution could serve admirably as a case for the defence. If one were called upon to argue for the pre-eminence of our language over all others in music, it might well be enough to repeat on its behalf what its adversary has said against it. But we have not reached that stage; let us not anticipate the argument.

'Our prosody, it is said, has no stress.' And yet it is impossible to change the value of a syllable without offending the ear.

'Our prosody, it is said further, is weak.' And yet from the verses of Racine, M. de Voltaire and Quinault, if well spoken, the ear derives a pleasure which M. Rousseau has surely felt as much as anyone.

But, we are told, our language has long syllables which are more or less short, and syllables which are neither long nor short. Denis d'Halycarnasse[2] [de Synth], Monsieur, said as much of Greek. If these words point to a radical defect, an anti-lyrical defect in the language, what of the praises M. Rousseau has heaped on the Greek language, which he finds so musical and so harmonious? Moreover, music itself has long notes which are more or less long, short notes which are more or less short, round, white, black notes, quavers, etc. How could such a striking relationship between language and music make them incompatible?

Let us pass on to a fresh charge, that our constructions are essentially didactic. M. Rousseau maintains that a musical phrase develops 'in a more pleasing and more interesting manner when the meaning of what is said, after a long period of suspense, is resolved by the verb and with the cadence, than when it develops to order'. This objection calls for more than one reply.

1. I have given this considerable thought but I cannot find any musical merit in inversion or understand the analogy of the final verb with the cadence.

2. I am more inclined to believe that, in a text written to be sung, far from keeping the meaning of the words in abeyance, one cannot explain it too early, in order to save the mind unnecessary reflection and work.

3. By relegating the verb to the end one no more keeps the meaning of the phrase in abeyance than if one places the noun at the end:

Misero Pargoletto
Il tuo destin non fai.

By placing the verb before the noun, the meaning of the phrase would not be explained any sooner.

4. It seems to me that M. Metastase [Metastasio], whose words have provided such

fine songs, makes very limited use of inversion and that his turns of phrase are quite similar to ours.

5. Finally, if the long sentences in which the meaning is held in suspense are particularly suitable for setting to music, our eight-syllable verses could also qualify; in the works of M. Greffet[3] one could find twenty or twenty-five verses of this kind. So our language, even in this respect, is not anti-lyrical.

Does it not seem to you, Monsieur, that one attributes to the written language too many defects which one finds in music? M. Glouch himself is guilty of this. He attributes the too frequent use of roulades, with which he reproaches the Italian song, to the abundance of vowels, but there is no need to 'roll' vowels, and the language is innocent of this abuse imputed to it. If Italian songs degenerate into roulades, it is because the composers defer to singers who are anxious to display their skill and also because audiences in Italy have acquired the habit of regarding the performances as a type of concert to which they only listen in parts. In consequence they are less able to appreciate how misplaced the roulade is in a tragic song; in consequence, one singer is made to sing at great length without any concern for his or her partner who, as long as the song lasts, is merely another member of the audience; in consequence, the 'ritornelli' are prolonged and the 'da capos' multiplied without considering the effect on the action or on the actors. None of these defects of Italian opera would be tolerated in France. With our refined and exacting taste, we consider the parts in relation to the whole and expect the music to contribute to the action on the stage. This is what has led me to think that we must develop operatic production beyond the point it has reached abroad; it is also perhaps what has kindled in M. Glouch the desire to place his talents at our disposal.

But does our language lend itself to a type of music which can satisfy both ourselves and people abroad? This question brings me back to my original subject and gives me an opportunity to put forward my own opinion.

I believe, Monsieur, that music is more independent of language than one imagines. I regard it as a language in itself, apart from all the others, a universal language, in essence unchangeable and only slightly influenced by the written word, if indeed it is influenced at all.

As this view is bound to arouse surprise, I shall omit nothing that might substantiate it.

The most profound, most accented language has comparatively few commensurable intervals in pronunciation, but this proportion exists and must exist in music, where every tone is subject to the laws of harmony and melody; how can one make something that always sings dependent on something that never sings?

Let us apply to the Greek language the principle which we are asked to accept and we shall see the result.

Almost all Greek words have an acute, grave or circumflex accent, which means, according to Denis d'Halicarnasse, that on each word the voice rose or dropped by a fifth, or simply ran through the whole interval within the two opposing accents. Do you think that the musicians submitted to this law of accents? Eh! in that case what would their melody have been like? It would have consisted necessarily of a series of high and low fifths repeated with each word! The very idea excludes any melody.

If vocal music is governed by inflections of speech, then great music must be essentially rhetorical. Do you think this theory can be sustained?

Was M. Rousseau, in the charming songs of *Le Devin du village*, aiming to be rhetorical? Speak these lines:

Si des galans de la ville, etc.,

then sing them and you will know the answer.

If each nation's music is a natural product, a necessary consequence of the language it speaks, why does music change, while the language remains the same? The Italians have sung in the French style; and we, who speak the language of Quinault, are far removed from that of Lully.

I regard the beginning of the *Stabat* as one of the finest pieces of music ever written. Are we indebted for it to the language and its accents? Is there any language in the world whose inflexions could be related to the intonations of the *Stabat*?

I have collected several songs by savages in Canada. Their melody is the same as ours; does this mean that their language must also be the same?

Eh! Is it not plain, Monsieur, that music, as I have said, is a language apart from all others? Every people, in order to make itself understood, has evolved a conventional language, the formation of which is the work of chance; for there is no reason why bread should be called bread rather than *artes* as in Greek. The main forms of music, on the other hand, are products neither of chance nor of convention; they derive from the laws of nature, in other words from our organic structure which makes them necessary, unchangeable and universal. The relationship between a musical combination of sounds and our senses is a mystery which defies rational explanation. No one can explain why such a concatenation of sounds should produce a melodious song or why from the rhythm expressed by this song a movement should emerge which carries our bodies with it; these effects cannot be rationally explained, but any mature person in any country and any climate can feel them. The most vulgar, brutish peasant has a feeling for songs and for rhythm: children are born with it. Eh! Can you not see them from their cradles responding to the nurses' singing, forgetting their impatience and their sorrows, turning tears into smiles of joy? The spoken language does not as yet exist for them but they already understand the language of music, they are sensitive to it, they have some inner notion of it; if one could believe in innate ideas, it would be in relation to music.

Music is independent of languages, because it exists without them. I cannot understand, I must confess, the basic distinction which people try to draw between vocal and instrumental music. The latter emanates, it seems, from the laws of harmony and melody alone, while the other, being dependent on inflexions of the voice, is an imitation of it. It is, in other words, an offshoot of language. But this simply means creating two art-forms instead of one.

The proof that vocal music does not derive its charm and its power from its relationship with language is that one can be entirely ignorant of the language of a country and still love its music. The Armenian, to whom M. Rousseau refers in his letter, did not understand Italian, but he could understand and enjoy the Italian airs sung to him.

Let us not look for differences where there are none. Vocal music is no more different from instrumental music than one instrument from another. Music is a goddess with a thousand voices, for each instrument provides her with one. Amongst all the vehicles through which she expresses herself, the human voice with its more limited range simplifies what an instrument executes. The voice gives the pure text, while instruments adorn and embellish it by playing round the theme. A song is like a nude, whereas the instrumental music which accompanies it is like a fabric draped in graceful folds about the nude in such a way as not to conceal its shapeliness.

But, one might ask, whence comes the difference between Italian songs and even modern French songs if not from the character of the two languages?—On the other hand, whence comes the difference between the modern and the ancient Italian songs, if the character of the music is determined by that of the language?

Between two violinists such as [Giuseppe] Tartini and [Domenico] Ferrari, for example, there is a greater difference in inflexion, style, and their way of making their instruments sing than there is between Italian and modern French songs. So it is not necessary to look to the language to explain differences in musical expression; the fact that music can be rendered with a certain amount of diversity does not make it any the less a universal language, just as the art of painting is no less universal because each painter has his own style.

I go further. For some years past certain actors in the *Comédie italienne* have been italianising their singing in a way that can easily be detected by a trained ear; either the public have not noticed this innovation or, if they have sensed it, they applaud it; both come to the same thing and prove that the rendering of Italian songs depends more on the music than on the words that go with it.

At the very moment when I was writing this, Monsieur, I chanced to hear an air by M. Grettri [Grétry] rendered by an Italian who puts much feeling and vigour into his singing. His rendering of the French air was not a whit subdued and never has this air been sung with greater effect. The author, who was present, was enchanted by it; the audience were all delighted and I even more than they; for added to my pleasure was the satisfaction of seeing something actually demonstrated which I had so long suspected.

With taste, intelligence and (what is no less essential) good faith, one could make various experiments which would confirm the view I have just put forward.

One could take melodies from our really beautiful comic operas and find Italian words for them, or *vice versa*, one could skilfully translate very beautiful Italian melodies into French; if one or the other were rendered musically, in the true sense of the word, then I would wager on the success of either translation. A beautiful song is a marketable commodity anywhere in the world; it is a diamond which retains its value and which everyone accepts as an ornament.

In the alliance between music and words, Monsieur, music plays the part of the favourites whom everyone treats as ordinary subjects but who in secret govern their masters. One symptom of the subservience of language is the frequent repetition of words in a song. I know that reason rebels against this custom as an abuse, but it is justified in music. As it is a recognized procedure to revert to the same phrases in a song, to repeat them several times in the same mode and in varying modes, the same words naturally recur in the same song; and once the ear has fallen under the spell of the notes, it loses many of its scruples about the privileges of language or of reason.

There is one point, however, where language impedes music, if it does not dominate it; this is in the observance of short and long syllables.

In principle, quantity in music seems at first sight absolutely essential, since it has a direct bearing on the need to make oneself understood; by changing the value of syllables one runs the risk of not being understood. But note, Monsieur, how this precept, so inflexible in theory, is trimmed and tailored in practice. One might say of it, as of verisimilitude in the theatre, that it is a secret known only to the masters just how far one can depart from it.

If necessary I can quote examples from every language to show how good music can violate the laws of versification. In the first couplet in the *Stabat* equal stress is placed on the four syllables of the words 'lacrymosa' and 'dolorosa'. The second couplet is scanned as follows:

Cujus animam gementem.

In the first air of [Pergolesi's] *Serva padrona* you will find words scanned syllabically, 'son tre cose', although 'tre' is definitely a short syllable in pronunication. (I am quoting at random and without having made any systematic investigation; if I confine myself to only a few quotations, it is to avoid making this letter too long.)

Rousseau's *Devin du village* is full of faults of versification. I have deliberately chosen this work, because its author can least be suspected of sinning from ignorance. M. Rousseau, who is an ardent champion of the privileged position of languages, must have felt that music also has its privileges and that they can sometimes take precedence, since the language he uses in this work is by no means so faultless as the language which he speaks and writes so well.

What general conclusion can one draw from all this? That observance of quantity is an impediment in music, from which it seeks to free itself as much as possible. But this impediment would be unimportant if a language existed with a vague, indeterminate, flexible and changing prosody which could be adapted to the needs of the composer. The individual words in this language would have no fixed or real value. Its long syllables would be more or less long, its short syllables more or less short, and many of them would be neither short nor long; they would resemble the syllables ut, re, mi, fa, sol, la, si, ut, which Italian, French and German musicians pronounce long or short as the melody requires.

You may have noticed, Monsieur, that, in outlining the characteristics of a prosody such as is really desirable for music, I have merely repeated word for word what M. Rousseau has said of our prosody; but I very much fear that M. Rousseau (who, in speaking thus, thought he was denying us certain qualities) may have assumed the existence of some which we do not have. As I have already said, I cannot admit that our prosody is indeterminate, since it is true that one cannot change the value of our syllables without offending the ear. Also I do not think, as M. Glouch does, that our language is more musical than all the others, but simply that it can adapt itself as well as any other to good music.

If I were called upon to ascribe to it qualities particularly suited to the art of the song, I could find them in the very qualities which, it has been alleged, are incompatible with music. Its mute terminations, for example, are directly related to the weak, or unstressed, notes in a musical phrase, on which the voice lingers before eventually fading into silence.

Our grammatical construction also favours music in so far as it is conducive to clarity of speech. The more a phrase is self-explanatory, the more readily the mind appreciates the relationship between the song and the words.

These, Monsieur, are the observations I wished to make. If this document is to be challenged, then I trust it will at least bring down upon its author criticisms which will enlighten him without causing him grief. It would be sad if even on subjects of minor importance one could not venture to express one's views without sacrificing one's peace of mind.

Last winter the fanciful and unjust reproach was laid against me that I had set out to discredit Rousseau. I take this opportunity of replying to that reproach by reiterating my faith in that great artist. I consider him one of the most astonishing men who has ever lived; perhaps no one in any of the arts has better deserved the title of man of genius. Far from denying what I had written in his praise by disagreeing with certain passages in his works, I have never ventured any criticism of him which was not implicit in my praise. The respect due to a great man must, while he is alive, silence all criticisms of the imperfections of his talent; but honest criticism, when the author can no longer take umbrage, is more of an honour than an insult to his memory, because it places the seal of truth on the praise which one has justly heaped upon him.

I have the honour to be, etc.

[1] Olivier Patru (born 1604 Paris, died 1661 Paris) was a lawyer and a member of the Académie Française. He was a friend of Boileau and Racine.

[2] Aelius Dionysius of Halicarnassos, a Greek writer at the end of the first century A.D.

[3] Greffet may refer to Antoine Gilbert Griffet de la Beaume [1756–1805], known as a dramatist and translator. He held a Government post.

[To Friedrich Gottlieb Klopstock.[1] *German*]

Vienna, 14th August 1773

Nobly Born,

Most Highly Honoured Councillor,

Father Denis[2] has informed me, that you desire to receive the verses which I composed on your *Herrmannsschlacht*. I would long since have done you this service, if I had not been geometrically assured that many would not find them to their taste, because they must be sung with a certain decorum which is not as yet very much in fashion; for, although you have excellent musical artists, music which calls for enthusiasm seems to me to be still quite unknown in your parts, the which I clearly perceived from the criticism which was directed at my *Alceste*[3] in Berlin. I am so great an admirer of your person that I promise you: (If you do not propose to come to Vienna) I will make a journey[4] to Hamburg next year, in order to make your acquaintance, and I give my assurance that I will sing to you not only much from the *Herrmannsschlacht* but also some of your sublime odes,[5] to make clear to you in how far I have measured up to your greatness or in how far I have obscured it with my music.

Meanwhile I am sending you a few songs, which are quite simple in style and easy to execute. Three of them are German in character and three with a more foreign flavour, and of the latter I have added two melodies in the old bardic style by way of experiment which can, however, always be thrown away. It will be necessary to choose a good pianoforte player for these, in order that they may appear to you less intolerable. I have the honour to continue to call myself with great respect,

Your Nobly Born's most obedient servant
Chevalier Gluck.

[1] FRIEDRICH GOTTLIEB KLOPSTOCK (born 2nd July 1724, died 13th March 1803), the famous poet, was a close friend of Gluck and his family. The *Herrmannsschlacht* appeared in 1769 and was dedicated to the Emperor Joseph II. Gluck committed to paper nothing of the composition on which his contemporaries passed very favourable judgments. He was in the habit of playing or singing it by heart to his visitors.

[2] JOHANNES MICHAEL COSMAS DENIS (born 27th September 1729, died 29th September 1800) was a useful intermediary between the literature of Protestant Germany and of Catholic Austria. He was a Jesuit. Mozart set to music his *Bardic Songs* about Gibraltar, although they seemed to him 'too extravagantly turgid for his delicate ears'.

[3] To which discussion of his *Alceste* Gluck is referring in his letter has not been established.

[4] The promised meeting with Klopstock in Hamburg did not take place.

[5] Klopstock's *Odes* with Gluck's music had not yet appeared in 1773. Gluck therefore sent them in manuscript to Klopstock. In 1775 the first ode, *Der Jüngling*, appeared in the *Musenalmanch*. Artaria published seven *Odes* in Vienna in 1787.

[TO FATHER GIAMBATTISTA MARTINI.[1] *Italian*]

Most Revered Father and friend!

I have learned through Signor Taiber [Teyber][2] of your Reverence's wish to possess my portrait. Sensible of the honour you pay me, I am all the more grieved that I cannot come in person in the hope of finding a skilled artist there, for I am certain that the pleasure of seeing you would make me more attractive.

H.E. the Count Durazzo,[3] Imperial Ambassador in Venice, who for many years has been my gracious patron wished to have a copy made of the portrait, which was made in Rome on the occasion of my last visit, and he commissioned a young pupil of his to adapt it to my present physiognomy and condition.

Of the compositions, which have been brought to your notice, I think only the *Orpheus* is known there. The others have found a certain amount of approval at our Court and I am now about to leave for Paris with the object of producing the latest of these, the *Iphigénie en Aulide*, at the great Opéra theatre. This is assuredly a bold undertaking and there will be serious obstacles, for we must face up to national prejudices against which reason is of no avail.

If I can be of any service here, you have only to command me. I have to thank H.E. the Ambassador for the opportunity of sending you the portrait, as soon as he returns to Venice. He loves and protects the fine arts and has a special regard for you, even without knowing you personally.

I am with the greatest respect
and friendship
Your Reverence's
most humble and devoted servant
Chevalier Christof Gluck.

Vienna, 26th October 1773.

[1] GIAMBATTISTA MARTINI was born in Bologna on 24th April 1706. After joining the Franciscan Order, he became Kapellmeister at the Church of the Order in Bologna as early as 1725. Four years later he was ordained as a priest. He was considered the leading authority in Italy on the history and theory of music; as he possessed not only an immense fund of knowledge but also a rare goodness of heart, students came to him from all parts of the country. Besides his compositions, his *Storia della Musica* [1757–1781] and *Exemplare ossia saggio fondamentale di contrappunto* [1774–1775] deserve special mention. Martini died at Bologna on 4th October 1784 [cf. G. Gandolfi: *Elogio di Giambattista Martini*, 1913].

[2] By Taiber is probably meant the violinist Franz Teyber [1756–1792], who lent Mozart a violin and a concerto for the feast of Saint Cajetan (letter from Leopold Mozart of 12th August 1773), or his brother, Anton Teyber [1754–1822.] However, Emily Anderson [*Letters of Mozart and His Family*, Vol. I, p. 344], identifies Mozart's Teyber not with Franz but with his elder brother, Anton.

[3] Gluck's *Iphigénie en Aulide* was first produced in Vienna on 30th October 1773.

[TO KING LOUIS XVI.[1] *French*]

[after 10th May 1774]

Sire,

When, following the example of the Greeks, Augustus, the Medicis and Louis XIV encouraged and supported the arts, they had a more important aim in view than that of providing further amusement and pleasure; they regarded that portion of human knowledge as one of the most precious links in the political chain;

they knew that only the arts are capable of making men gentle without corrupting them and of rendering them prone to submission without debasing them.

From the moment you ascended the throne, Sire, you showed that you were moved by the same principles and the same views. While Your Majesty works tirelessly for the betterment and happiness of your subjects, you do not spurn the homage I venture to pay, and, in giving me the first signs of your protection of the arts, you bring happiness and glory to a stranger who yields to no Frenchman in zeal, in appreciation and in devotion to your sacred person.

It is with these sentiments together with the most profound respect

that I am,

Sire,

Your Majesty's very humble and very obedient servant,

Chevalier Gluck.

[1] Louis XVI, grandson of Louis XV, came to the French throne on 10th May 1774. He was guillotined on 21st January 1793.

[Contract with M. Marchand. *French*]

I, the undersigned, acknowledge having given of my own volition, by these presents, the score of my opera *Orpheus et Eurydice* in manuscript to M. Marchand, giving him the power to have it engraved for his own profit, in toto or in part, as he may think fit, on the understanding that no one will trouble him in the gift I have made him, ceding to him all my rights in this work granted by the licence I obtained from the King, which, in the event of any forgery by the merchants [?], I will cede to him, so that he may act in my name; he will be responsible for any expenses he may incur.

Made in Paris, this 10th July 1774

Chevalier Gluck

[To Queen Marie Antoinette.[1] *French*]

[before 2nd August 1774]

Madame,

Of the many benefactions which you have lavished upon me, the most precious in my eyes is that which enables me to remain in the midst of a nation which is all the more worthy to possess you as it is sensible of your great virtues. Honoured with your protection, it is to this advantage that I undoubtedly owe the applause I have received. I have never claimed, as several have seemed desirous of reproaching me, any wish to give the French lessons on their own language nor to prove to them that until now they had no author worthy of their admiration and gratitude. There exist here pieces to which I gave the praise they merit; several of their living authors are worthy of their reputation. I have thought that I might try setting to French words the new type of music which I adopted in my three last Italian operas. I have noted with satisfaction that the accent of nature is the universal language: M. Rousseau employed it with the greatest success in its simple style. His *Devin du village*[2] is a model which no author has yet imitated. I do not know to what extent I have succeeded in mine, but I have Your Majesty's approval, since you permit me to dedicate this work to you; for me that is the most flattering success. The genre I am trying to introduce seems to me to restore to art its original dignity. The music will no longer be confined to the cold, conventional beauties, to which composers have been obliged to adhere.

It is with sentiments of profound respect that I am,
Madame,
Your Majesty's very humble and very obedient servant,
Chevalier Gluck.

[1] MARIE ANTOINETTE was the wife of Louis XVI, a daughter of Maria Theresia, and for a time a pupil of Gluck's in Vienna before her marriage. She did much to promote his music in Paris. She too was guillotined in 1793.

[2] Rousseau's LE DEVIN DU VILLAGE was first produced on 18th October 1752 for the Court at Fontainebleau and was repeated on 1st March 1753 at the Paris Opéra.

[TO COUNT MERCY-ARGENTEAU.[1] *French*]

Paris, 11th August 1774

Excellency!

I cannot find words to convey to Your Excellency the gratitude I owe you for the zeal with which you have so kindly protected my interests. But I do not believe that I could live in Paris on an income of less than 10 to 12 thousand livres, for I must have a carriage for my wife and a decent house; moreover, if I am to settle in Paris and give up my establishment in Vienna, this sum should be allotted to me in a fixed and certain manner, independent of any circumstance, even a possible change of administration at the theatre. I would then give one opera gratis every year, excepting if I should fall ill, and I would also take upon myself to give advice and guidance to any young composers who chose to consult me about their works, in order that a standard of good taste might be set up which would never again be debased. I would endeavour to make the orchestra, as far as possible, more perfect, and would give advice to the singers, and I would do everything in my power to provide the best theatrical productions in Europe. As for titles, I have no ambitions except to be near the King or the Queen, only I must have the necessary authority to remedy certain abuses, which hinder the perfection of our productions. For the rest, I leave everything to the clear-sightedness of Your Excellency, and I am sure that you take my interests as much to heart as I do myself.

I have the honour to be with profound respect

Your Excellency's very humble and very obedient servant,

Chevalier Gluck.

[1] FLORIMOND COUNT MERCY-ARGENTEAU, born 20th April 1727 in Liège, devoted himself from his youth to the diplomatic service, being attached first to the Embassy in Paris, then in Turin, and returning as Austrian Ambassador to Paris, where he was accredited simultaneously with the Marquis de Stainville, but from 1780 onwards he was sole representative. In 1790 he became Statthalter of the Austrian Netherlands. Later he was Ambassador in London, where he died on 25th August 1794 [cf. Comte de Pimodan: *Le Comte F.-C. de Mercy-Argenteau*. Paris, 1911].

[TO COUNT MERCY-ARGENTEAU. *French*]

Paris, 16th August 1774

Your Excellency!

I do not know how I can find words to express my gratitude for what I owe you. Your Excellency has arranged everything most admirably: the subjects will suggest themselves as I produce operas, for in order to form a singing school one must make other arrangements; nevertheless I shall begin giving all my attention to Mlle Rosalie [Levasseur][1] and I hope that she will become quite admirable.

If the Court does not return until the beginning of next month, I would prefer to come to Compiègne, for I would have more time to arrange my affairs in Vienna, but if Your Excellency finds it more suitable that I await the return of the Court, I will remain with pleasure until then, and on this I await your orders; I make so bold as to enquire again of Your Excellency whether I can tell my friends of the favour I have just been granted, or whether I must wait till the affair has been completed with all necessary formalities; I have difficulty in keeping silent, for these arrangements give me all the more pleasure as I will have the prospect of being always in a position to pay my respects to Your Excellency in Paris and from time to time to make some good music together.

I have the honour to be with the most profound respect
Your Excellency's
very humble and very obedient servant,
Chevalier Gluck.

[1] Rosalie Levasseur was born at Valenciennes on 8th October 1749. From 1765 to 1785 she was a popular singer at the Grand Opéra in Paris and won particular acclaim in parts she played in Gluck's operas. For a time she was Count Mercy-Argenteau's mistress. While in Paris in 1777 Gluck lived in her house in the rue des Fossoyeurs. After Gluck's death she lived with his widow in Vienna till she too died and Mlle Levasseur returned to Paris. She died at Neuwied on 6th May 1826.

[Johann Gottfried Herder[1] to Gluck. *German*]

Highly esteemed and honoured friend, you will find enclosed a musical drama,[2] which at first reading will doubtless make an unfavourable impression on you. So with your kind permission I will explain something of the purpose of it.

The great conflict between poetry and music, which has created such a gulf between these two arts, is the question at issue: which of the two should serve? which rule? The musician wishes his art to rule, likewise the poet, and so they frequently stand in each other's way. Each wishes to provide a beautiful whole and often overlooks that he must only provide a part, in order that the whole may emerge in the effect achieved by both.

Could it be that the musician would give way and merely follow and that this is your purpose in your musical creations?

Or might it be the poet who gave way, who merely gave indications and outlines, who, as it were, merely interpolated words and clarified the otherwise vague sensations created by music?—that is the object of this experiment. He should only be what the inscription is to a painting or sculpture, an explanation, a guide to lead the stream of music by means of the words he intersperses.

Hence, honoured friend, the disjointed effect, the effect of isolation and barrenness in reading. It should not be read but heard. The words should merely lend animation to the emotional framework of the music, which should speak, act, move, continue speaking, and should follow only the spirit and general outline of the poet.

But to which composer should the Muse now turn? Not to one for whom the old law of music—that everything should be made in the round—is like an arm-chair in which he periodically rocks himself to sleep. To him who fills each scene with action, feeling and ideas and makes it speak, as when Portia and Brutus must pour out their souls in speech—in short, to Gluck.

It would be pointless for me to say what effect was produced on me by the few pieces I have heard and in which I came to know your great simplicity. Unfortunately I know only a few of them. But if, noble friend, a kindly spirit moved you in reading to look at this poem, set it in its action, if only in certain scenes and passages—I know what I am asking! What I wish! But I will not ask. A happy or unhappy demon, who is present when the piece is read, must decide.

After all, Plutarch's life of Brutus and, for instance, Shakespeare's *Julius Caesar* contain everything on which this drama is a mere commentary in musical hieroglyphics.

With immeasurable respect,
Herder
Schaumb.-Lippscher Consistorial-Rath.

Buckeburg 5 Nov. 1774.

[1] JOHANN GOTTFRIED HERDER was born at Mohrungen in East Prussia on 25th August 1744. In 1762 he went to Königsberg to study medicine but soon changed to theology. In 1764 he became a teacher at the German Cathedral School in Riga, where, in the following year, he became preacher at the Vorstadt-Kirche. In 1769 he travelled by way of Nantes to Paris and made further journeys in the years that followed. From 1771 to 1776 he was parson at Bückeburg. In 1776, at Goethe's instigation, he was called to Weimar as General Superintendent and he died there on 18th December 1803.

[2] The opera manuscript sent to Gluck was called *Brutus*. It had already been produced at Bückeburg on 27th February 1774, set to music by Johann Christoph Friedrich Bach (1732–1795). As Herder was not satisfied with this composition he turned to Gluck, whose answer has not been traced, and to Johann Fr. Reichardt, who had written on Herder's work with great enthusiasm but was not in favour of setting it to music a second time [cf. Günther: *J. G. Herder's Stellung zur Musik*, 1903, pp. 52ff.; G. Schünemann: 'J. Chr. Fr. Bach', *Bach-Jahrbuch*, 1914, pp. 97ff.].

[PRO MEMORIA ON GLUCK'S AGREEMENTS WITH THE ACADÉMIE ROYALE DE MUSIQUE. *French*]

[1775]

Pro Memoria

FIRST ARTICLE

The Chevalier Gluck has received from the Académie Royale de Musique three thousand livres for his Opera *Iphigénie*, and three thousand which he has received on behalf of the poet; he has been promised a gratification, which he hopes to receive, all the more as his journey here and back, with the expenses he has incurred during his stay in Paris, amounts to at least six thousand livres.

Second Article

It has been agreed that for all the operas he will make, he will have a sum of six thousand livres; he is under no obligation to indemnify the poet, but if the poet supplies his poem *gratis*, he will still have only six thousand livres for his work and he will ask nothing for the words; thus in the case of the *Siège de Cythère*, the Académie Royale will be responsible for indemnifying the poet, as was done for the opera *Orpheus*.

Third Article

As until now he has fulfilled his obligations against the fee of six thousand livres which had been granted him, he wishes to know if he can draw *pro rata* upon the sum due to him since the 8th of October of the year 1774, in the event of his contract not being renewed.

Fourth Article

If the Académie retains him on contract, he is obliged to compose a further three operas, which are: *Alceste, Electra, Iphigénie en Tauride*, or in place of one of these an opera in the style of the *Siège de Cythère*, to which number his promise is confined, as his age and his health do not permit him to promise more, and in this latter case he would come in the spring of the year 1776 to give two operas simultaneously, one during the summer for the 'doubles',* the other, which would be *Alceste*, for the height of the season, and he would thus be in a position to prepare the actors for the roles which they will play; he believes, furthermore, that when he has completed the six operas which he is to provide, the revolution in music will have been accomplished.

As he is on the point of leaving for Vienna, he begs to be informed without delay what, with reference to these articles, is planned for him.

* 'doubles' = high holidays.—Trs.

[Power of Attorney for Franz Kruthoffer. *French*]

In the presence of the undersigned royal Counsellors, notaries at the Chatelet in Paris, M[re] Christophe de Gluck, Chevalier of the Holy Empire, resident in Paris, rue Villedot, has made and constituted

CHRISTOPH MARTIN WIELAND
Engraving by J. F. Bause from the painting by May

B. J. SAURIN
Engraving by R. d'Elvaux from a pastel by Robineau (1788)

FÜRST WENZEL ANTON KAUNITZ-RITTBERG
Engraving by J. G. Haid (1774) from a painting by Johann Nepomuk Steiner

as his Attorney, Sr Francois Kruthoffer, Secretary to H.E. the Ambassador of their Imperial and Royal Majesties, giving him the authority to negotiate, on his behalf and in his name, with such persons as he shall think fit and to sell and surrender to them at such prices and charges and on such conditions as he may find the most advantageous:

1. The entire score of the opera entitled *The Siege of Cythera*, of which the aforementioned constituent is the author, with all appurtenances;

2. The engraving plates of the score of the opera entitled *Iphigénie*, of which the aforementioned constituent is also the author, as well as the plates of the arias extracted from the same opera, altogether everything that may form part of it; in consequence, to pass and sign all documents concerning any such sale or cession, to agree upon a price for the said objects, to receive all or part of the said price, to grant and agree upon all question of duration or delays, to act always as the assenting party, to be responsible for surrendering all the objects included in the aforementioned sales, to give receipts for all money paid and all valid expenses, and generally, by virtue of all the aforesaid, to do everything that the said attorney may require of him, even if not provided in this document, providing the constituent gives his full agreement and will supply acts of ratification on demand, obliging. . . .

Made and passed at Paris, in the office, in the year one thousand seven hundred and seventy-five, the ninth March, and signed by

[autograph signatures:]

[In the margin, facing the last lines:] Chevalier Gluck

Fourcaut Deherain

Sealed on the stated day and year.

[Agreement with Antoine de Peters. *French*]

We, the undersigned, Antoine de Peters, on the one hand, and François Kruthoffer, on behalf of and acting as attorney for M. le Chevalier Gluck as agreed in the presence of Me Dehairin, notary in Paris, on the 9th of this present month of March, on the other hand,

Do recognise and are agreed

1. That the payment acknowledged to have been made by the said Sr de Peters to the said S[r] Kruthoffer of the sum of five thousand pounds as the price of the sale and the transfer, negotiated this day before the said M[e] Dehairin, of the operas and rights of the said S[r] Chevalier Gluck, consists of two bills from the said S[r] de Peters in favour of the said S[r] Chevalier Gluck, the one for two thousand pounds

payable in September next, and the other for three thousand pounds payable in April seventeen hundred and seventy-six, the value received in specie;

2. That the said Sr de Peters will in no way embarrass the S[r] le Marchand with regard to the engraving he has made of a *Book of Airs* containing arias taken from the Opera *Iphigénie* arranged for two violins or flutes, but on condition that there are no words under the aforesaid arias.

Made in duplicate between us at Paris this 28th March seventeen hundred and seventy-five.

De Peters F. Kruthoffer

[Agreement with Antoine de Peters. *French*]

Before the undersigned Royal Counsellors, notaries at the Chatelet in Paris, appeared Sieur François Kruthoffer, Secretary to H.E. the Ambassador of their Imperial and Royal Majesties, residing in Paris at the hotel of H.E. the Ambassador, rue de Vaugirard in the parish of Saint Sulpice, in the name of and as attorney for M. Christophe de Gluck, Chevalier of the Holy Empire, especially authorized to act with regard to these presents, this authority having been vested in him before M[e] Deherain, one of the undersigned notaries, and his colleague on the 9th of the present month of March, the original certificate of this power of attorney as represented by the aforesaid S[r] Kruthoffer is attached herewith after having been signed and found genuine by the undersigned notaries:

The same has by these presents sold, ceded and transferred and promised to guarantee against any troubles and hindrances in general and of any kind to M. Antoine de Peters, Esquire, Painter to the King of Denmark and His Serene Highness Monseigneur the Prince Charles of Lorraine, residing in Paris, rue du Hazard in the parish of St. Roch, and accepting, as vendee for him and his trustees,

1. the complete score of the opera entitled *The Siege of Cythera*, of which the said Sr de Gluck is the author, with all appurtenances,

2. the complete score of the opera entitled *Iphigénie*, of which the Sr de Gluck is also the author,

3. the engraved plates both of the said opera *Iphigénie* and of the arietta and the separate arias which were added, altogether everything that might form part of the said two operas, without excepting, reserving or retaining anything.

4. Finally the right held by the said Sr de Gluck to have engraved and printed the said operas and appurtenances by virtue of the licence acquired by him in the Grand Chancellery of France for the engraving and printing of all his musical works without exception, completed or still to be completed;

In order that the said S[r] de Peters may enjoy, make and dispose of all the said objects and appurtenances in complete propriety and as if they were his own as from this date, the said S[r] Kruthoffer has vested in the said S[r] de Peters, with the aforementioned guarantee, all the rights of the said S[r] de Gluck.

This sale is herewith made against the sum of five thousand pounds [livres], which the said Sr Kruthoffer acknowledges having received from the said Sr de Peters in current coins of the realm, of which he acquits and discharges him.

The said Sr de Peters, for his part, acknowledges that the said Sr Kruthoffer has surrendered to him all the engraved plates, both of the opera *Iphigénie* and of the ariettas and other separate arias deriving from the opera, of which he acquits and discharges him.

As regards the score of the opera entitled *The Siege of Cythera*, the said Sr Kruthoffer promises to deliver it or have it delivered to the said Sr de Peters within one month from this day.

The said Sr Kruthoffer promises furthermore to deliver within eight days to the said Sr de Peters the original in parchment of the licence granted to the said Sr de Gluck for the engraving and printing of his works, or a collated copy of the same and of its registration at the chamber of advocates.

And for the execution of these presents, the parties have chosen the addresses stated below, in which places, notwithstanding . . . promising . . . obliging . . . renouncing. . . .

Made and approved in Paris, in the office in the year seventeen hundred and seventy-five, the twenty-eighth March, and signed by

[Autograph signatures:]

F. Kruthoffer De Peters

Fourcault Deherain.

[FRANZ KRUTHOFFER TO GLUCK. *French*]

To the Chevalier Gluck in Vienna, Paris, 31st March 1775.

A few days after your departure I decided, Monsieur, to conclude with M. de Peters the final arrangement concerning your operas *Iphigénie* and the *Siège de Cythère*, by virtue of the power you have given me in this respect. Before taking the necessary steps I pledged M. de Peters to arrange with S. Le Marchand[1] all that might be necessary on the one hand to expedite his business and on the other to replace the short airs for two violins which had been taken from *Iphigénie*. M. de Peters accepted this with the best will in the world, but M. Le Marchand did not think fit to reply. I, for my part, being sure of M. de Peters's way of thinking and relying on your assurance to me that you have given nothing in writing to the aforementioned Sr. Md. [Marchand] which might authorize him to take any other airs from the opera *Iphigénie* than those engraved last year for two violins, and not wishing to lose any more time in completing this affair, I hastened to submit the contract with M. de Peters to a Notary, by which contract I transfer to him in your name the full and entire ownership of the said operas on the conditions laid down between you and him, and with one further condition in a separate document under private seal that the aforesaid M. de Peters would not trouble the aforesaid Sr. Marchand in the sale of his volume of airs for two violins.

This operation completed, it only remained to transfer the copyright of the opera *Iphigénie*, which you have partially ceded to Sr. le Marchand. I urged him to proceed accordingly. He agreed. But I learn to my surprise that he had written permission from you and bearing your signature, which authorizes him to extract from *Iphigénie* such airs as he might consider suitable, other than those mentioned above. I cannot conceal from you, Monsieur, that this assertion, which is contrary to what you told me, came as a shock to me. I was reluctant to attach any credence to it but was obliged to give way on seeing the document in question. It is dated the 6th March last and is signed and approved by you.

I am bound to tell you frankly that the facility with which you thus commit yourself in writing can in general harm your interests; and in the present instance it can be a source of embarrassment to me. On your testimony that no such permission had been given, I drew up the contract with M. de Peters, making but one reservation to cover the *Book of Airs*, on which the stipulations are quite precise, and, after all this trouble has been taken, S. Md. [Marchand] comes forward with a written permission, the existence of which had not even been suspected, and announces in the public papers a new *Book of Airs* taken from this opera and arranged for the harpsichord. You will agree, Mr., that an incident of this kind is designed to displease persons who conduct their affairs without reservation and without obliquity. The debit of this new *Book of Airs* must do an injustice to the present proprietor, the more so as he had planned to have a similar suite of ariettas taken from it and he would be legally justified in suing you for appropriate compensation. But judge now the honesty of M. de Peters and the conduct of Sr. le Md. [Marchand]—M. de Peters out of regard for you, Monsieur, was willing to let this article pass and extend your permission to the new Book, his sole conditions being 1) to substitute his permission for yours, it being just that an extract from any work whatsoever appearing at a time when one-third of it is in private ownership, permission with regard to it must emanate from the last owner, 2) that M. de Peters may in his turn take airs from the opera *Orfeo* should he wish to do so.

These conditions, the fairness of which will not escape you, Monsieur, were rejected by M. Marchand. As his refusal could have no solid foundation, one can only ascribe such strange conduct to recrimination or a leaning to chicanery. This is how things stand at present. I do not guarantee that the goodwill of M. de Peters will be maintained indefinitely; if M. le Md. suffers any inconvenience, he must ascribe it to his own obstinacy,* and you are too just-minded not to see at the first glance that M. de Peters and I have done all that honesty and integrity could do to carry out your wishes.

There remains one final clause which I must bring to your attention: Under the contract the copyright of *Iphigénie* has had to be given to M. de Peters. As this copyright was allegedly ceded to Sr. le Md. in a private agreement which is in your hands, it is essential that I have this private agreement in my possession either to return to Sr. le Md., in the event of the said copyright being restored to M. de Peters, or as a guarantee if the other, as a result of his perpetual inconstancy, were unwilling to accede to this partial performance. I beg you therefore to send me this counterletter without delay. I have reason to believe that le Md. has already asked you for it directly. Take good care not to give it to him, for this would merely render still more confused a transaction which, instead of causing me a thousand fruitless *démarches* and unpleasant disputes, would have been simple and would have been terminated in one day, had one not been compelled to deal with people who deliberately bandage their eyes in order not to see the light.

However disagreeable and unsettling this affair may be, I am none the less anxious to acquit myself well in it in order to justify the friendship and confidence with which you honour me. I beg you to make use of my services in any circumstances in which I might be of use to you in any way; I would respond with a zeal equal to the complete and sincere attachment with which I have the honour to be. . . .

[1]LE MARCHAND was Hautbois des Mousquetaries et de l'Académie Royale de Musique. He started as a music publisher around 1768 in the Cloître St Thomas du Louvre aux 3 Célèbres, moved in 1774 to the rue Fromenteau

au maison du Sellier and in 1778 to the rue de Grenelle St Honoré. About 1783 his business was taken over by Des Lauriers.

* The text has 'ententement'. 'Entêtement' would make good sense.—Trs.

[To Franz Kruthoffer.[1] *German*]

[added in Kruthoffer's handwriting:
Replied Paris 17 May 1775]

Vienna, 15th April 1775

Most esteemed friend!

At the time when I asked you to conclude my affairs with Mr Peters, I had not even dreamt that you would have so much worry on my account. This distresses me so much that I would rather lose all the money than see you further involved in such inconvenience. Mr Marchand has written to me and complains as usual of the great injustice that has been done to him. I am sending you my reply, which, when you have read it, please forward to him. Should he persist in his obstinacy, then, if you think fit, to meet the loss Mr Peters might be persuaded to bear part of the advance of five thousand livres, for I am absolutely determined that you should have no further trouble in the future on my account. I only wish that I could make good what has happened so far. Mr Marchand's declaration which you demand from me does not exist; I did not ask for it, because I could not suspect that he would ever be capable of becoming a rogue. You teach me, however, to be more careful in future with such people. The matter is known to everyone and he can be confronted with enough witnesses, if it should be necessary. I beg you to give my respects to Mr Peters and to warn him that perhaps the last Allegro in the overture will be changed, so that he should not have it engraved till it is decided whether it remains.[2] My wife and Nanette[3] send you their warmest regards, and also to Mr de Blumendorff.[4] Write us something cheerful, for here in Vienna the climate is very wild and melancholy. We have a hard frost and snow and envy you the fine weather in Paris. Adieu! Do not tire of my friendship, for you are not prodigal with it. I will always remember the troubles I have caused you and will endeavour by my appreciation to convince you that I am,

Most esteemed friend,

Your most devoted servant,

Chevalier Gluck.

PS. Let me know if you have found or should find a good way out with those 4 [Quartets] by Mr. Aspelmayer[5] which I submitted to you.

[Address] To Monsieur
Monsieur Kruthoffer
Secretaire de son Excellence
Mr: L'Ambassadeur Impériale á Paris

[1] FRANZ KRUTHOFFER, according to Georg Kinsky, was born around 1740 in Heidelberg, where his father was a forestry official of Prince Karl Theodor. After completing his law studies, he took up the career of private secretary. While still a young man he became Secretary to the Prince of Hessen-Rheinfels in Paris, then from 1768 onwards Secretary to the the Imperial Ambassador. In 1794, during the French Revolution, the Ambassador's palace was requisitioned by the French War Ministry and Kruthoffer was arrested. He spent a year in prison. After the Imperial Embassy was reopened in Paris, Kruthoffer entered Austrian Government service. He appears to have left the service about 1805. As far as we know, he died some time after 1815.

The highly illuminating letters reproduced here are all that remain concerning the affairs with Mr Peters and the publisher Marchand.

[2] 'THE LAST ALLEGRO IN THE OVERTURE' refers to the engraving prepared by Peters of the new version of the ballet-opera *Cythère assiégée*, which was first produced on 1st August 1775. The composer, who was seriously ill in Vienna, was not present. The printed score does not contain the overture, a revised version of the *Sinfonia to Paride ed Elena* of 1770; it was added in orchestral parts (cf. C. Hopkinson: *A Bibliography of the Works of Gluck*. London, 1959).

[3] MARIANNE NANETTE GLUCK was the daughter of Gluck's sister, Maria Anna Rosine (born 2nd April 1718 Reichstadt), who from 1758 to 1761 was married to a Captain of Horse in the Hungarian Hussars, Claudius Hedler. Nanette was born in 1759 (or 1760) and died of smallpox in Vienna on 22nd April 1776, the day before the *première* of *Alceste* in Paris, which Gluck, her uncle and father-by-adoption, was attending. As we know from contemporary accounts, she had an excellent soprano voice and had been trained by the famous castrato, Giuseppe Millico (1737–1802).

[4] FRANZ VON BLUMENDORF was employed in the Chancery of the Austrian Embassy in Paris from 1770 until 1785, when he succeeded Secretary to the Embassy Georg von Barre as *Chargé d'Affaires*, a post he held till the Embassy closed down in 1792. Finally in 1801 he became Commercial Counsellor at the Imperial Chancery in Vienna and in 1817 *Archivar der älteren Akten* (Archivist of older documents). He died at the age of eighty-eight on 13th July 1826 in Vienna.

[5] FRANZ ASPELMAYER (born 1721, died 21st May 1786) was a Court Musician and composer of ballet with the Italian Opera in Vienna. Hugo Riemann describes him as 'one of the first Viennese composers, who followed in the footsteps of the Mannheimer school in the sphere of orchestral and chamber music'. The postscript probably refers to the 'Six quartets', opus 6, which

appeared in Paris and in the publication of which Gluck was to act as intermediary.

[To the publisher Le Marchand. *French*]

Vienna, 15th April 1775

I am distressed to learn of the difficulties that you have had in connection with your affair, as I am convinced that Mr Kruthoffer and M. Peters have always been most honest and reasonable and I regret that you have not accepted with a good grace the arrangements they wished to make with you. I do not wish to reach any decision, for I have seen a letter in which complaints are again made against you. I cannot believe that your feelings of friendship for me would allow you to be the cause of annulling the contract I made with M. de Peters, so I beg you *not* to place any obstacle in the way of the execution of my agreement with M. Peters. I have been told that I gave you written authorisation to borrow airs from the opera *Iphigénie* other than those for two violins which were engraved last year. Having sold my *Iphigénie*, I cannot in all honesty give such an authorization. So if you have anything in writing from me—which I do not recollect, or the contents of which I have not understood, or which I wrote at a moment when I was preoccupied with something else—I beg you to return this document to M. Peters, for you would not wish me to pass in Paris for a dishonest man. Thank heaven, I am not yet dead, and I will still have many opportunities of being of use to you and of compensating you. If you attach any value to our friendship, then see to it that I hear no more talk of quarrels and that everything is settled. I need my head for my work, for, between ourselves, I will arrive next year with three operas instead of the two I had promised you. You can see that I have no time for disputes and that I must work like a dog. Be sensible, for I have the means whereby, on my arrival, you can make a reasonable profit. My wife and daughter embrace you——. Send me news of the operas.

I am always,

Your very dutiful friend and servant,

Chevalier Gluck.

PS. I hope to hear without delay that your affairs with M. de Peters have been arranged amicably. Do your utmost to settle this affair once and for all.

[ANTOINE DE PETERS TO FRANZ KRUTHOFFER. *French*]

Monsieur,

I sent a message to Mr Berton[1] this morning to enquire of him when I might have the score of the opera *Siège de Cythère*. He replied that he knew nothing of it and that, moreover, M. Gluck had sold this piece to the Royal Academy of Music. I must confess, Monsieur, that all this is new to me. I only know that M. Gluck, before leaving for Vienna, charged you to procure it, and I therefore beg you to let me have this work, otherwise, as you will readily understand, I cannot make the full payment agreed between you and M. Gluck. Furthermore, if my *Siège de Cythère* is not in my hands in time to be engraved for the first performance, I shall demand the compensation which is or will be due to me. Have the goodness, therefore, to see that my expectations are satisfied. For the rest, I will bow to circumstance and will send for the copyist in the hope that M. Berton will be able to lend me one act of the *Siège de Cythère*.

I have the honour to await your reply and to be,

Monsieur,

Your very humble servant

A. de Peters

21st April 1775

[1] PIERRE-MONTAN BERTON, born on 7th January 1727 in Maubert-Fontaine near Rocroy (Ardennes), received his musical training in the Cathedral School at Senlis and in Paris, where he was engaged at the age of eighteen as a tenor at the Royal Academy of Music. He then sang and conducted in Bordeaux, returning in 1755 to Paris, where he became a Master of Music. From 1761 onwards he was Director of Opera in Paris, first with Trial (died 1771), then with Antoine d'Auvergne (1713–1797), till de Vismes took over from him in 1778. Berton, who was appointed General Administrator of the Opéra in 1775, died on 14th May 1780 in Paris. He wrote, *inter alia*, the *divertissements* for Gluck's *Cythère assiégée*, which were included in the performances in Paris but not in the printed score. The 'final *divertissement*', which in the score follows the 'final chorus' (Quartet and chorus: 'Içi mille plaisirs'), consists of ballet movements and other pieces taken from earlier works by Gluck—*Semiramide, Il re pastore, Iphigénie en Aulide, Paride ed Elena*. Page 192 of the printed score carries the following footnote: 'All the *divertissements* from the beginning of the march to the end of the score were composed by M. Gluck, and the *divertissements* played in the Opera House were composed by Mr. Berton.' The *Mémoires secrètes* contain this observation (VIII, 141): ' . . . as M. Gluck found it necessary to leave for Vienna earlier than he had expected, he did not have time to write the music for the last act; he was, therefore, obliged to engage Sr. Berton to complete the work for him; hence there is, of necessity, an appreciable disparity between the two compositions'.

[FRANZ KRUTHOFFER TO M. LE MARCHAND. *French*]

[30th April 1775]

M. le Ch^r^. Gluck has just sent me the attached letter in which he explains his wishes concerning what remains of his agreement with M. de Peters: it will make clear to you, Monsieur, that my sentiments and the *démarches* which I made are in complete conformity with M. le Chr. Gluck's wishes. I was too fully acquainted with them to be in ignorance, and, now that he himself has confirmed them, I have reason to think that you will no longer ascribe to partiality what in principle was founded on justice. Consider, Monsieur, how you can fulfil the wishes of M. le Chr. Gluck. My intervention will perhaps not be agreeable to you, in which case you can deal directly with M. de Peters, who has been advised that you are to remit to him the document in question, on which I have no comment to make, in view of the fact that M. le Chr. Gluck has already dealt with this in the letter he wrote you. I am convinced that you attach too much value to M. Gluck's friendship not to settle this matter as soon as possible, which should not have dragged on so long: for myself I will be greatly obliged to you.

I have the honour to be—

[Kruthoffer]

[TO ABBÉ ARNAUD.[1] *French*]

Vienna, 12th May 1775

Monsieur and very dear friend!

We are all astonished that you have not replied to my daughter's letter. Is it possible that Grétri[2] could have taken my place in your affections? Is it necessary to forget one person in loving another? You give so much of your time to your acquaintances and friends that all make claims on you; do likewise with your affections so that I shall always be able to keep a small place in your heart and I shall await before long a few kindly words from you, such as we have come to expect of you and give me so much pleasure. If you do not write to me soon, I promise to take my revenge when I arrive in Paris, for I will not let you hear a single bar of my *Alceste*, on which I am working at present. In this respect I beg you to press M. Comte or Marquis, who intended to do *l'Olimpiade*,[3] to send me the poem as soon as possible, for, if it is well done, I would begin at once to set it to music, and tell me, I beg you, whether I can count on him or not. My wife and my daughter send you a thousand tender regards, and I remain always

Your very humble and very obedient friend and servant

Chevalier Gluck.

PS. I beg you to let me know whether M. de Plessi will finish my portrait[4] for the Salon, or not.

[1] FRANÇOIS ARNAUD was born on 27th June 1721 in Aubignau near Carpentras. In 1752 he came to Paris, in 1765 became Abbot of Grandchamps and later Reader and Librarian to the Count of Provence and a member of the

Academy. In the dispute between the Gluckists and the Piccinnists he took the side of Gluck. Arnaud, who together with Suard published the *Variétés littéraries* (1768–1769), died on 2nd December 1784 in Paris [cf. E. de Bricqueville: *L'Abbé Arnaud et la réforme de l'opéra au XVIIIe siècle*, 1881].

[2] ANDRÉ ERNESTE MODESTE GRÉTRY was born on 8th February 1742 in Liège. After a superficial study of music in his native town and in Rome, he went, on Voltaire's advice, to Paris, where he wrote some epoch-making comic operas. Apart from a brief period as Inspector at the newly-founded Conservatoire, he held no official positions, as he wished to devote all his time to creative work. In 1802 Napoleon appointed him a Chevalier of the Légion d'Honneur, and, as he had lost his fortune during the Revolution, granted him a pension. Of his many operas the most successful were *Barbe bleue* and *Richard Cœur de Lion*. Grétry died on 24th September 1813 at Montmorney near Paris [cf. H. de Curzon: *Grétry*, 1909; E. Closson: *A.-M. Grétry*, 1920].

[3] The text-book of the OLYMPIADE mentioned here is presumably the one which Nicolas Etienne Framéry produced from a libretto by Pietro Metastasio. The opera had its *première* with music by Antonio Sacchini on 2nd October 1777 in the Comédie italienne in Paris.

[4] The painting by JOSEPH DUPLESSIS, the French Court Painter, was completed. It is a half-length portrait, which shows Gluck seated at the piano. The original hangs in the Belvedere Gallery in Vienna, to which it was left by Gluck's widow in her will (see frontispiece).

[TO FRANZ KRUTHOFFER. *German*]

[In Kruthoffer's handwriting:
Replied Paris, 23rd June 1775]

Vienna, 30th May 1775

Most esteemed friend!

I have received no answer to my letter to Mr Marchand; should I receive one, I will follow your advice completely. If you think fit, have a word with the Bailly du Roullet about this matter; perhaps he can bring Mr Marchand to see reason. In that case I will advise him in advance, for I am anxious that the matter should be settled once and for all. If you or Mr Peters, to whom I send my respects, should wish a theatre ticket at any time, then please address yourself to the Bailly du Roullet, to whom I will write accordingly. I have written to Mr Berton that he is to transmit to Mr Peters the alteration in the Overture, in the event of its being produced. As far as the final divertissement is concerned, I deliberately omitted to make one, because it is an *hors d'œuvre* and my piece concludes with the final chorus. Should Mr Peters, however, attach importance to introducing something of the kind, then I will ask Mr Berton to try to work something out, although I believe the piece will be strong and long enough as it stands, without incurring further expense. My regards to H. v. Blumendorff and Mr [Joseph] Kohaut.[1] Please tell him from me that I will write to him as soon as possible. If you see Mr La Motte,[2] tell him to write to his mother, if he does not wish her to die.

I remain,
Most esteemed friend,
Your most obedient servant,
Chevalier Gluck.

PS. Please let me have some news of the theatre.

[Address:]

To Monsieur
Monsieur de Kruthoffer,
à
Paris

[1] JOSEPH KOHAUT, born around 1736 in Bohemia, was a brother of Karl Kohaut (cf. p. 68), who was an operatic composer in Paris and described himself as 'Ordinaire de la Musique de S.A.S. Monseigneur le Prince de Conty'. Three trios by him for harpsichord, violin and bass-viol (published by Gerardin) appeared in 1767. He died about 1793 in Paris.

[2] FRANZ LA MOTTE (Lamotte), born 1751 in Vienna (?), died 1781 in Holland, was a violin virtuoso who was admired, amongst others, by Mozart. He made very successful appearances in Vienna, from 1769 onwards in Paris and in 1776 in London.

[TO FRIEDRICH GOTTLIEB KLOPSTOCK. *German*]

Vienna, 24th June 1775

I hope you have received the arias as requested from the Graf von Cobentzl [Kobenzl],[1] which I sent on this occasion to you in order to save the cost of postage. I was compelled to leave out the annotations because I found it impossible to express myself as I wished. I think you would find it equally difficult if you had to inform someone by letter how and with what kind of expression he should declaim your *Messiah*. All this is a question of feeling and is not easy to explain, as you know better than I. Although I am doing the spade-work, I have not thus far been able to act, for hardly had I arrived in Vienna when the Emperor left and he has not yet returned. Moreover one must still observe the regulation quarter of an hour if one is to achieve anything. At large Courts there is seldom occasion to settle anything worthwhile. I hear, however, that an Academy of Fine Sciences is to be established here and that the income from its papers and almanacs is to form part of the fund to meet the costs. When I am more fully informed of the affair, I will not fail to report everything to you. Meanwhile love me a little until such time as I am again so happy as to see you. My wife and daughter send you their compliments and are happy to have news of you.

I remain,
Your most devoted
Gluck.
from Vienna.

[Address:]
To Monsieur
Monsieur Klopstock
à
Hamburg
in der Konigsstrasse

[1] JOHANN LUDWIG JOSEPH GRAF VON KOBENZL (1753–1809) was Austrian Ambassador in Copenhagen, later in Berlin and St Petersburg. From 1801 to 1805, as Court and State Chancellor, he was virtually the Director of the Austrian monarchy.

[TO BAILLI DU ROULLET.[1] *French*]

Vienna, 1st July 1775

This is a letter in three acts; you will find it somewhat vulgar but I am forgetting fine manners and speaking only to a friend, to whom I am at least as attached as to my wife.

Act I. Siège de Cythère

To begin with, I think Mr Berton is something of a wretch, because he has made no reply to two letters I have written to him, and, as he has been imprudent enough to present *Orphée* again on the stage, I can only believe that he cares little whether my works are well or badly produced. I have even very little hope that the *Siège de Cythère* [the real title of the opera was *La Cythère assiégée*] will give any pleasure, particularly if the end of the second act is not produced with great precision and if the actors and the choirs do not respond to it warmly. If you see that the work is being spoiled, I beg you, together with the Ambassador, to see that it is removed from the theatre and I will then present it myself when I arrive in Paris. Then we shall see how it should be produced.

Act II. The Opera buffa or Rewarded Loyalty[2]

You tell me that the author is a poor devil who must be paid. So be it. But one must arrange a price with him, as, according to my contract, I receive only 6,000 livres for the opera, assuming that the poetry belongs to me. You can come to some agreement with Mr Berton on this. Moreover, this is an opera which should only be presented every Thursday and by the second cast; although the work will be weaker than the other operas, it will have its merits on the day on which it is given and for the actors who must perform it. But tell the author that he must not forget to introduce choruses only where the situation permits.

Act III. Alceste

In the fifth scene of the first act I had removed the second verse of Alceste's monologue: 'Voilà donc le secours que j'attendais de vous'; it should be restored as in the original. The divertissement in the second act should not, I think, be too long, otherwise it will be out of proportion to the rest of the opera, and I also think that the dance, during the choruses, must be general and very gay, not a *pas de deux* or a solo, because I believe that only gaiety must predominate, and any other dance not of a general nature would spoil the situation. *I wish your opinion on this point.*

I am delighted that you find my arrangement to your taste, but I do not find your dénouement at the end of the third act a very happy one. It would be suitable for an opera by Chabanon,[3] Marmontel,[4] or the Chevalier Sain[t] Mar[d],[5] but it is no good for a masterpiece like *Alceste*. What the devil do you think Apollo is doing here with the arts? They are only in place in his company on Mount Parnassus; here interest in the catastrophe is merely distracted. Suddenly, like a flash of lightning, a dénouement occurred to me which I find infinitely better and which will set the seal on the beauty of your work. Here it is: Apollo: 'Your misfortunes have moved the gods, and Fate, in answer to your pleas, consents to revoke its harsh commands. Go and console your subjects, who are mourning the loss of Alceste, etc. etc., and live happily from now on.' *Apollo withdraws and Admetos and Alceste sing a couple of verses together expressing their gratitude to him.* Last scene: a large room or an illuminated open space, the chorus and the dancers grouped in attitudes of great sadness. *The people still believe that Alceste is dead and know nothing of what is happening in the wood.* The children are surrounded by the dancers, on whom they gaze sadly. *Evander [Evandros] in a duet with a leader of the chorus says:* 'What will become of us? Alceste no longer lives! Admetos has met a dreadful fate! I tremble . . .' The other: 'I am turned to ice! Terror and horror will bring consolation!' (Both: 'What unhappy wretches we are! Who can help us?') The chorus in a long verse: 'Weep, Oh native land, Oh Thessaly! Alceste is dead'. A few verses of lamentation are exchanged between the leader of the chorus and Evandre, then the choir again: 'Weep, Oh native land!', etc., etc., as in the Italian original. After this whole scene, Admetos and Alceste appear.

All this must be said with surprise and urgency.
Admetos: Oh, my friends.
Alceste to his children—Oh, my children. (They run up to them.)
Chorus: Heaven.
(Admetos: Our sorrows are at an end.)
Alceste (to the children): At last I see you again.
Chorus: Oh, unexpected happiness! Oh, eternal power!
Admetos: Disperse the clouds of sadness; be joyful and let us bless the gods for their sublime goodness.

Alceste and Admetos sing a few verses together, then the whole chorus as I have already indicated. Thereafter only a chaconne as dance. And that is the end, for, after having heard the opera, the public could not possibly appreciate anything further. People wanted to hear or see nothing after *Iphigénie*, and this is something quite different! I myself become almost mad when I go through it all. One's nerves are strained for too long a time and one's attention is held from the first word to the last. This opera is a cask of frozen wine, the spirit of which has withdrawn to the centre; it is truly exquisite but with too much body to be drunk in any quantity. I pity the poet and the musician who tried to create a second opera of the same kind!

The first act only lasts forty minutes, the third, up to the arrival of Apollo, twenty minutes, so *Alceste* will never be a winter opera. I am well content with this. We will give it soon after my arrival, otherwise, if I had to wait longer, I would go mad. For a month now it has given me no sleep; my wife is in despair; it seems to me that I have a hive of bees constantly buzzing in my head. Believe me, these types of opera are very vicious; I am now beginning to understand the shrewdness of Quinault[6] and Calzabigi in filling their works with secondary characters, thus enabling the spectator to relax. Such an opera is not enjoyable entertainment but a very serious occupation for anyone who hears it.

As soon as you hear any news, you will pass it on. In doing *Iphigénie en Tauride*, be guided by my observations. Do not press anyone else to write operas for me, for I have already decided on my third, which I will bring with me to Paris. I will not tell you the subject yet, because you might dissuade me. I feel that you have too much power over my mind and I will only tell you the subject when I am too far advanced to be able to turn back. I believe . . ."

[1] FRANCOIS LOUIS GAUD LEBLOND BAILLI DU ROULLET was born in Normanville (Eure) in 1716. He became an officer in the Guards and later a Commander of the Order of Malta. His main works were the libretti of *Iphigénie en Aulide* and *Alceste*. Du Roullet also wrote a five-act comedy in verse, *Les effets du caractère*, which was produced in the Théâtre Français on 5th January 1752. His *Lettres sur les drames-opéras* was published in 1776 and, in collaboration with Baron Tschudy, he wrote the libretto for Salieri's *Danaïdes* (Paris, 1789). For a time he was an attaché at the Embassy in Vienna. He died in 1786 in Paris.

[2] The plan for an opera entitled *Rewarded Loyalty* did not come to fruition.

[3] MICHEL PAUL GUI DE CHABANON was born in 1730 on the island of San Domingo. He was a mediocre poet, a highly reputable scholar and a clever musician. As a scholar he wrote a number of good studies on Greek poetry. Several of his tragedies were presented and in the 'Concerto des Amateurs', which was conducted by the Chevalier de Saint-Georges, he played the violin.

[4] JEAN FRANÇOIS MARMONTEL was born in Bort in the Limousin province on 11th July 1723. In 1763 he became a member of the Academy in Paris and in 1783 its permanent Secretary. In the dispute between the Piccinnists and the Gluckists he sided with Piccinni and wrote an *Essai sur les révolutions de la musique en France* (1777). Marmontel, who also wrote several libretti for Piccinni and Grétry, died at Abbéville on 31st December 1799.

[5] RÉMOND DE SAINT-MARD was born in Paris in 1682. He became known through his *Réflexions sur l'Opéra* (The Hague, 1741). He died in Paris in 1757.

[6] PHILIPPE QUINAULT was born in Paris in 1635. He was Lully's librettist and was one of the few men of his time who realized that a good opera libretto must also be good poetry. He died on 26th November 1688 (cf. F. Lindemann: *Die Operntexte Ph. Quinaults*. 1904)

[TO FRANZ KRUTHOFFER. *German*]

Vienna, 31st July 1775

Most esteemed friend!

I understand from his letter that Mr Peters considers my *Siège de Cythère* an incomplete work, as I had explained to him before that my piece ends with the last chorus. A ballet which Mr Berton wishes to perform is, whatever one may call it, for me an *hors d'œuvre*, and it seems to me as if my piece were too short and an act by another composer had been added to make up the required time. This would mean that my opera was no longer an incomplete work! Mr Peters may, with regard to Marchand, be right to complain of *Iphigénie*, but where the *Siège de Cythère* is concerned he is wrong, because the Academy paid me for it as a completed work. I will tell you something more: in future I will have no more ballet airs in my operas apart from those which occur during the action of the opera, and, if people should be dissatisfied with this, then I will do no more operas, for I will not let myself be reproached in all journals that my ballets are weak, mediocre, etc., and so the scoundrels shall hear no more by me and my operas will always end with dialogue.

Concerning Marchand, please have the goodness to explain the whole affair to Mr Bailly du Roullet. He will make him see reason. I have advised him that you will speak with him. I beg you also to pass a message from us to Mr [Joseph] Kohaut and tell him that his brother [Karl][1] called on me, that I found him extremely well-disposed and that I do not doubt that his affairs will be concluded very soon. I expect another visit from him, which he has promised to make.

One more commission: my Nanette has lost the roll of Indian cloth and I wish to have another sent for her. As it is a small parcel, could it not, with your intervention and that of Herr von Blumendorff, be sent here by courier? Or must I inconvenience H.E. the Count? Let me know what can be done. My women-folk send you and Herr von Blumendorff a thousand compliments, in which I join and remain ever

Your most esteemed friend
and most humble servant
Chevalier Gluck.

[Address:]
To Monsieur
Monsieur de Gruthoffre
Chez son E. Mr: L'Ambassadeur
Le Comte de Mercy
à
Paris

[1] Karl Ignaz Augustin Kohaut, the brother of Joseph Kohaut, was born in Vienna in 1726 and was the last of the well-known Old Vienna

FRIEDRICH GOTTLIEB KLOPSTOCK
Engraving by Geyer from the portrait by Juel (1780)

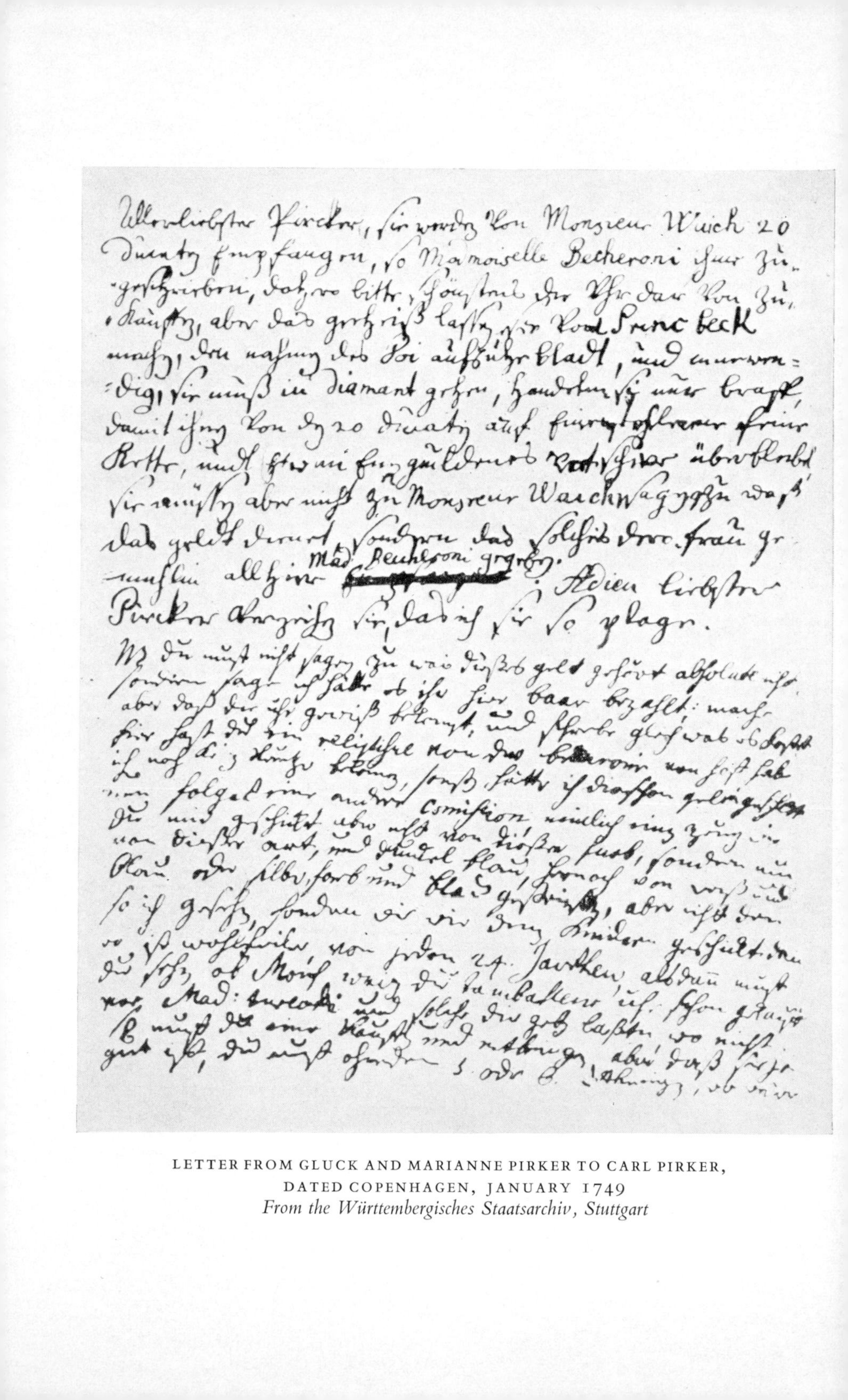

LETTER FROM GLUCK AND MARIANNE PIRKER TO CARL PIRKER,
DATED COPENHAGEN, JANUARY 1749

From the Württembergisches Staatsarchiv, Stuttgart

lute-players. He was a secretary in the Court and State Chancery of Foreign Affairs in Vienna. He died in his native city on 6th August 1782.

Presumably Kruthoffer had enclosed with his letter to Gluck the following letter from the publisher Antoine de Peters:

[Antoine de Peters to Franz Kruthoffer. *German*]

[Paris] 19th July 1775

Monsieur,

Attached is a letter which I beg you to despatch by courier to Mr de Birkenstock.[1] You would also oblige me if you added his rank to the address. I cannot for the moment remember it. I confess that I have much trouble on my hands and that I am tired of all the misfortunes and unpleasantness which I am suffering over the *Siège de Cythère*. After much difficulty and many requests I finally succeeded in obtaining the piece. I sent M. Meryglev[2] to the shop to make the correction[s] on the engraving either in the form of alterations or to carry out a general inspection of the score. There was such confusion that I was obliged to have recourse to the copistà of the opera, who assures me I will need five or ten days to examine this score note by note. This will cost me another couple of louis. I assure you that I am tired of spending money from my own pocket, and all this is due to the obstinacy of M. Berton, who has completed his engraving, and the *divertissements* are given to M. Le Marchand. Judge what effect this will have on the public. How many reproaches there will be from this side and that to the effect that this work is not complete, that it is too dear at 21^{r}, assuming that the ballet airs are not included, and I do not know what to reply: that, Monsieur, is my situation, which, I believe, you cannot find very agreeable. I hope we shall have the pleasure of entertaining you. Until then, I have the honour to be very perfectly

Monsieur
Your very humble and obedient servant
A. de Peters.

[1] Johann Melchior Edler von Birkenstock (born 11th May 1738 at Heiligenbach/Eichsfeld, died 30th October 1809 in Vienna) was a member of the Royal Prussian Academy of Arts in Berlin and an active teacher. He held the office of Court Secretary and belonged to the Committee of Book Censors. His valuable library was sold by auction in 1813.

[2] Nothing further is known of M. Meryglev.

[To the Bailli du Roullet. *French*]

Vienna, 14th October 1775

I am deeply grateful to Madame de la Ménardière[1] and to you for the interest you both took in my illness and in my recovery; I shall never forget as long as I live the debt I owe you for the friendship you show me and for the interest you displayed in all that concerns me. My wife also sends her thanks and her compliments to you both. She is in reasonably good health, although she did not have a moment of relaxation during my illness and suffered almost as much through my illness as I did. She had kept all the letters you had written me and gave them to me all together when I recovered. So I should have many things to write to you about, but I am not able to satisfy you, for I am still very weak. I will therefore answer only the most essential points. I shall only be able to leave here towards the end of March or the beginning of April, for, if I were to leave during the winter, I would inevitably catch once again the cold which I am now quit of. This will not prevent us from giving *Alceste* after Easter, for as I progress with the work I will send it to be copied and distribute the various parts. Thus on my arrival I will be able to start with rehearsals and in fifteen days I will be able to teach all the cast their parts. The *Siège de Cythère* could be presented during the summer. The Buffon opera is, in my view, too mediocre, and I think that it could only be presented on Thursdays during the winter. I agree that the poetry is very weak, but the music is amusing and has an originality which should produce more effect than the execrable fragments which are invariably performed. Mr Ghibert's act, which you advise me to compose, makes good reading but, as regards setting it to music, I find it the most unpleasant thing in the world. To begin with, the choruses and the dance are performed by young students, whom we do not have, and the leading characters do not have the same effect. Alexander is always on the stage and is the most foolish character in the world. In Noverre's[2] ballet he was absent and he appeared most appropriately to surprise the two lovers. This was effective. Here Alexander and his officers are mere supernumeraries. Campaspe has only a romance to sing at the end, so you see the poverty of the piece as a whole, which will never be able to produce a major effect. As for *Armide* I visualize a new method, for I am not going to remove one verse from Quinault's opera. But in many scenes one must be able to trot or, to put it still better, gallop with the music in order to conceal the coldness and *ennui* contained in the piety which fill the soul, and when I study the fifth act I have to weep despite myself, so realistic and tender is the situation. If my plans are successful, your old-style music is destroyed for ever; but at the same time I am determined to do nothing more, for either I would have a breakdown or I would go mad. My nerves are too sensitive not to give way in the end.

Now I reply to the proposal made by you and our dear friend the Abbé Arnaud that I should settle in France. In the first place, I could not leave the service here, although I can do nothing without the consent of the Queen, otherwise I would be regarded everywhere as immoderate. Secondly, I would not like to be in France when the change of administration takes place, because I would not wish to be suspected of having intrigued for a post and of having been the cause of those at present employed losing their employment and myself obtaining it. Thirdly, as I feel that I am no longer strong enough to write operas, I could not contribute to the perfection of music in France and to the success of the new administration except by working with Gossec[3] or all those who have musical talents, as Mr Laborde[4] [sic] and Mr Berton are doing at present. This would enable many musicians to use their minds and their talents and would produce good composers of opera more rapidly than if I alone composed my operas. I beg you to pass on my observations to Mr l'Abbé Arnaud, for he is so close a friend and always represents my interests with so much warmth that it would be wrong of me to hide my ideas from him, and besides he will give me nothing but good advice. Tell him that his friendship is still very precious to me, that my wife and my daughter send him a thousand compliments, and that I beg him to arrange for Mr du Plaissi [Duplessis] to send me my portrait which we here are curious to see. I have nothing to say in reply to his letter, except that I thank him for all the feelings of friendship which he has for me and that I love him with all my heart and that I look forward to the time when I will be able once again to chat with him. I beg you also to give my thanks to all those who have taken an interest in my illness, principally M. Durancy.[5] I am still too weak to reply myself to all my friends. As to yourself I say nothing, for I feel that any words I might use could not convey the feelings with which I am imbued towards you.

PS. Do not forget the air from *Alceste* at the end of the second act.

[1] Of Madame DE LA MÉNARDIÈRE and Monsieur GHIBERT nothing is known.

[2] JEAN GEORGES NOVERRE was born in Paris on 29th April 1727. After appearing as a dancer in Paris at the early age of sixteen, he went to Berlin in 1748 as a solo dancer, starred in Dresden in 1749, then became Ballet Master at the Opéra Comique in Paris. He held the same position in London, Lyons, Stuttgart, Vienna and Milan and finally, from 1776–1780, at the Opéra House in Paris. Noverre was the first to introduce dramatic action into pantomime ballet and made an important contribution to the development of the art of choreography. He put forward his ideas in his *Lettres sur la Danse et sur les Ballets* (1760) [cf. H. Abert: 'Noverre und sein Einfluss auf die dramatische Ballettkomposition'. *Jahrbuch*, (*Peters*), Leipzig 1908].

[3] Francois Joseph Gossec was born in Vergnies in Hennegau on 17th January 1734. In 1751 he went to Paris, where Rameau obtained for him a conductor's post with the orchestra of the Intendant-Général La Pouplinière. After his death he went in the same capacity to Prince Conti in Chantilly. In 1770 he founded the famous 'Concerto des Amateurs' and in 1773 he reorganized the 'Concerts spirituels', which he directed, alone and in collaboration with others, until 1779. From 1780 to 1782 he was Deputy Director of the Opéra House and remained a member of the Directorate until 1784, when he was made Director and Administrator of the 'Ecole royale du chant'. In 1795 when this school was expanded to become the 'Conservatoire de Musique', he was given a post as Inspector and at the same time became a member of the newly-founded Academy. Gossec, who composed a number of vocal and instrumental works, ranks as one of the outstanding French operatic composers. From 1815 onwards he lived in retirement at Passy near Paris, where he died on 16th February 1829 [cf. F. Hellouin: *Gossec et la musique française à la fin du XVIIIe siecle*, 1903].

[4] Jean Benjamin de Laborde was born in Paris on 5th September 1734. He was a pupil of Dauvergne and Rameau. He became a Chamberlain to Louis XV and later Intendant-Général. He wrote several comic operas and an *Essai sur la musique ancienne et moderne* (1780), which is one of the best of the older histories of music. On 22nd July 1794 he was guillotined in Paris.

[5] Mlle Durancy (Magdeline-Céliste Fieuzal de Frossac) was born in Paris 21st May 1746. She was a member of the Paris Opéra. We are told that 'Mademoiselle Durancy supplée surtout dans la scène, pour laquelle elle a une véritable intelligence' [O. Uzanne: *Les mœurs secrètes du XVIIIe siècle*. Paris, 1883, p. 192.] She died 28th December 1780.

[Statement by Franz Kruthoffer. *German*]

Account with M. le Chevalier Gluck

Receipts	[livres][1]	*Expenditure*	[livres]
Received from M. le Ch. Gluck—	48.—.—.	1774 to M. Diedenheffer—	48.—.—
Received from M. de Peters—	2000.—.—.	27 Nov. for transport of a trunk, a case and a basket from Le Petit Luxembourg to—St.—	4.18.—
		1775 March	
		10. transporting plates of *Iphigénie* from M. Marchand's to M. Gluck's—	4.12.—
		14. to M. Eberts a bill—	258.10.—
		30. desp. of a case with two portraits of M. Datez. Postage—	9.16.—
		Letter postage—	10.—.—

April		
25	Postage of a letter from M. le Ch. Gluck—	1.10.—
April		
10	postage of a letter from M. le Ch. Gluck—	1. 4.—
15	Postage of a letter—	1. 5.—
		4.10.—
—	La Lanterne Magique Critique du Sallon[2]—	1. 4.—
Nov.		
5	to M. Rilliot[3]—	1721.—.—
		2048.—.—

Total 2048.—.—.

Made this 10th November 1775

Kr[uthoffer]

[1] The account is made out in livres (1 livre=20 sous). One livre would be worth about one shilling and tenpence today.

[2] The publication referred to is a pamphlet, *La Lanterne Magique aux Champs-Elysées ou l' Entretien des grands peintres sur le Sallon de* 1775 (o.O.u.I.) 8°. There is a copy in the Bibliothèque Nationale, Paris.

[3] M. Rilliet, a Parisian banker.

[To the Bailli du Roullet. *French*]

To Monsieur
Monsieur le Bailly du Roullet,
rue de melée à Paris.

Vienna, 22nd November 1775

My very dear friend, It gives me infinite pleasure to hear from you that you sympathize with me, but if it prejudices your health I wish you to love me a little less; for nothing is more precious than your health, and I am very relieved not to have had your illness, for that would have affected me too strongly. I hope that with your syrup we shall laugh in future at all the illnesses that threaten us. I am also very relieved that you have not abandoned work on your *Iphigénie*. It would have been too great a loss to be deprived of a poem written by someone so full of knowledge of the theatre, of genius and of taste. As for your *Alceste*, I shall only be in a position to say which of the two dénouements I shall choose when I have finished the accompaniments of all three acts, when I will be able to judge how everything links up and runs together. In the meantime I can tell you that the poetry seems to me very good. I hope to be able to send you by the courier for the month of January both the music and the poem, so that you could then have them copied and extract the parts for the orchestra and for the singers.

As to *Armide*, I will only decide upon the music in Paris, for I wish to consult with you beforehand whether we leave the poem as it is or whether we make cuts. I hope soon to receive the end of the second act of *Alceste* with the other alterations already included. For the rest, I think it will be difficult to settle in Paris, for there will be many obstacles to be overcome if the project is to succeed. Since I returned to Vienna, I have tried to sell my garden but up to the present I have found no one who is willing to bite; things never go as one wishes.[1] Marchand has written and begged me to grant him a deferment of his debt and I have agreed, so I beg you not to importune him for the present. As regards my journey, I shall take counsel with My Lady Moon and I believe that she will not stand in the way of my arriving in Paris towards the middle of the month of March, which would give sufficient time to present *Alceste* after Easter. I beg you to give my most tender regards to Madame de la Ménardière and to tell her that we rejoice with all our hearts that she is restored to health. My wife and my daughter always have tears in their eyes, when I read you letters to them. They send you a thousand compliments and sing your praises as if you were their most cherished lover. Do not forget, I pray you, to give my respects to Mr L'Abbé Arnaud and to Mlle Rosalie [Levasseur] and all the company round the table. I think it will be necessary to warn Mr Berton that we reckon to give *Alceste* after Easter. Since you do not wish compliments, I say nothing, save that I am ever yours.

[1] The garden in question was doubtless a part of Gluck's property on the Rennweg, which he had purchased in 1768 from Freiherr von Sander and which he appears to have given in (part?) exchange for a country house in Perchtholdsdorf in 1781 [cf. K. Kobald: *Altwiener Musikstätten*, 1919].

[To Franz Kruthoffer. *German*]

[In Kruthoffer's handwriting:
Replied from Paris on 15th Dec. 1775]

Vienna, 29th November 1775

Most esteemed friend!

I am deeply obliged to you for sending the brochures and the criticism of the *Siège de Cythère*, which seems to me witty and has my approval. I also duly received the bill of exchange and am also obliged to you for this; with the next courier I shall send something of *Alceste*, because I propose to produce this opera after Easter, so you can sound Mr Peters—to whom I send my respects—whether he feels inclined to undertake it, because, on account of his honesty, I would prefer him to any other. I hope that by the middle of next March at the latest I shall be able to embrace you and also Herr von Blumendorff. Meanwhile, my wife, niece and I send our regards and I remain as ever

Most esteemed friend
Your most devoted servant
Chevalier Gluck.

[Address:]
A Monsieur
Monsieur de Kruthoffer
à
Paris

[To the Bailli du Roullet. *French*]

Vienna 2nd December 1775

I am much obliged to you for the news you give me, which greatly amuses me, in particular that I will prevent you from producing *Iphigénie* if Mr l'Arrivé[1] does not play in it. When will you abandon your scruples concerning *Alceste*? Would you become pale and thin as at the time when we gave *Iphigénie*? I will certainly not tolerate it and I am resolved to cure you for ever on this point. Firstly, you write for the lyrical theatre and not a tragedy for the comedians. This changes infinitely one's manner of approach. Though excellent masters in the making of tragedies, neither Racine[2] nor Voltaire[3] has ever been able to make an opera, and no one has measured up to this task as well as you. It is sometimes necessary to laugh at rules and to make one's own rules in order to produce good effects. The old Greeks were men like us with a nose and a pair of eyes. One must not always be *servile pecus* and submit to their rules but, on the contrary, one must break with their habits, sever the chains with which they wish to bind us, and try to become original in our own right. Those persons who wept and who found the dénouement bad, when you read them your work, are sensitive, have a sound instinct, judge with their souls, that I agree, but are they infallible? My wife and I also wept when you read us your work, and, with all that, when I grasped the thing in its entirety, I found many places which were not in keeping with the musical effect, but you mock me when you say that the third act belongs to me; you must think me very foolish or very vain. Do you believe that if one gave fifty pictures to a man, arranged according to his taste, he could, by arranging them a little differently, imagine that he had painted them? The injustice you do to yourself makes me angry and I will make you angry in your turn by praising my dénouement and criticizing yours. According to your dénouement, the opera with the chorus who, *nota bene*, are actors and very interesting in the piece with the other characters—so it begins with pomp and some grandeur—your chorus are always active and the piece revolves very much around them in the first two acts, for they do not wish to lose so perfect a King and a Queen; now to the third act, where the chorus who took so much interest in preserving their sovereigns are seen no more and are quite forgotten. I say that the piece cannot finish before these poor people have been consoled. It is useless to tell me that Apollo brings them back; this seems to me an *hors d'œuvre* and one that is dragged in by the hair. Moreover, Apollo must play the sorcerer, for, when he changes the scene in the wood into a magnificent setting, another magic word is needed to transport the people there, who suddenly sing their chorus without being prepared gradually for their happiness. In my dénouement everything is prepared naturally, without any need to have recourse to miracles, and the piece finishes with the same pomp and grandeur but without the help of any alien spirit or artistry, as it had begun. It is not on account of the music that I hold to this, for the music here is of little consequence and very short, but because, in reading and re-reading the opera, I have never succeeded in persuading myself that it progresses naturally and that it can produce any effect. If all this still does not reassure you, I will convince you or you will convince me otherwise when I arrive in Paris. I beg you to continue writing to me on many things even if I do not reply, for I must work at present if I am to send you the first and second acts by the courier who leaves on the first of January next. You write that Mlle Rosalie [Levasseur] wishes to leave, in another letter Mlle la Guerre[4] also. With whom is one to present operas? I foresee that *Alceste* will be the last opera I will be able to give, for without troops one cannot fight battles. My wife, the little one and I send our compliments to Madame la Ménardière, to you, and to Mr l'Abbé. Adieu, my admirable friend, I embrace you with all my heart.

[1] HENRI L'ARRIVÉ was born in Lyons on 8th September 1733. Reber, the well-known Director of the Opéra House, discovered his excellent bass voice and took him into the Opéra chorus. From 1755–1786 he was a prominent solo member of the Paris Opéra and was particularly successful in Gluck's operas. He retired to Vincennes, where he died on 7th August 1802.

[2] JEAN RACINE was born in La Ferté-Milon near Valois on 21st December 1639. He was the leading French dramatist. He died in Paris on 22nd April 1699.

[3] FRANÇOIS-MARIE AROUET DE VOLTAIRE, the most influential Frenchman of the eighteenth century, was born in Paris on 21st November 1694. After an adventurous youth, he lived from 1734 to 1749 at Château Cirey. In 1746 he became a member of the Academy. From 1750 to 1752 he was at the Court of Frederick the Great. In 1758 he retired to Ferney near Geneva. He died in Paris on 30th May 1778.

[4] MARIE JOSEPHINE DE LAGUERRE was born in Paris in 1755. In 1774 she joined the Paris Opéra as a member of the chorus. Two years later she made her début in Laborde's *Adèle de Panthieu*. In the same year she sang with brilliant success in Gluck's *Alceste*. After the departure of Sophie Arnould (1778), she and Rosalie Levasseur sang all the leading roles. As a result of dissolute living and dipsomania, she met an early death on 14th February 1783 in Paris.

[TO THE BAILLI DU ROULLET. *French*]

To Monsieur le Baily du Rouillet,
Rue Melée à Paris

Vienna, 13th December 1775

I have given much thought to Mr Berton's remarks and, looking at things closely, I believe that I will not be able to produce any other piece next year apart from *Alceste*, because, having been ill for four months, I lost much working time and until I leave I shall have to occupy myself solely with *Alceste,* which requires infinite care. Moreover, *Armide* is so full of actors and actresses that I do not know where we shall find them; for the part of Armide we should have either Rosalie [Levasseur] or la Guerre [sic], for the part of Arnaud Mr le Gros,[1] for Hate Mlle du plan[2] or Durancy, Mr Gelin[3] as the aged kinsman of Armide, but the other characters are so heavy and the public so touchy that I do not know to whom they should be given. *Nor could I risk the opera buffa,*[4] *for that would require at least ten actors and actresses, amongst whom I would need Mr le Gros and l'Arivée, otherwise I would give the critics the most delightful opportunity to band together against me as they did for the 'Siège de Cythère', where they treated me like a small schoolboy without having a single word to say in my defence, and I decided to get as far away from their claws as possible. As I do not live in Paris, all these writings damage my reputation in Germany and Italy, for here everything is taken literally, whether for or against an author. So at the same time as I am killing myself to try to amuse Messieurs les Francois, they seek to deprive me of such little reputation as I had acquired before coming to Paris.*

I hope to send you (without fail) the first act with next month's courier. You might suggest to Mr Berton that, if Mr l'Arrivé wished to take on the part of High Priest, he would surely give the public as much pleasure, or even more, as in the part of Agamemnon, for his recitative is the most striking piece in the whole opera, and its success would be assured when I had communicated to him my intentions; failing him, the part will have to be given to Mr Gelin. *Evandre* will be he who played the part of Olgar in the *Siège de Cythère*,[5] and the chorus-leaders Mlle Chateauneuf[6] and a girl who understudied Rosalie [Levasseur] in *Iphigénie*,[7] who has a nice voice and whose name I do not remember, but I beg you to tell Mlle Rosalie that she should be careful only to learn her part as a whole, because she cannot possibly appreciate the nuances and the beginning without me; otherwise both she and I would find it infinitely more difficult to correct a bad habit which she had acquired in my absence. The choral parts will have to be allotted, because the chorus is always in action and must know its parts by heart like the *Pater Noster*.

Our respects to Madame de la Ménardière and to you.

[1] JOSEPH LEGROS was born in Monampteuil near Laon on 7th September 1739. In 1764 he was engaged by the Opéra House in Paris. He was a famous tenor with an excellent voice. He also made his mark as a composer. In 1783 he retired from the stage. From 1777 to 1791 he was Director of the 'Concerts spirituels'. He died in La Rochelle on 20th December 1793.

[2] Of MLLE DUPLANT we are told: 'Les rôles à Biguette sont toujours rendus par Mlle Duplant qui fait également illusion par sa vie, sa taille et sa corpulence volumineuse' [O. Uzanne: *Les mœurs secrètes du XVIIIe siècle*. Paris, 1883, p. 192.]

[3] Nothing further is known of Monsieur GELIN.

[4] The comic opera was presumably *'La rencontre imprévue, comédie en trois actes melée d'ariettes, tirée de l'ancien théâtre de la Foire* par M. Dancourt [Florent Canton, 1661–1726], comédien de leurs Majestés. La Musique est de Mr le Chev. de Gluck. Les ballets sont de la composition de M. [Gasparo] Angiolini [1731–1803]'.

According to Zinzendorf's diary, it was first produced on 7th January 1764. The libretto [Austrian National Library, Vienna, 128 F.377] bears the date 1763. Between 1768 and 1774 Le Marchand published from it 'Six Ariettes nouvelles avec symphonie. Tirée de la Rencontre imprévue tel que les a chanté a Vienne Monsieur Godard'. The work was first produced in Paris on 1st May 1790 at the Comédie Italienne under the title *Les jeux de Medine ou le rencontre imprévue.*

[5] The name of the TENOR who sang the part of Olgar is not known. In *Alceste* the part of Evandre was sung by Tiret.

[6] Mademoiselle DE CHATEAUNEUF had sung Carite in *Cythère assiégée* (*Siege of Cythera*).

[7] It is not known which singer Gluck had in mind.

[TO FRANZ KRUTHOFFER. *German*]

[In Kruthoffer's handwriting:
Replied Paris 17 January 1776]

Vienna, 31st December 1775

Most esteemed friend!

I am deeply obliged to you for the very pleasant wishes you sent me and also the packets all of which I duly received. I must trouble you again with the present packet, which contains the two acts of *Alceste*, and the enclosed letters for forwarding. As regards the affair of Mr Peters, to whom I send my regards, I could not do better than leave it in your hands, because I am convinced that you are a true friend to both of us. So I place my whole trust in you to deal with this business. I beg you to kiss Herr v. Blumendorff on my behalf; my old lady and my little lady both send you their kindest regards and wish you to remember them. I remain,

Esteemed friend,
Ever your most humble servant
Chevalier Gluck.

[TO ABBÉ ARNAUD. *French*]

To Monsieur l'Abbé Arnaud de l'Académie des Quarantes et de Beaux Arts à Paris

Vienna, 31st January 1776

Monsieur,

I am much obliged to you, my dear friend, for the perseverance you show in all that concerns me and for your friendship towards me, which never seems to falter, but you can at least be sure that my esteem for you and your knowledge of the fine arts could never be greater. I will tell you in a few words that I had conceived several scenes of the opera *Armide* when I fell ill, and thereafter, having heard of the intrigues which had grown up around the *Siège de Cythère*, I stopped working on it, for I cannot comprehend the animosity of a public against a stranger who is quite ready to kill himself in order to amuse them and enlighten them on many things. It could be given as it is, but I confess that it is very weak in many places and that it would be more effective if reduced to three acts, and if I can reduce the choruses and the actors to thc expression and the action I have conceived, you have a terrible work after which another would be difficult to bear, but I confess that I am not satisfied with the dénouement. The opera will resemble a beautiful portrait, the hands of which are crippled. Mr le Baily [du Roullet] rightly says that the action ends with the death of Alceste, but Euripides, who, I believe, also knew the rules of the theatre, brought in Hercules after his [Alceste's] death to restore her to Admetus, in this way avoiding strangling the piece by dint of the rules. In order that the grief of the people at her death should produce its effect, there must be a place apart from that in which the catastrophe has taken place, for the military music is only effective at the spot appropriate to it; that is why the music with the drum is not suitable for the church. We will decide on this when I arrive in Paris; I shall make my arrival as early as the season permits. In the meantime, accept my humble respects and those of my wife and my niece, who, like me, are enchanted by you.

[To Friedrich Gottlieb Klopstock. *German*]

Most highly honoured Sir,
Most esteemed friend!

A friendship which shares our grief gives us unhappy mortals our greatest comfort. I know that I will have this comfort from you, most esteemed friend! I have lost my Nanette. Your German maiden with the good and noble heart, who was so proud of your good opinion and your friendship, is no more. In the springtime of her life she withered like a rose, and I lose with her all the joy of my old age. Oh, how deeply I feel this loss! At the very time when I should have reaped the harvest of a happy upbringing, she was taken from me, taken during my absence, denying me the last awareness of her innocent soul before it departed this life. How barren, how lonely I shall be from now on! She was my sole hope, my consolation and the life and soul of all my work. Music, which otherwise is the occupation nearest to my heart, has now lost all attraction for me; or should it ever mitigate my sorrow, then it must be dedicated to the memory of this beloved creature. Is it asking too much of your friendship to wish to move your sensitive soul with my loss, to hope that your sublime Muse will stoop to strew a few flowers on the ashes of my beloved niece? With what delight I would exploit this great consolation! Fired by your genius I would then endeavour to express my grief in the most moving tones. Nature, friendship and more than a father's love would be the springs of my emotions.

Do not leave me to sigh in vain, noble friend, for this gift so worthy of your beautiful soul. In Vienna, to which I am about to return, I shall await your answer with longing. Then, each time I think of you, my heart will be filled not only with emotions of the most sincere friendship but also with the most grateful appreciation, and both will perpetuate the perfect veneration with which I have the honour to be

Most highly esteemed Sir and friend
Your entirely devoted servant
Ritter Gluck.

Paris, 10 May
1776

[To Franz Kruthoffer. *German*]

[In Kruthoffer's
handwriting: Replied Paris
16 July 1776]

Vienna, 30th June 1776

Most esteemed friend!

I am deeply obliged to you as also to H. v. Blumendorff for the brochures[1] you sent, which amuse me greatly. Please continue to send me everything and all anecdotes relating to the opera. I make over to you the bill for Mr Berton. You can leave the opera as it stands; the little that Mr Gosseck [sic] may have done for it can be of no consequence. This will make the opera no better and no worse, because it is the end of it. With regard to Marchand, I have already written to the M. Bailly [du Roullet], who will try to keep this intriguer quiet. My wife sends you her compliments and hopes next spring or next summer to enjoy your pleasant company in Paris. With my best respects to Mr v. Blumendorff, I remain

Your most devoted friend and
servant
Chevalier Gluck

PS. The courier has escaped me this time, so I am writing by post from Vienna

[Address]
To Monsieur
Monsieur de Kruthoffer
chez Son Excellence Mr. le Comte de
Mercy Ambassadeur de L:L: M:M:
J:J: [their Imperial Majesties] et Royal
à
Paris

[1] Amongst the pamphlets which appeared in 1776 the *Lettre sur les drames-opéra*, by de Roullet, *La soirée perdue à l'Opéra* and *Le souper des enthousiastes*, by the Abbé Arnaud, are worthy of special mention.

[Christoph Martin Wieland[1] to Gluck. *German*]

Weimar, 13th July 1776

I am quite ashamed, most venerable man, to have kept silent so long after your friendly, confidential letter from Paris and to appear before you still with empty hands. In the state of mind in which I received your letter I was able to weep with you, to feel deeply and mourn your loss, but to put something into words that would be worthy of the departed angel and of your pain and your genius, that I could not and will never be able to do. Apart from Klopstock only Goethe[2] is capable of it. It was to him that I had recourse and showed your letter, and the very next day I found him possessed by a great idea, which was working in his soul. I saw it emerge and looked forward with infinite pleasure to its final realization, difficult as this seemed to me. But what is impossible to Goethe? I saw that he was brooding over it lovingly. Only a few quiet days alone, and what I had glimpsed in his soul would be consigned to paper. But Fate denied him and you this comfort. About the same time his position here became more and more disturbed and his attention was taken up by quite other things. Then, some weeks ago, enjoying as he does the complete confidence and special affection of our Duke,[3] he was obliged to accept a post in the Privy Council; since then all hope is virtually gone that he will be able to finish the work he had started in the near future. He himself, I must add, has abandoned neither the will nor the hope, and I know that from time to time he gives it earnest thought, but in a situation in which he is not his own master for one single day, what can the prospects be? You can see, however, dearest Sir, why I have delayed writing to you from week to week, for always I was hoping to be able to send you, together with the enclosed testimonial of Karl August's love for you, either the whole piece which Goethe intended to dedicate to the memory of your beloved niece or at least a part of the same. Goethe himself did not lose hope and reassured me; I am also certain, knowing that splendid mortal as I do, that it will still be produced and, however belated it may be, your genius and the spirit of your departed one will find joy in it, of this I am certain. But I could not possibly delay giving you this news any longer and so accounting for my strange silence.

There are moments when I heartily wish that I could produce a lyrical work, which would be worthy to receive life and immortality from Gluck. At times I feel it is in my power. But this is no more than a passing feeling, not the voice of genius. Moreover, I am lacking in subjects, which would be suited to lyrical drama and at the same time could produce a major effect. Perhaps, my dearest Ritter Gluck, you know of one which you would like to see written and then to work upon. Should I be mistaken in this, then let me know your mind and I will try to wake the Muse once more. At one time *Antony and Cleopatra* was much in my thoughts, but, even if I could work my way into it, this is no subject for Vienna, where, I do not doubt, this excess of love would seem too monotonous. The three greatest subjects—*Orfeo, Alceste* and *Iphigénie*—you have already set to music, and what still remains that would be worthy of you? Undoubtedly there are still interesting subjects and situations—but would I be able to execute them? Yes, if I could work at your side, under your supervision, warmed by your fire, inspired by your power over all the forces of music! But here in Weimar!

This letter from Karl August has been in my hands for some time. Forgive me for having withheld it from you for so long. I have told you the reason, but it can hardly excuse me in his eyes and yours.

May you be able to find some compensation in Vienna, if only this nepenthe, this magic draught which Parthenia offers to the dying Admetos! And O! may we ere long be happy enough to see and hear you here! Then I will see the man face to face and be able in his presence to unburden myself of some at least of the emotions, which the little I have heard of his splendid works (only inadequately performed) has aroused in me.

[1] Christoph Martin Wieland (1733–1813) probably made his first contact with Gluck during a visit to Swabia. He was one of Gluck's most fervent champions, who knew his operas well and who, under Gluck's influence, wrote his 'Versuch über das deutsche Singspiel', *Teutscher Merkur*, 1775.

[2] Johann Wolfgang von Goethe (1749–1832) was inspired by Nanette Gluck's death to write his monodrama, *Proserpini*. It appeared in 1778 in the *Teutscher Merkur*; it was performed independently in Ettersberg in 1779, when it was 'wantonly inserted in the *Triumpf der Empfindsamkeit* with disastrous results', and finally in 1865 with music by Carl Eberwein (1786–1868).

[3] Carl August Duke of Sachsen-Weimar (1757–1828).

[To the Bailli du Roullet. *French*]

[July-August 1776]

I have just received your letter of the 15th January, in which, my dear friend, you exhort me to work diligently at the opera *Roland*.[1] This is no longer possible, for as soon as I heard that the Directors, who were not ignorant that I was at work on this opera, had given the same text to Signor Piccinni,[2] I cast into the flames all I had completed of it. Perhaps it was not worth much, and in that case the public will be greatly obliged to M. Marmontel,[3] who in this way has spared them the misfortune of hearing bad music. Moreover, I do not feel fit to enter into a contest. Signor Piccinni would have too great an advantage over me; since, besides his personal merit, which is undoubtedly great, he would have the advantage of novelty, for Paris has already had from me four operas—whether good or bad matters not; in any case, they exhaust the imagination. Moreover, I have marked out the path for him, and he has only to follow it. I say nothing of his patrons; I am sure that a certain politician of my acquaintance[4] will have three-fourths of Paris to dinner and supper, in order to make proselytes, and that Marmontel, who is so good at stories, will acquaint the whole kingdom with the exclusive merit of Signor Piccinni. I pity M. Hébert[5] sincerely for having fallen into the clutches of such people, one of whom is a blind admirer of Italian music, and the other the author of so-called comic operas; they will make him see the moon at midday.

I am truly put out about it, for M. Hébert is a worthy man, and that is why I do not hesitate to give him my *Armide*, on the conditions, however, which I mentioned to you in my previous letter, and of which the essential points are, that when I come to Paris I must have at least two months in which to train my actors and actresses; that I shall be at liberty to have as many rehearsals as I think necessary; that no part shall be doubled; and that another opera shall be in readiness in case any actor or actress shall fall sick. These are my conditions, without which I will keep *Armide* for my own pleasure. I have written the music for it in such a way that it will not grow old quickly.

You say in your letter, my friend, that none of my works will ever compare with *Alceste*. I cannot agree with this prophecy. *Alceste* is a perfect tragedy, and I do not think it often fails of its full perfection. But you cannot imagine how many shades and manners music is capable of, and what varied paths it can follow. *Armide* is so different from *Alceste*, that one would hardly believe they were by the same composer; and I have put into it what little power remained to me after *Alceste*. I have striven to be, in *Armide*, more painter and poet

JOHANN GOTTFRIED HERDER

Engraving by F. Anderloni from the painting by Gerhard von Kügelgen

JEAN-BAPTISTE ANTOINE SUARD
Engraving by C. Pradier from a portra
by Gérard

LOUIS-JOSEPH FRANCŒUR
Engraving by Mme Lingée after Moreau le Jeune

than musician; of that, however, you will be able to judge yourself when you hear the opera. With it I expect to close my career as an artist. The public, indeed, will take as long to understand *Armide* as they did to understand *Alceste*. There is a kind of refinement in the former that is not in the latter; for I have managed to make the different personages express themselves in such a way that you will be able to tell at once whether *Armide* or another is singing. I must end, or you might think me either a charlatan or a lunatic. Nothing sits so badly on a man as praise of himself; it only suited the great Corneille.[6] When I or Marmontel blow our own trumpets, people laugh in our faces. For the rest, you are right in saying that the French composers are too greatly neglected; for I am very much in error if Gossec and Philidor,[7] who understand the style of the French opera so well, could not serve the public better than the best of Italian composers, if people were not too enthusiastic over whatever is new. You say further, dear friend, that *Orfeo* loses in comparison with *Alceste*. But, good heavens! how is it possible to compare two works that have nothing in common? The one can please as well as the other; but put *Alceste* on the stage with your worst players and *Orfeo* with your best, and you will see that *Orfeo* will bear away the prize; the best things become insupportable in a bad performance. Between two works of a different nature there can be no comparison. If, for example, Piccinni and I had both composed a *Roland*, then people would have been able to judge which was the better; different libretti must necessarily produce different compositions, each of which might be the most beautiful of its kind; in any other case—*omnis comparatio claudicat*. Indeed I must almost tremble at the idea of a comparison between *Armide* and *Alceste*—two poems so diverse, of which one moves to tears and the other stimulates exquisite sensations. If such comparisons are made, I do not know what to do, except to pray God to give the worthy city of Paris its sound common sense again.

Adieu, my dear friend, I embrace you, etc., etc.

The editor prefaced the letter with the following words: 'As you are doubtless aware, Monsieur, the famous Chevalier Gluck had charged me to set to music the words of the opera *Roland*, During his absence a secret cabal, ever jealous of his successes, engaged M. Piccinni to work concurrently on the same subject. M. Gluck, when he learned of this, wrote to one of his friends —du Roulet—the following letter, a copy of which has just fallen into my hands.' At the end of the letter there is the following comment: 'N.B. This letter, written in the confidence of friendship, was not intended, as one can see, for publication. It was printed without the consent of M. Gluck or of the person to whom it is addressed.'

[1] The text of the opera ROLAND, which with Piccinni's music had its *première* on 27th January 1778, was by Philippe Quinault and was condensed into three acts by Marmontel.

[2] NICOLA PICCINNI was born in Bari near Naples on 16th January 1728. From 1742 onwards he attended the Conservatorio Sant' Onofrio, where he became a favourite pupil of Leo and Durante. In 1754 his first opera *Le donne dispettose* was produced in Naples and a further 130 followed in the course of the years. In 1756 he married the singer Vincenza Sibilla, who had been his pupil but at his wish abandoned the stage. His comic opera *Cecchina nubile* (*La buona figliuola*) had an enormous success when it was first produced in Rome in 1760. It was performed not only on every stage in Italy but throughout Europe. In 1773 he fell out of favour with the unpredictable public of Rome, which became enamoured of Pasquale Anfossi, a composer who was not to be compared with Piccinni. The turning-point in his life came when he moved to Paris in 1776 at the instigation of the Du Barry and the Neapolitan Ambassador Caraccioli (see below).

His first work in French was *Roland*, which, in spite of efforts by the Gluckists to discredit it, was an enormous success. In 1778, when an Italian troupe performed at the Opera House, alternating with a French company, he had an opportunity to present his best Italian works, in which his imagination was not inhibited by a foreign language. His *Iphigénie en Tauride*, which was performed two years after Gluck's, had a cool reception. Gluck, who had a high opinion of him, had proved his superiority. After Gluck's return to Paris a new rival to Piccinni emerged in Sacchini. During the French Revolution he returned to Naples. In 1798 he again settled in Paris, where he lived in modest circumstances. Shortly before his death a sixth Inspector post was created for him at the Conservatoire. He died on 7th May 1800 at Passy near Paris [Ginguené: *Notice sur la vie et les ouvrages de Nicola Piccinni*. 1801].

[3] MARMONTEL probably informed Gluck of Piccinni's plans in order to interrupt the former's work on *Roland*.

[4] The diplomat referred to by Gluck was DOMENICO CARACCIOLI, who was born in Naples in 1715 and eventually became Ambassador in Turin, London and Paris, where he arrived in 1771. Ten years later he became Viceroy of Sicily at Naples, where he died in 1789.

[5] HÉBERT was Director of the Opera.

[6] PIERRE CORNEILLE, the great French dramatist and creator of the French classical tragedy, was born on 6th June 1606 in Rouen, became a lawyer and in 1647 a member of the Academy. He died in Paris on 1st October 1684.

[7] FRANÇOIS ANDRÉ DANICAN PHILIDOR was born in Dreux on 7th September 1726. He was no less famous as a chess-player than as a composer. He began his musical career in 1745 with a *Lauda Jerusalem*, with which he hoped to win the position of Chief Intendant, but, as the Queen did not like his music, he was not appointed. In 1759 he emerged for the first time as a dramatic composer and met with so much success that for several decades he was the leading representative of the Opéra Comique. When *Le sorcier* was

produced in 1764, he made history by being the first composer to be called on to a Paris stage. His *Tom Jones* (1765) included what was then an unheard-of innovation, namely, a quartet 'a capella'. In collaboration with Favari, he produced the first engraved score of Gluck's *Orfeo* in 1764. He died on 31st August 1895 in London [cf. G.-E. Bonnet: *Philidor et l'évolution de la musique française au XVIIIe siècle*. 1921.]

[To Chr. M. Wieland. *German*]

Vienna, 7th August 1776

Most highly esteemed Sir and friend,

Your letter of the 13th July was to me a gift which was all the more agreeable because I had awaited it with great impatience. Although time has lessened my pain, as it is wont to subdue all human passions, even joy, yet your letter did not come too late to fill the void left by the loss of my child. The friendship of a Wieland, Klopstock and other such men is sufficient to compensate and console anyone with feeling for all the sorrows of this world. You give me hope that I may gain in Herr Goethe a new friend of this kind, and my joy is now complete. While I cannot expect either from you or from Herr Goethe a poem on the good, snow-white, departed soul of my little one, however much I might wish it, your Muse, dearest Wieland, will never be unfaithful to you, unless you yourself wished it so; and Goethe, whose writings, like yours, I have read and devoured, Goethe, of whom Klopstock said to me, 'This is the great man', can surely not be prevented by any official duties from becoming inspired and from laying one of his roses upon a grave that merits roses. Is anything impossible for you and Goethe? Give my respects to this excellent man and tell him that I would have prepared the songs from his *Erwin*[1] for the theatre here, if the people had not been lacking to execute the same.

Instead of forgetting your *Antonius*[2] and his *Cleopatra*, rather forget the thought that this excess of love would shock people in Vienna, where, in any case, there is now no German opera. I would gladly work with and for you, if you were willing to send me your poetry; in Weimar, under such a Prince, in such good company with Goethe and others, you cannot possibly lack encouragement. All I would ask is that, instead of the usual confidants, choruses should be introduced, of Romans on Antony's side and of Egyptian women on Cleopatra's, for confidants or other secondary characters make the play dull, because they are too uninteresting; a further reason is that it is seldom easy to find more than one good soprano singer. Choruses, however, produce life and, if they fill the scenes, particularly at the end, they make a splendid effect.

It may be that my relations with Vienna and Paris will permit me to make a pleasure-trip through Germany. Then Weimar will be one of the first places I shall visit in order to see there one of the finest collections of great men and draw fresh inspiration from the source.

I beg you to hand the enclosed to His Serene Highness[3] and to say as much concerning it on my behalf as you think fit, in order to keep me in the favour of this illustrious Prince.

Farewell, and may you enjoy all the blessings of life which you so richly deserve!

Gluck.

[1] Goethe's *Erwin und Elmire* appeared in 1775 as a play with songs. It was first produced in Frankfurt-am-Main on 13th September 1775 with music by Johann André (1741–1766); it was frequently performed before the Court in Weimar with music by Anna Amalie Duchess of Sachsen-Weimar (1739–1807) [cf. S. E. Böttcher: *Goethe's Singspiele 'Erwin und Elmire', 'Claudine von Villa Bella' und die Opera Buffa*. Marburg, 1912.]

[2] Wieland's translation of Shakespeare's *Antony and Cleopatra.*

[3] Carl August Duke of Sachsen-Weimar.

[To the Musicians of the Paris Opéra Orchestra. *French*]

Vienna, 14th August 1776

Gentlemen,

I am told that you perform the opera *Alceste*[1] with a surprising degree of perfection and with extraordinary zeal: I cannot find words to express the pleasure I feel at this evidence of your friendship for me on this occasion; I beg you to believe that I will neglect no opportunity of showing my appreciation. In the meantime, my dear friends and companions, accept my most heartfelt thanks, and, if I may venture to beg of you a further token of your friendship, do all you can to make a success of M. Cambini's[2] opera, for I am told that, apart from his other talents, he is a very honest man, something that is very rare amongst our colleagues in the century in which we live.

I remain always, Gentlemen and dear friends, your very humble, etc.

The editor prefaced this letter with the following comment: 'As regards letters, here is quite an original one from our friend Gluck; it is causing a lively stir at the Opéra, where it is regarded as very tactless of the German Orpheus to pretend that integrity is hardly compatible in this day and age with musical talent. Moreover, the Chevalier Gluck has left it somewhat late to engage the support of his dear friends for the opera, *The Romans*, which, if performed alternately with *Alceste*, would have been a mere shadow on the stage, since this unfortunate work by M. Cambini has fallen through.'

[1] Gluck's ALCESTE, which had its première on 23rd April 1776, was still such an outstanding success on 30th July 1776, which should have been the last performance, that it was repeated. On 14th September 1776 Gluck himself was present at the thirty-eighth performance.

[2] GIOVANNI GIUSEPPE CAMBINI was born in Leghorn on 13th February 1746. He was a pupil of Padre Martini. After an adventurous career he went to Paris in 1770, where he found a patron in Gossec and met with some success as a composer. He died in 1825 in the poorhouse at Bicêtre. Gluck is probably referring to his three-act ballet, *The Romans*, the libretto of which was by Michel de Bonneval. The 'entrée' is in the archives of the Paris Opéra.

[TO FRANZ KRUTHOFFER. *German*]

[In Kruthoffer's handwriting:
Replied Paris, 17th September 1776]

Vienna, 29th August [1776]

Most esteemed friend!

Am much obliged to you for the package you sent. We have not yet received the atlas from the architect, because the courier does not know where his lodging is. We hope to discover this soon. My wife, who joins me in sending kindest regards to Herr von Blumendorff and yourself, begs you to send the two rolls of gauze, if it is of the right colour, at the earliest opportunity. Concerning Marchand, I have given him *The Pear Tree*,[1] in the hope that he may some time become an honest man, although I see that neither good nor ill helps to improve him, as I never hear anything further from him. Write and tell me when the score of *Alceste* will be finished. Even here I am plagued from Paris about this. I hear that Mr Noverro [Noverre] has been engaged by the Opéra; if this is so, then next year, if with God's grace I am still alive, I will be able to produce *Le Siège de Cythère* again, because this opera with appropriate dances will look quite different and I have no doubt it would succeed. Your story about Mlle Arnoud (Arnould)[2] made us laugh heartily. As you will remember, I have always said: when the public has once understood *Alceste*, then this piece will make a deep and lasting impression, and it now seems as if I had guessed aright. *Armide* will have difficulty in holding its own beside it, for the poem is not so sensitive as *Alceste* and it contains many episodes; but, if Mr Janson's[3] subscription materializes, I will hardly be in a position, if only out of gratitude to the public, to withdraw from this work. If I have merited this honour, then it is not so much on account of the good music—for good music has been and will be made by many before and after me, but because I have shown them the way to complete their operas and because I have developed an actress and an actor of whom they thought nothing; it is, if I may say so, a reward that was deserved. Moreover, Mr Janson receives the greatest honour from it.

I remain,
Most esteemed friend,
Your most humble servant
Gluck.

[1] Gluck had given Le Marchand the publishing rights of the new version of his one-act comic opera *Le Poirier* (THE PEAR TREE) *ou L'Arbre enchanté*, which he had originally written for Schönbrunn in 1759 and which had been performed on 27th February 1775 at Versailles on the occasion of a visit by the Archduke Maximilian, youngest brother of Marie Antoinette. The performance by the Comédie Italienne was not a great success (*Mémoires secrètes*, XXIX, 294). Le Marchand published the orchestral parts and an extract from the work for piano.

[2] MADELEINE SOPHIE ARNOULD (born 14th February 1744 in Paris, died 18th October 1802 also in Paris). An outstanding soprano, she belonged to the Académie de Musique from 1757 to 1778, was Gluck's first *Iphigénie* and *Eurydice*, but was then superseded by Levasseur. Sophie Arnould 'was known for her wit, which was frequently sharp and caustic'. Her intimate relationship with the Duc de Brancas, Count of Lauraguais, gave rise to many rumours [cf. Ed. and J. de Goncourt: *Sophie Arnould d'après sa Correspondence et ses mémoires inédites*. Paris, 1877].

[3] JEAN BAPTISTE AIMÉ JOSEPH JANSON (1742–1803) was a 'cellist who gave a series of concerts in Vienna in 1779.

[TO FRANZ KRUTHOFFER. *German*]

[In Kruthoffer's handwriting:
Replied Paris, 17th October 1776]

Vienna, 30th September 1776

Most esteemed friend!

I have received everything in good order. My wife sends you her warmest thanks for the cloth and her regards to you and H. von Blumendorff. You have forgotten to send the twelve volumes of [*Le Nouveau*] *Spectateur* [sic] and you give me no news. Another time consider your letter in advance so that you do not wait until the last moment to write to me. If Mr Peters finds himself unable to engrave *Alceste*, then give same to Marchand so that it is soon finished, for the Emperor keeps asking me when he will get a copy of the score. I no longer know what answer to give. It is almost a year since it became known that I would give *Armide*, and Mme Laurenti[1] is not taking any trouble to find 'protectores' [guarantors], who could help her to produce her *Armide*, for without 'impegno' [without guarantee] the Administration will hardly accept her opera, because it is costly and her husband has not yet worked for the public theatre. It is an important point; she must do as Mr Floquet[2] has done. He sought 'protectores'; the public in Paris is sympathetic and his poverty contributed as much to his success as the music itself. She must take action; now is the right time, because the administration does not know what to produce next. I wrote to the Bailli [du Roullet] asking him to speak to Mr Berton in my name and to do everything possible to make a success of this. That is all I can do. I cannot force her, for this would be interpreted as impertinence and arrogance. On the other hand, I would like nothing more than that the opera should be presented, in order that I should be released from the everlasting nagging with which I am bombarded every post day to bring *Armide* with me, which in many places I find very shallow. I have put forward a proposal to the Administration that I will postpone my *Armide* until next Carnival, 1778, so that I incur no reproaches. This is what I have done at your request, and I remain,

Most esteemed friend,
Ever your most devoted servant
Gluck.

PS. Please to give my respects to Mr Hoppé,[3] to whom I am greatly obliged for the letter he sent.

[1] MME LAURENTI remains something of a mystery. This and the following letter suggest that friends in Paris had made an appeal on behalf of the widow of a composer Laurenti, who had written an opera, *Armide*, and whose widow was trying, despite the fact that 'her husband had not worked for the public theatre', to have the work accepted by the Académie de Musique. Gluck supported this project and had proposed to the Director of the Paris Opera, Berton, that the production of his own *Armide* should be deferred until spring 1778—an unselfish trait in his character, which also came out on other occasions.

[2] As a result of the lukewarm reception given at the beginning to *Alceste*, the Directors of the Opéra had considered staging another performance at the end of May 1776 of the ballet *L'union de l'amour et des arts*, by ETIENNE JOSEPH FLOQUET (1750–1785), which had met with considerable success in

September 1773 (cf. vols. VII and IX of the *Mémoires secrètes*). In the last year of his life Floquet made an attempt, which completely failed, to follow Gluck's *Armide* with another setting of Quinault's poem by himself. This failure is said to have hastened his death.

[3] HOPPE, like Kruthoffer, was a Private Secretary to the Ambassador Mercy-Argenteau; he accompanied the Count to Brussels in 1791 and remained with him until he died in 1794.

[TO ABBÉ ARNAUD. *French*]

To Monsieur l'Abbé Arnaud
de l'Académie Françoise, Paris.

Vienna, 31st October 1776

Monsieur,

I have at last divined the reason for your silence towards me: it is the return of M. l'Ambassadeur of Naples to Paris. You know that he is my enemy, having very different views on music from mine. So it suits you to prefer the friendship of a titled man to that of a simple musician like myself. My feelings towards you are none the less constant and you will always remain my hero. I have read in the gazettes that you gave an admirable discourse on the Greek language.[1] If it is printed, I beg you to send me a copy by the courier of M. l'Ambassadeur of our Court. It is not sufficient for me that I know you to be a great man, I wish the whole of Europe to pay you homage. Concerning great men, the portrait by your M. du Plessis is highly regarded here by the connoisseurs, but the hands are criticized. I wish he could finish them and so crown his reputation in this country. I ask your advice on this, whether I should bring the portrait back to Paris, the condition being, however, that he completes it soon. Letters from Paris tell me that almost everyone is pleased with *Alceste*. I flatter myself that you are also; to me your approval is worth that of a whole nation.

I am,
Monsieur,
Ever your very humble and
very obedient servant,
Gluck.

PS. My wife sends you a thousand compliments. The word *Sussola*, of which the Chevalier Planelli[2] speaks, signifies a postchaise which ladies use in Naples and which is painted with much taste, much as are your 'carrosses de gala'.

[1] The DISCOURSE BY ARNAUD, to which Gluck refers, was given when he joined the Academy. Its title was: *Du caractère des langues anciennes comparées avec la langue française*.
[2] CHEVALIER ANTONIO PLANELLI was born in Bitonto near Naples on 17th June 1747. He studied chemistry at Altamura but then turned to writing. His *Dell' opera in musica trattato* (Naples, 1772) won especial favour with his contemporaries. He died in Naples in March 1803.

[TO FRANZ KRUTHOFFER. *German*]

[In Kruthoffer's handwriting:
Replied Paris, 14th November 1776]

Vienna, 31st October 1776

Most esteemed friend!

I do not know what to think, not having received a letter from you by the last courier. I hope you will not be angry with me. I have received a letter from Mr Berton, in which he writes that he knows the opera by Mr Laurenti and that he does not find the same sufficiently good to be produced at the Opéra. I will send you his original letter with the next courier, but in the meantime I am giving you a means of sounding Mr Berton himself. It is a bill for 1000 livres, which you will have the goodness to cash for me and keep the money till I arrive. On this occasion you could also say something yourself of the needy condition of the poor widow [Laurenti]; the spoken word often makes a stronger impression than writing. I would also ask you to pursue the opera *Alceste* as much as possible. My wife sends you and H. van Blumendorff her best regards, as I do, who, moreover, have the honour to be

Most esteemed friend
Your most humble servant
Gluck.

PS. I beg you to forward the enclosed letters to their addresses.

[TO NICOLAS ETIENNE FRAMERY. *French*]

[November 1776]

In the *Mercure de France* of the month of September 1776 there is a letter from a certain Monsieur Framery[1] on the subject of M. Sacchini, who would be much to be pitied, if he had need of such a defender to uphold his reputation. Almost all that M. Framery can think to say of M. Gluck, M. Sacchini,[2] and M.

Milico[3] is false. M. Gluck's Italian *Alceste* has never been presented at Bologna nor in any other town in Italy, because of the difficulty of producing it if M. Gluck is not present to direct his work.

He only presented it in Vienna in Austria in 1768.[4] When this opera was repeated, M. Milico sang the part of Admetos.[5] It is true that M. Sacchini inserted the disputed passage into his aria 'Se cerca se dice' etc.;[6] this musical phrase is in M. Gluck's Italian *Alceste*—'Ah! per questo gia stanco mio cuore'—printed in Vienna in 1769. We wish to point out further that there is yet another passage at the end of the same aria, taken from the aria 'Di Scordamo' in *Paride ed Elena*[7] [*Paris and Helen*], which was also printed in Vienna. M. Framery does not know that an Italian composer is frequently compelled to accommodate himself to the whim and the voice of the singer, and it is M. Milico who obliged M. Sacchini to insert the aforesaid phrases into his opera. M. Gluck himself reproached his friend Milico for this. For at that time M. Gluck had not yet presented his *Alceste* in Paris but he had it in mind to do so. M. Sacchini, genius that he is and full of good ideas, has no need to steal from others, but he was sufficiently accommodating towards the singer to borrow these passages in which the singer believed that he shone most. M. Sacchini's reputation has been established for a long time; it has no need to be defended, but it may be that it is damaged by parodying arias in French which were composed for the Italian language, bearing in mind the difference between the two melodies and the two prosodies. M. Framery, being a man of letters, could surely do better than confuse in this way the national character of the French and the Italians and introduce a hermaphrodite music by transposing arias, which, though tolerated in comic opera, are not suited to grand opera.

[1] Nicolas Etienne Framery was born in Rouen on 25th March 1745. He was Surintendant de Musique of Count Artois, poet, composer and writer on music, and died on 26th November 1810. He was a Piccinnist, as is shown by his letter to the Editor of the *Mercure de France*, to which Gluck's letter was a reply.

Framery's letter, which appeared in the *Mercure de France* in September 1776, ran as follows: Monsieur, I do not know if you are in any way acquainted with a small brochure entitled *La Soirée perdue à l'Opéra*. It contains one phrase which appears to have attracted the attention of the public. It is the only one that interests me and the only one that I will quote. Here it is:

'That is an agreeable chorus (said one interlocutor), but it is stolen from the opera *Golconde*—Wait, Monsieur, at the end of the second act there is one of the finest arias ever heard in any lyrical drama, and in this aria the most moving and the happiest inflexion which art has yet borrowed from nature. Well! this same inflexion, this same trait is found in the *Olympiade* of M. Sacchini. But you must needs know that long before the birth of M. Sacchini's *Olympiade* and of the opera *Golconde, Alceste* had already seen the light and, indeed, broad daylight; that is to say, it had been presented, engraved, and published. Oh! you do not know how many thefts have been committed at the expense of poor Chevalier Gluck; it was found, and rightly so, much easier to rob him than to imitate him, etc.'

Is it not true, Monsieur, that, when one accuses a man like M. Sacchini so openly of plagiarism against a man like M. Gluck, one must be very sure of one's facts?

I know that the Italian *Alceste* was presented a dozen years ago in the small theatre at Bologna. I do not know, nor does anyone in Italy, if this opera is engraved, which is not customary in that country, but, if it is or even if it has only been published, nothing is easier than to convict M. Sacchini of the crime with which he is charged. Let M. Gluck's original aria be published in France (if so desired, I will pay the cost of the engraving) and then it will be demonstrated that M. Sacchini, forgetting the reputation he has firmly established throughout Europe, falsely gave himself out to be the creator of a form of expression which belonged to another opera performed in a small town.

A brief historical exposition would perhaps throw light on many things. Towards the end of the 1773 season M. Sacchini was commissioned to arrange a pasticcio of the *Olympiade*, that is to say, an opera composed of different pieces by different authors. M. Millico, who played the part of Megacle, asked the *maestro* to give him an aria of his own on these famous words: 'Se cerca, se dice,' etc. M. Sacchini had already done an *Olympiade* at Rome and another at Milan, but, as Italian composers are not in the habit of keeping their music (still less that of others), M. Sacchini specially composed the aria in question, which is written in a clear, simple, moving style—in short, in a style entirely different from that of the *Alceste* aria; but the trait in question is there.

M. Millico, delighted with the aria and with his success, comes to Paris, lodges with his friend, M. Gluck, sings this scene wherever M. Gluck directs it, has it sung by Mlle Gluck, and leaves with them for Vienna.

Now, you must know, Monsieur, that the French *Alceste* is entirely different from the Italian *Alceste* where the music is concerned. Almost all the arias were entirely rewritten. *Alceste* cannot, therefore, date much before the birth of the *Olympiade*. Every workman is known by the works of his trade. I transpose arias and I claim to have expert knowledge in this. I can therefore declare without fear of contradiction that the aria in question was composed for the works. A transposed aria does not have the same elegance or the same grace: it is almost impossible to be mistaken in this.

Does anyone wish to confound me? I have indicated the means; let the original aria be engraved, if it exists.

If M. Gluck is the hero of the Anonyme, M. Sacchini is mine; it is for me to come to his defence, when he is not in a position to defend himself; his glory is sufficiently dear to me that I should continue to uphold it. I have sacrificed my evenings to it, together with such little pretension as I might have had to literary merit in the Colony (*La Colonie*), a sacrifice which I make today in the *Olympiade*.

No one can imagine how difficult is the task I have undertaken, and, when the task has been accomplished, I shall have done everything for M. Sacchini's reputation and nothing for my own. I shall always suffer reproaches, particularly with regard to style, because all the pains I have taken will count for nothing. But I shall console myself with the pleasure of having been instrumental in causing genuine music to be played in our great theatre.

It is, therefore, not generous of the Anonyme to seek to warn the public in advance of a work which has not yet been submitted for their judgment.

I have the honour to be, etc.

Framery.

[2] ANTONIO MARIA GASPARO SACCHINI was born in Pozzuoli near Naples on 23rd July 1734. He joined the Conservatorio Sant' Onofrio and was a pupil of Durante together with Piccinni. In 1756 he made his *début* with the intermezzo *Fra Donato*. In 1762 he moved to Rome and in 1763 became Director of the Ospedaletto, a conservatoire for girls in Naples. In 1771 he left Italy and travelled via Munich and Stuttgart to London, where he had a number of successes between 1772 and 1782. Then he went to Paris, where, to begin with, he produced several older operas with French librettos, and, under the influence of Gluck's *Dardanus* (1784), wrote his most important work, *Oedipe à Colone*, which had its *première* on 4th January 1786. He died in Paris on 8th October 1786 [cf. Chr. J. Jagemann: 'Nachrichten von dem berühmten Kapellmeister Sacchini', *Neuer teutscher Merkur*. 1796. Part 9, p. 67].

[3] GIUSEPPE MILLICO was born in Terlizzi near Naples about 1730 (1739?). He was a famous castrato who was greatly admired not only by Gluck, whose niece he taught, but also by J. P. A. Schulz. He lived for several years in Vienna, then went to London and Berlin. In 1780 he returned to Naples, where he was engaged at the Court as a singer. He died in 1802.

[4] The *première* of the Italian ALCESTE had taken place in Vienna on 16th December 1767. The first performance abroad was on 1st February 1775 at the Castle Theatre at Christianborg under the direction of Paolo Scalabrini, who had been with Gluck in the Mingotti troupe.

[5] The part of Admetos was sung at the *première* by Giuseppe Tibaldi.

[6] The text of the aria 'Se cerca, se dice' is from Metastasio's *Olympiade*.

[7] Gluck's *Paride ed Elena* was first performed in Vienna on 3rd November 1770.

[TO FRANZ KRUTHOFFER. *German*]

[In Kruthoffer's handwriting:
Replied Paris, 19th February 1777]

Vienna, 15th January 1777.

Most esteemed friend!

Please speak with Herr von Blumendorff so that he gives his brother a small reprimand, because, after I had enquired three times at his house, he sent the reply each time that nothing had arrived for me, and only on 11th January he sends me the packet without offering any plausible excuse for this delay, which is why I have received your letter thirteen days later. I send you the contract, although it is not worth while drawing up a document for such a trifle. I also do not believe that Mr Peters will use any such thing against me. I would ask you further, most esteemed friend, to give me reliable information as to why, on whose account and on what account Piccinni has been called to Paris and what he is receiving in the way of emoluments. Send me some entertaining news. I hope that the roads will soon be good and that I shall be able to embrace you personally. I remain

Your most devoted servant
Gluck.

[Address:]
To Monsieur from Vienna
Monsieur de Kruthoffer
Chez S. E. Mr. L'Ambassadeur
Imperial:
à
Paris
au petit Luxembourg

[To Franz Kruthoffer. *German*]

[In Kruthoffer's handwriting:
Replied Paris, 19th February 1777]

Vienna, 31st January 1777

Most esteemed friend!

Your letter was written with such a flavour of Klopstock that it really gave me the idea of completing *Hermannsschlacht*. You see what force your letters have. The contract with Mr Peters requires some interpretation, for, if I no longer come to Paris, then he should not pay anything. It must be understood to mean the time when I should arrive in Paris. I can write you nothing more; I do not know whether the courier has already left or not. Regards from my wife and myself to you and to H. V. Plumendorff [Blumendorff]. Write and give me all the news; at this time everything must be humming with theatrical affairs,

Your most devoted servant
Gluck.

[To Franz Kruthoffer. *German*]

[In Kruthoffer's handwriting:
Replied Paris, 18th March 1777]

Vienna, 3rd March 1777

Most esteemed friend!

I am obliged to you for the news you sent me in your letter: I hope, with God's help, to be able to embrace you for certain this year and perhaps soon, for I learn that they are thinking of presenting *Siège de Cythère* again, which requires my presence. With regard to the Italian *Alceste*, I had almost expected Marchand to play one of his tricks. Mr Eberts[1] has asked me for twenty-five copies for despatch. He has received them and I am forwarding to you his own letter, which will acquaint you more fully with the facts than if I wrote to you. My wife and I send our best regards to H. V. Blumendorff and you and we hope soon to take many walks with you. Meantime I remain

Most esteemed friend
Your most Humble servant
Gluck.

[1] The twenty-five copies of the *Alceste* score were copies of the Italian score which were printed in 1769 by Johann Thomas von Trattnern in Vienna and which bore the important dedication to the Grand Duke Leopold of Toscana, later Emperor Leopold II. Mr Eberts is perhaps the Paris engraver and banker Johann Heinrich Eberts, who is frequently mentioned in the journals of his teacher, the well-known copper-engraver Joh. Georg Wille.

[To Franz Kruthoffer. *German*]

[Vienna] 30th March [1777]

On this occasion, dearest friend, I can write nothing, for the courier is leaving too soon, having barely arrived. I hope for certain to embrace you in the month of April or at the beginning of May,[1] with God's help. Adieu. Keep a little affection for me. Our regards to H. v. Blumendorff.

[Address:
A Monsieur
Monsieur de Kruthoffer
Chez S.E.M. L'Ambassadeur
Imp. et Roy.
à
Paris

[1] Gluck did not arrive in Paris until the 29th with his wife. 'Mr le Chevalier Gluck, author of the operas *Orphée, Iphigénie* and *Alceste*, arrived on the evening before last; he is lodging in the rue des Fossoyeurs . . .', the *Journal de Paris* announced on 31st May. Early in July the rehearsals of *Armide* began, and after long and careful preparations the first performance of this masterpiece took place on 23rd September. The return journey began in February of the following year (*Mémoires secrètes*, XI, 72); on 1st March, after a laborious journey, Gluck arrived back in Vienna.

[To Jean François de Laharpe,[1] *French*]

[October 1777]

It is impossible, sir, for me to do anything but agree with the intelligent observations on my opera that appear in the number of your journal for the fifth of this month; I find in it nothing, absolutely nothing, to contravene.

I have been simple enough to believe, till now, that music, like the other arts, embraces the whole sphere of the passions, and that it cannot please less when it expresses the troubles of a madman and the cry of grief, than when it paints the sighs of love.

> Il n'est point de serpent ni de monstre odieux,
> Qui, par l'art imité, ne puisse plaire aux yeux.

I have thought that this rule should hold in music equally as in poetry. I have persuaded myself that song, when it thoroughly takes the colour of the feeling it is to express, should be as various and as many-sided as feeling itself; in fine, that the voices, the instruments, the tones, even the pauses, should strive after one end—expression—and the agreement between the words and the song should be such that neither the poem should seem to be made for the music nor the music for the poem.

However, this was not my only error; I thought I had noticed that the French language was less rhythmical than the Italian, and that it had not the same definition in the syllables; I was astonished at the difference between the singers of the two nations, as I found the voices of the one soft and pliable, those of the other stronger and more suited for the drama; and so I had decided that Italian melody could not link itself with French words. Then, when I came to examine the scores of their old operas, I found that in spite of the trills, runs, and other inappropriate devices with which they were overladen, there were yet so many genuine beauties in them that I was prompted to believe that the French had within themselves all that was required to do good work.

These were my ideas before I had read your observations. Now, however, you have lightened my darkness; I am wholly astonished that in a few hours you have made more observations on my art than I myself in a practical experience of forty years. You prove to me that it is sufficient to be a well-read man, in order to speak on everything. Now I am convinced that the Italian is the most excellent, the true music; that the melody, if it is to please, must be regular and periodic, and that even in a moment of confusion, where we have to do with the vocal utterances of several persons swayed by varying passions, the composer must still maintain this regularity of melody.

I agree with you that of all my compositions *Orfeo* alone is supportable; and I sincerely beg the forgiveness of the gods of taste for having deafened the hearers of my other operas; the number of their representations and the applause the public has been good enough to bestow on them do not prevent my seeing how pitiable they are. I am so convinced of it that I wish to re-write them; and as I see that you are passionate for tender music, I will put in the mouth of the furious Achilles a song so tender and so sweet, that all the spectators will be moved to tears.

As for *Armide*, I will be very careful to leave the poem as it is; for, as you very perspicaciously observe, 'the operas of Quinault, although full of beauties, are yet not well adapted for music; they are fine poems but bad operas'. So that if they are written to bad poems, which, according to your view, will make fine operas, I beg you to introduce me to a poet who will put *Armide* in order, and give two airs to each scene. We will between us settle the quantity and measure of the verse, and when the syllables are complete I will take the rest on my own shoulders. I, for my part, will go over the music again, and conscientiously strike out, according to reason, all the loud instruments, especially the kettle-drums and trumpets; I will take care that nothing shall be heard in my orchestra but oboes, flutes, French horns, and muted violins. And there will be no more question whence the text of the airs was taken; this can no longer matter, since we have already taken up our position.

Then will the part of Armide no longer be a monotonous and fatiguing shriek; she will no longer be a Medea, a sorceress, but an enchantress; I will make her, when in despair, sing an aria so regular, so periodic, and at the same time so tender, that the *petite maîtresse* most afflicted with the vapours will be able to listen to it without the least damage to her nerves.

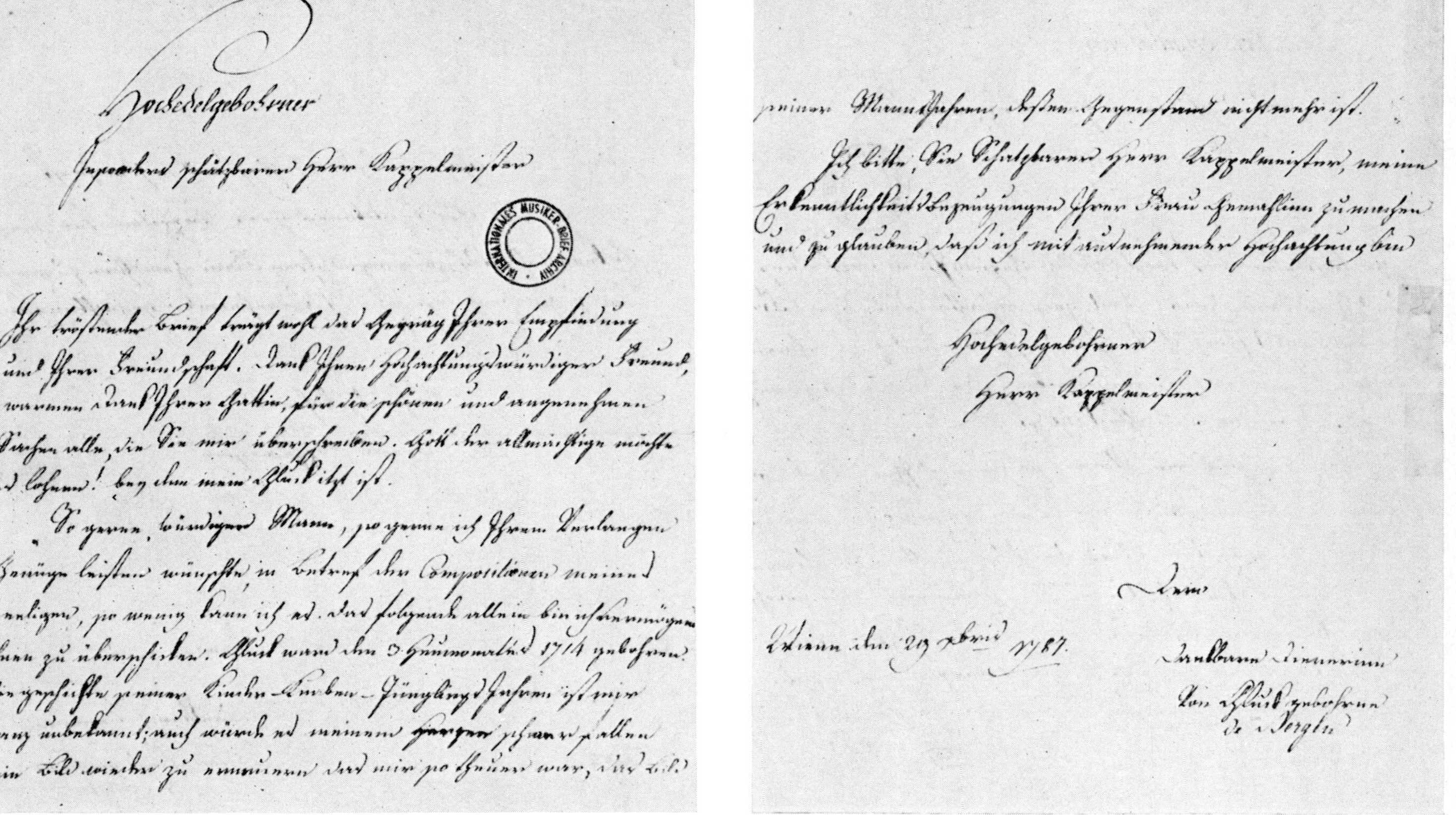

LETTER FROM MARIANNE GLUCK TO J. F. REICHARDT, DATED VIENNA, 29 DECEMBER 1787

From the original autograph in the Internationales Musiker-Brief-Archiv, Berlin

WOLFGANG HERIBERT FRH. VON DALBERG
From a silhouette in the Schiller-National-Museum, Marbach

FRANÇOIS ARNAUD
Engraving by L. Valperga (1785) from a painting by J. S. Duplessis

If some wicked person should say to me, 'Sir, be careful that Armide mad does not express herself like Armide amorous,' I will reply: 'Sir, I do not wish to frighten the ear of M. de La Harpe; I do not wish to contravene nature; I wish to embellish it; instead of making Armide cry out, I want her to enchant you.' If he insists, and shows me that Sophocles, in the finest of his tragedies, dared to show to the Athenians Oedipus with his bloody eyes, and that the recitative or the kind of *arioso* by which the eloquent plaints of the unfortunate King were rendered must have expressed the deepest sorrow, I will retort that M. de La Harpe does not wish to hear the cry of a man in suffering. Have I not well grasped, sir, the meaning of the doctrine laid down in your observations? I have done some of my friends the pleasure of letting them read your remarks.

'We must be grateful,' said one of them as he handed them back to me; 'M. de La Harpe has given you excellent advice; it is his confession of faith in music; do thou likewise. Get all his works in poetry and literature, and search out in them everything that pleases you through your friendship for him. Many people maintain that criticism does nothing more than upset the artist; and to prove it, they say, the poets have at no time had more judges than now, and yet were never more mediocre than at present. But get the journalists here together in council, and if you ask them, they will tell you that nothing is so useful to the State as a journal. One might object to you, that, as a musician, you had no right to speak about poetry; but is it not equally astounding to see a poet, a man of letters, who wants to have despotic opinions on music?'

That is what my friend told me; his reasons seemed to me very well founded. But, in spite of my regard for you, I feel, Monsieur, after due reflection, that I cannot possibly become involved, without incurring the fate of the expositor who, in the presence of Hannibal, gave a long discourse on the art of war.

[1] JEAN FRANÇOIS DE LAHARPE was born in Paris on 20th November 1739. He was a poet and critic. He made several sharp attacks on Gluck's music. He died in Paris on 11th February 1803. The article by Laharpe, to which Gluck's letter was a reply, appeared on 5th October in the *Journal de Politique et de Littérature* and ran as follows:

[LAHARPE TO *Journal de Politique et de Littérature. French*]

On Tuesday the 23rd M. Gluck's *Armide* appeared for the first time. At the moment of writing this article, one can only take account of the effect of this first performance. It was very mediocre. The first act and part of the fifth were applauded. The three others were given a very cold reception. Such is the general impression. As regards the details, the chorus 'Poursuivons jusqu'au trépas l'ennemi qui nous offense etc.', appears to have given satisfaction, a chorus preceded by a word of which the musician has made such a happy use: 'Un seul guerrier! un seul! un seul!' This cry of astonishment passes from mouth to mouth at the moment when Armide learns that a lone warrior has set her prisoners free. This is an ingenious idea and it is a creation of the musician. Another chorus which to my mind is much finer is that of Hate in the third act:

Plus on connoit l'Amour, et plus on le déteste:
Détruisons son pouvoir funeste;
Brisons ses traits, éteignons son flambeau.

After this infernal imprecation, which is terrifying in its effect, the musician places in the mouths of the demons words which the poet gives to Hate:

Infortunée Armide,
Suis l'Amour qui te guide
Dans un abyme affreux.

Mournful and sinister chords, following upon a furious storm of sound, make a most apt variety and arouse in advance sympathy and pity for Armide's misfortunes. This again is a truly dramatic idea, which stems from the musician.

The duet between Renaud and Armide in the first scene of the fifth act is of the very highest quality, full of tenderness and charm. It is one of the very small number of vocal pieces which one perceives from time to time in M. Gluck's compositions.

The monologue, 'Plus j'observe ces lieux, etc.', was successful largely by virtue of the accompaniments. The arias in the fourth act seemed pleasant but common. They are shepherdesses who sing but these shepherdesses are fantastic, and the music should have a fairy-like quality instead of resembling an ordinary pastoral. The *décor* must be held solely responsible for the absurdity of making these alleged shepherdesses enter a cloud through a doorway, at the moment when the magic ring makes them disappear; it is the first time anyone ever thought of putting a door in a cloud.

In the rôle of Armide, apart from the duet of which I have just spoken, this passage roused applause:

Le perfide Renaud me fuit;
Tout perfide qu'il est, mon lâche cœur le suit.

There we have one of those cries of grief which are amongst M. Gluck's great media and which, well placed and well treated, give to the recitative a wealth of expression which it did not possess before him. But when these cries are repeated too often, when one hears them constantly as in *Iphigénie* and in *Alceste*; when even in the arias they take the place of those vocal passages which are both moving and melodious, which penetrate to the soul without frightening the ear, and which one so admires in the fine arias of the Italians and their pupils; then one is deafened rather than moved; this harsh disturbance of the organs interferes with the emotion of the soul; one observes that the author has too often put all his expression into the noise and all the means at his disposal into the cries. This affectation to counterfeit nature is very different from an art based upon an embellished imitation, which must please by its resemblance. I do not wish to hear the cry of a man in pain. I expect from the musician as an artist that he will find accents of grief without making them unpleasant; I wish him to flatter my ear while penetrating my heart; I wish the charm of the melody to mingle with the emotion I feel. I wish to carry away in my memory his harmonious lamentation, which should still resound long after in my ears, arousing in me the desire to hear it again and to repeat it myself. But if I have merely heard cries of despair and convulsive moans, I may find it very true to life, but so true that I will not return to it.

The part of Armide, almost from one end to the other, is one monotonous and fatiguing shriek. The musician has made her a Medea and has forgotten that Armide is an enchantress, not a sorceress. Moreover, he has been very badly served here by the poem, which is full of dramatic beauty but in a measure which is not at all favourable to music. This eternal recitative is, of necessity, without effect. I appeal to all spectators of good faith, to all those who know this famous monologue by heart,

'Enfin il est en ma puissance, etc.'

This piece, if declaimed with moderation, would make a very lively impression. It produced none, absolutely none with M. Gluck's music. Now, what could be more absurd than to ally two arts, one of which weakens the other? Let us recall Armide's dream,

'Et par un charme inconcevable,
Je me sentois contrainte à le trouver aimable,
Dans le fatal moment qu'il me perçoit le cœur.'

Declaim these beautiful verses and they will delight you; listen to them in the opera *Armide* and they will freeze you. Look at the first scene, that sublime reply by Armide, who, after being regaled for a long time with the glory of her charms, which triumph over all the Crusaders, cries:

'Je ne triomphe pas du plus vaillant de tous.'

Let a good actress speak this line and it will fill you with delight: in the opera, when this line was sung, it was no different by one iota from the long chorus which has just been sung by Armide's attendants and with which it should present such a striking contrast. I am giving an account of what I experienced, as I have already done when I spoke of M. Gluck's first productions. While paying homage to his talents, I took the liberty of pointing out with much reserve all that his works left to be desired. Heatedly contradicted by his enthusiastic supporters, I set about reading what had been written on this subject by men whose talents and knowledge are not disputed, amongst others the author of the *Essai sur l'union de la Poésie et de la Musique*,[1] an excellent work, full of sound views and illuminating principles. I was quite flattered, I admit, to see that the ideas of the most enlightened men coincided with my feelings and their science with my instinct. Encouraged by this accord, I venture here to make my profession of faith in music. I well know that this means running great risks, and of all forms of tolerance which people have been demanding for so long, tolerance in music is perhaps the most difficult to attain. But what encourages me is my feeling of certainty that, whatever methods may be adopted to oppose me, I will not be engaged in a war and that those who might feel inclined to do so will do it alone. At ease on this score, I believe that an article of such importance in the history of the arts must not be omitted from this journal.

M. Gluck is undoubtedly a man of genius, since he has written *Orphée* and several pieces in his other operas which are worthy of his *Orphée*. His operas are the first to be constructed on a pattern which is both musical and dramatic, whether he himself designed this pattern, as his supporters claim in his honour, or whether he followed that of Calzabigi in *Orphée* and that of Count Algaroti in *Iphigénie*. However that may be, these operas were the first to be purged of the defects found in the Italian and French operas. The dramas of Metastasio, very pleasant to read, like those of Quinault, always presented on the stage a double or triple intrigue, which destroyed unity and so destroyed interest. Almost all his arias were placed at the end of scenes in order to preserve the custom whereby the singer or virtuoso emerged from the theatre after having sung her or his aria. Thus detached from the dialogue, these arias had become all too often a brilliant *hors d'œuvre* in which the musician employed all his artistry in order to show an actress's vocal chords to the best advantage. And yet this same *hors d'œuvre* was, and even still is, the only thing that sustains the Italian opera, because little interest is aroused by a drama divided into two or three episodes, besides which the excessive length of the spectacle and the naked simplicity of an insipid recitative also do not attract much attention.

On the other hand, French opera, with its surfeit of ballets, usually divorced from the action, and with its lack of arias was little more than an eternal recitative; one found harmony only in a few choruses by Rameau and melody in his dance airs, the most perfect ever composed.

Orphée, devoid of all these faults, could not but succeed in Italy and in France; in Italy because, apart from its beautiful music, one found for the first time a coherent whole, a spectacle confined within the limits of a reasonable duration, a drama holding the interest by its unity, despite faults of verisimilitude, and finally a recitative which was better contrived, stronger and better adapted to the scene; in France, because one heard for the first time in our lyrical theatre those expressive airs applied to dramatic situations, because for the first time in this opera and in *Iphigénie* before it, formal song formed part of the scene, which previously was dominated either by the soporific uniformity of recitatives or the din of choruses.

Such is the welcome revolution of which M. Gluck is the author and for which he deserves everlasting honour. But by a strange quirk of Fate and by a kind of contradiction between what he did in the beginning and what he is doing today, he may be retarding the progress of an art which he had at first stimulated. Let me explain myself. It may be that the very nature of his talent impels him to flights of harmony rather than to the invention of song and that, being strong and fertile in the instrumental part, he is weak and poor in melody, which, however, like style in poetry, is the happiest and rarest quality in music; it may be that certain specific ideas have become allied to his natural talent; it may be that he had the ambition to create a theatrical music all his own and so to avoid any comparison; it may be that all these causes were joined together; however that may be, it is certain that, with the exception of *Orphée*, M. Gluck in his other compositions seems to have set out to banish the song from lyrical drama, and he appears to be convinced, as his supporters constantly assert, that the song is contrary to the nature of dialogue, to the development of the scenes, and to the action as a whole.

Such a religion could not prosper in Italy; people there love music too much. Moreover, he has only risked his *Orphée* there, an opera which contains music. But in France, where he made his debut with *Iphigénie*, which was highly successful, he may have thought that he would find it so much easier to establish his system, as those Frenchmen who had seen the Italian opera had been mainly impressed by its defects. M. Gluck could find great advantages in building on a completely new pattern. Although there are some fine songs in *Orphée*, those of Galuppi,[2] of Jomelli,[3] of Sacchini and of Piccinni, those admirable airs which are sung from one end of Europe to the other, those masterpieces of emotion and melody in which the composers carry the expression of feeling to its highest pitch and so eschew the false ornaments with which the Italians have so justly been reproached, these great works might offer a comparison in which all the superiority would not have been on the side of the author of *Orphée*. But if the song is removed, if the opera relies upon a livelier recitative, on better constructed and more picturesque choruses with pieces of obbligato recitative to bring out the skill of the accompaniments, it is clear that M. Gluck has created a new art, that he stands alone in his sphere and that his place is unique.

The course he has followed in successive compositions makes these ideas very probable. There is little song in *Iphigénie*; the airs are weak and poor. There is still less in *Alceste*. Finally, he decided to work on an old opera, cut into five acts, full of long monologues, in which there is not a single air suitable for a formal song, if it is not in the ballets; and when all musicians are agreed in thinking that Quinault's operas, though full of beauty, are planned in a manner that is not very favourable to music, M. Gluck alone is unaware of this difficulty. What is one to conclude from this strange enterprise except that the author is persuaded that airs full of expression, which alone are suited to dramatic songs, are not at all necessary for lyrical drama and that with choral recitative, with harmony, one is certain to arrive at a perfect spectacle?

Listen to the maxims propounded by his supporters and you will find confirmation of this doctrine. They admire in him the art of following the exact sense of the words, which, they say, is alone in conformity with the spirit of the scene. They are accustomed to see in the Italian airs only the defects which frequently disfigure them, and where an art is abused they conclude that it does not exist. They agree that many of these airs are in the simplest and purest taste, expressing all the passions of tenderness, grief and jealousy and designed to move as much as to please, but they persist in maintaining that these airs which depict passions in general cannot express a particular situation and that, if they bring tears to the eyes of a concert audience, they will chill a theatre audience. Such is their doctrine. I confess that it will never be mine.

I think, on the contrary, that it is in the expressive melody of these airs that the primary power, the main charm of the music resides; that in every opera provision should be made in each scene for one or two of these airs designed to explain the situation of the character, unless the scene is such as to make a duet, a trio, a quartet or a chorus more natural and in keeping with the action; that this modern melopoeia, this 'noted' declamation which is to replace the formal song, is sometimes expressive, all too often monotonous and shrill, and generally very inferior to natural declamation, and it should not be used unless it is needed to state something factual and to introduce the song; that sound as such, being a rapid and fleeting sensation, can only make a strong impression if it is reproduced in a variety of forms without damaging the overall unity of the plan, in those repetitions which the ear waits for and hears again with so much pleasure—in short, all the riches of regular and periodic song.

The objection has been made that it is not natural to sing an air of this kind in an impassioned situation, that it is a way of arresting the scene and damaging the effect.

I find these objections completely illusory. To begin with, if one is to admit the song, then one must admit it at its most beautiful and it is no more natural to sing badly than to sing well. All the arts are founded on conventions, on certain basic factors. When I go to the Opéra, it is to hear music. I am not ignorant of the fact that Alceste did not bid farewell to Admetos by singing an aria, but, as Alceste is on the stage to sing, if her grief and her love are communicated to me in a very melodious aria, I will enjoy her song and at the same time become interested in her misfortune. For I have come for that, just as, when I go to see *Zaïre*[4] at the Comédie Française, I expect to weep over the unhappiness of love and to hear charming verses.

Furthermore, why should an air of this kind, with whatever breadth of expression the music finds in it, arrest the action? Why should it chill me, if it is well placed, if it expresses the feelings of the character, if it never deviates from the main motif? And what other means has the character to bring his situation home to me and move me deeply? Is it this recitative, which, more often than not, makes me wish he would talk? This aria, which is to be forbidden him, is what I am waiting for in order to be moved. I am waiting to hear what is in his soul, for song is his language. Let us consult actual experience. What! in *Lucile*, in *Silvain*, in the *Colonie*,[5] where, by a bizarre alliance, music follows on the words, a melodious and emotional air moves me to tears, and I would not succumb to the same illusion if a formal song followed upon a recitative! I shall never be able to understand such an improbable reasoning.

Let us go further. So great is the appeal of good music that it pleases even when it is misplaced. Nothing, surely, is less reasonable than the famous duet of Orpheus and Eurydice. What intolerable torments! For their grief is certainly devoid of all reason. But this duet is so beautiful that improbability is forgotten, and, if the music produces this effect, even when it is out of place, can one say that it will arrest the action when it is well placed?

I will say then to M. Gluck, in conclusion, 'I prefer your *Orphée*. It has pleased you, since that time, to write as little melody as possible. You have given up that truly lyrical plan of a drama interspersed with airs, which you yourself have expounded to us. You have come back to *Armide*, which is a very fine poem and a bad opera, to establish the reign of your melopoeia, sustained by your choruses and your orchestra. I admire your choruses and the resources of your harmony. I could wish you to be more prodigal in your melopoeia, and that it were more adapted to the French phrase; that it were less broken and less noisy; and above all, I could wish for some arias. For I like the music one sings and the verses one carries away.'

'I am not unaware that this opinion is strongly opposed to that of several of your friends, whom I like and esteem infinitely. But as, in order to like and esteem each other, it is not necessary to hold the same opinions on music, I hope they will pardon my ignorance, and that they will be content to regard me as a free-lance, who, being of good faith, can never be sectarian, and whose heresy is not dangerous.'

[1] FRANÇOIS JEAN MARQUIS DE CHASTELLOUX, author of the essay referred to (which was published in Paris, 1763) was born in Paris in 1734, and also published a translation of Algarotti's *Saggio sopra l'opera* in 1773. He died in Paris, 28th October 1788.
[2] BALDASSARE GALUPPI (born on the island of Burano near Venice in 1706) was senior conductor at San Marco and Director of Music at the Ospitale degl'incurabili in Venice from 1762 onwards. He also conducted in London and St Petersburg and had a European reputation as a composer of opera.
[3] NICCOLO JOMMELLI (born at Aversa/Naples on 10th September 1714, died in Naples on 25th August 1774) composed in Italy and Vienna and, from 1753 to 1769, in Stuttgart. He became known as a composer both of opera and of church music.
[4] ZAÏRE, tragedy by Voltaire (1732).
[5] LUCILE, opera by Grétry (Paris, 1769). SILVAIN, opera by Grétry (Paris, 1770). LA COLONIE, i.e. Sacchini's opera, *L'Isola d'Amore* (Rome, 1766), was given in Paris, in a French translation, under this name in 1775.

[FROM ANTOINE FABRE[1] TO GLUCK. *French*]
[before 16th October 1777]

Monsieur,

I had not read the remarks of the *Journal de Littérature*; your letter, inserted in the Paris journal, made me anxious to read them. What was my surprise to find that I did not see things from the same viewpoint as you. One might be tempted to believe that the remarks attributed to M. de la Harpe [sic] are by a musician and that your letter was written by a journalist. These little sarcastic asides, the knack of evading the question, all these subtleties seem quite unlike a famous artist. You seek to escape as if you felt you were wrong: or is it perhaps that musicians are like pretty women who want to be loved without scrutiny?

Your ideas could not be more apposite: the song and the periodic song are frequently misplaced. You have done a great service by restoring to its function of expressing nature an art which even the greatest masters have sometimes abused; Italy herself pays you this tribute. But have you not sometimes gone too far in wishing to follow the intemperance of the passions and the convulsive movement that accompanies them? Reasonable people will be very much of your opinion: if in sacrificing all else to pure singing one stifles interest, if absurdity, which is perhaps too common, has substituted agreeable songs for a powerful situation, if an abandoned lover sings a rondeau, a romance or merely a brilliant aria, who would not regard such extravagances as an artistic abuse? But this is not the question. All we are concerned about is whether an air written purely and formally (despite the show of ridicule invoked by it) is not susceptible of great expression. I believe that there are many examples to prove that it can be; you yourself have produced airs, the beauty and warmth of which cry out to be sung. All one need know is how to write and how to place them; with regard to this, you and the greatest *maestros* in Italy have supplied the proof. If today attempts are made, I know not why, to prove the contrary, is there not some justification for being scandalized by the comments of those whose enthusiasm, whether feigned or misguided, is so biassed that, if it were a general affair, it would do injury to the nation? How is it possible, Monsieur, to argue that passion is constantly unbalanced and without repose? It is well known that great movements must not be confined by measure, cadence, etc., and that there must be the recitative obbligato in which you so excel; but when Nature, tired of effort, reverts to one sole interest, to one feeling which is the amalgam of the crowd of emotions to which one has been subject, it is this one feeling which remans in all its force and to which Nature returns and is reduced despite herself. Do you then believe that an air, which is well measured, has a good motif, is well executed and completed, does not add to the situation, does not add to the dramatic expression the charm of a delightful song? I confine myself to this observation; too many ideas would involve me in other details: but you are in a better position than anyone to follow these principles to their conclusions and to judge whether they harm the theatrical process.

I am neither a poet nor a musician, yet I have ventured to write on subjects which are perhaps beyond my competence. But has an amateur not some right to speak his mind? Does he not pay for that? Without the amateurs, what would become of the arts? It seems to me unjust to pour scorn upon people who write on an art in which they are not professionals. Is it not enough merely to consider if the observations made are reasonable and honest, without busying oneself with other things? Although I might appear in some respects to hold a view opposed to yours, I am, with the greatest respect, etc.

Fabre.

PS. I beg you to excuse me if I reply seriously to a joke. I thought that out of respect I could not adopt a mischievous tone with you. The only serious passage in your letter is when you quote Sophocles. You will allow me to tell you that I would like Oedipus with bloodshot eyes no better than the heart in *Gabrielle de Vergy*,[2] a disgusting spectacle, which, however, people go to see.

[1] Probably ANTOINE FABRE D'OLIVET, who was born on 8th December 1768 at Ganges (Hérault). He was employed in the War Ministry and took an active interest in music. None of his works appear to have survived. He died in Paris in April 1825.

[2] GABRIELLE DE VERGY. Tragedy in five acts by P. Laurent Buirette de Belloy (born St Flour 1727, died Paris 1775). The romance of the Duc de la Vallière and the anecdotes of the Court of Philippe Auguste by Mlle de Lussan provided the author with the theme of his tragedy. When it was printed, he added (1) a historical memoir on the house of Coucy, (2) another on the 'Chatelain de Coucy' and the 'dame de Fayel'. In the final *dénouement* Mme Vestris made a tremendous impression with her melodramatic performance. She remained for some time rigid with emotion, then burst into heartrending sobs. At the first performance in 1777 several women fainted and had to be carried out of the boxes. One line is frequently quoted from this tragedy:

'Hèlas! aux cœurs heureux les vertus sont faciles.'
(Alas! virtue comes easily to the contented heart.)

[TO JEAN BAPTISTE ANTOINE SUARD.[1] *French*]

[October 1777]

Monsieur,

As I regarded music not only as the art of entertaining the ear but also as one of the greatest means of moving and exciting the senses and as, in consequence, I adopted a new method, I turned my attention to the stage, I sought deep and strong expression, and I strove above all to link all the parts of my works together. I found, to begin with, that the singers, both male and female, and a large number of musicians were against me, but all people of intellect and culture in Germany and in Italy, without exception, gave me ample compensation with the praise and marks of esteem they accorded me. The same has not been true of France; if there are people of culture whose approbation should indeed console me for the loss of the others, there are also many who have come out against me.

It seems that these gentlemen (the journalists) are happier when they write on other matters; for if I may judge by the welcome the public has given to my works, the said public does not lay much store by their phrases and their opinions. But what think you of the new attack which one of them, M. de La Harpe, has made on me? He is a humorous doctor, this M. de La Harpe; he speaks about music in a way that would make all the choir-boys in Europe shrug their shoulders; he says, 'I wish', and he says, 'My doctrine'.

Will you not say a few words to him, sir, you who have already defended me so well against him? Ah! I beg you, if my music has given you any pleasure, give me the opportunity of proving to my friends in Germany and Italy that, among the men of letters in France, there are some who, in speaking of the arts, at least know what they are talking about.

I have the honour to be with great respect and appreciation, Monsieur, your very humble and very obedient servant.

Le Chevalier Gluck.

[1] Jean Baptiste Antoine Suard was born in Besançon on 15th January 1754. He was a member of the Academy and an enthusiastic champion of Gluck, for whom he repeatedly took up the cudgels. He died on 20th July 1817 in Paris. Suard's reply to this letter from Gluck ran as follows:

[J. B. Suard to Gluck. *French*]

[before 23rd October 1777]

Monsieur,

It seems to me that you are placing a high price on the criticisms which have been made of your sublime compositions in showing that you are sensitive to them; you do me much honour by entrusting me with the task of avenging you.

I find it most pleasant to defend what I admire, but what need have you of defenders? One could count your adversaries with ease, whereas your admirers are without number. Your works have charmed Italy, Germany and France, and your triumphs have placed you above eulogy or criticism.

Allow me to tell you, Monsieur, that you have been more fortunate than any reformer could expect to be. Never has genius achieved so great a revolution with more striking and more rapid success.

You have taught the Italians that, while they have theatrical music, they did not yet have dramatic music, that a multitude of beautiful arias of all kinds did not make operas, and that, although they have the richest and most flexible language with an abundance of poems which are moving, sublime and passionate, they still do not have true tragedy.

But it was not in Italy that you were able to achieve the revolution you had in mind. You felt that, in the arts as in the customs of a people, it was easier to lead to truth and greatness those who were still far removed from that goal than to lead back those who had strayed from it. Your eyes turned to France; you chose a moment when we, tired of our old music, were groping for something that might appeal to us. You were not in the least put out by the curse which M. Rousseau placed on our language; you considered it worthy of the greatest riches music has to offer. You saved us from the almost inevitable contempt into which we were about to sink by adopting what would merely have been an adapted and degraded version of Italian music, because we had neither a sufficiently well-established language, nor sufficiently brilliant and flexible voices, nor a sufficiently informed taste to preserve all its finesse and grace. Finally you came and gave us a truly national music; you produced actors, singers and an orchestra for us; you turned our Opéra into the first lyrical theatre in Europe. All this could only be regarded as deserving the eternal gratitude of any Frenchman who loves his country and the fine arts. But

Les plaisirs de l'esprit font aussi des ingrats.

Such great things cannot be accomplished without experiencing a little persecution: this is the price of fame. And, when one considers how your success must shock the prejudiced, humiliate the pretentious and antagonize self-seekers, it is surprising that you met with so little resistance.

You are astonished, Monsieur, that, after finding none but supporters and friends amongst the men of letters in Italy, you should have found so many here who seek to discredit you. If you care to reflect a little, you will easily find the reason. In Italy, where music fulfils a more widespread need and arouses a livelier interest than elsewhere, the people as a whole have more feeling for it and are better informed. They love their music because it gives them pleasure, and they wish for nothing beyond it. But better-informed men are aware of the defects as well as the beauties of this music; they realize that on the stage it has neither the dignity, nor the warmth, nor the wealth of expression which is required for tragedy, that, instead of stimulating interest, it stifles it; they see with dismay how the most moving of all the arts is constantly debased and degenerates into a mere profession, with routine taking the place of learning, with artistic caprice in place of genius and pleasant noises instead of true melody; they see with indignation that success depends on the voice of a soprano or on the *prima donna*, and that the ovations of the public are reserved for a striking passage on the violin or the organ; the singers, fêted and spoiled, grow rich, while the composers, neglected and abused, remain poor. These are the complaints which have been made for the past fifty years by all Italian men of letters, without exception, who write on music, men such as Muratori,[1] Gravina,[2] Apostolo Zeno,[3] Metastasio, Tartini, Marcello,[4] Conti,[5] P. Martini, Chevalier Planelli, Don Eximeno[6] and even Jomelli himself, who lamented the fact that he was obliged, like the other composers, to sacrifice to an idol which he despised. No man of note in Italy has attempted to clear music of these charges. It is somewhat strange, one must admit, that it should be Frenchmen, who have never seen an Italian opera and who know nothing about art, who have taken it upon themselves to come to the defence of music.

Our men of letters, with very few exceptions, are not great lovers of the arts, do not cultivate them and do not live with artists. They go to hear a new opera as they go to see the pictures in the Louvre, so that they can talk about them at dinner, place the artists in various pigeon-holes and prove that, given intelligence, one can speak well on any subject. When Italian music was first introduced in France, the most distinguished amongst them gave it an enthusiastic welcome and defended it both rationally and emotionally. Unhampered by those day-to-day, routine prejudices which tie most men to the things they have always loved and admired, they quickly sensed the superiority of this music over the slow-moving, monotonous psalmody which, until then, we had heard in our lyrical theatre. It was preferred primarily because it was better, but also, to a certain degree, because it was considered a good thing to like it. It placed one apart from the crowd; one could boast of having a more refined taste; one adopted the dignified pose of a connoisseur; and we know how much influence variety can exercise, often unbeknown to us, over our judgments and even our pleasures.

This first germ of prejudice was joined by another. We are as prone to generalize as to pass judgment, and in the arts, as in the sciences, one is all the more inclined to make systems if one has amassed relatively few facts and made few detailed observations. Impressed by the degree of perfection which the Italians had attained in their music, certain intellectuals concluded that no further progress could be made and that, if we wished to have fine opera, we must follow in their footsteps. As the great riches of Italian music are at their most resplendent in the arias, it was assumed that the whole power of the art resided in the aria, and it is on this pattern that theories were evolved and rules formulated. As distinguished talents were revealed by several composers and well-merited success was achieved by following more or less the Italian pattern in our comic operas, the logic of these theories seemed to be borne out.

When you came and announced a form of opera based on a plan which conflicted with these premature theories, the supporters of the system rose up in arms against you; you were judged in the first instance before being heard, then people were reluctant to hear you lest they should be compelled to revise their first judgment. They looked for qualities in your work which you had deliberately excluded, and ears were deafened by prejudice to those qualities which you had put in their place. Add to this the spirit of independence which makes us reluctant to join in praising a production which we do not yet know. We like to find fault, and, as the wise La Bruyère[7] has said, the pleasure of criticizing prevents us from being moved by very beautiful things.

I am speaking here only in general terms, with no thought of attributing to any of these motives the derogatory opinion of your talents expressed by those men of letters who have been most outspoken against you. I know several of them, whose characters I respect, whom I love as persons, for whose genius, gifts and works I have infinite respect, who have a sincere love of the arts, and who are endowed by nature to respect talent in others because their own command respect.

I would be flattered to share their feelings and their opinions in all things, but I am never astonished by the extreme divergences of taste even amongst men who have most of it, especially in those artistic spheres where the appeal is to the senses and imagination rather than to the mind and reason. When men of this stature form an opinion, it is undoubtedly based upon a manner of seeing and feeling which is essentially their own, and none has the right to call them to account for it. But, if they thought fit to make it public, it would be with all the respect which men of superior intelligence owe to truth, to interest in the arts, and to themselves.

I confess, Monsieur, and with regret, that M. de la Harpe has not conformed to this principle in the account he has given of your *Armide*, and I am the more surprised by this as he speaks on subjects within his competence in a spirit of justice, which is often very exacting but always enlightened and almost always impartial. At first he had shown a profound and sincere admiration for your works, and this admiration was only tempered by slight criticisms which gave added weight to his praises. He appears, it is true, to remain an admirer, since he regards you as a man of genius, as the creator of a truly lyrical plan, but he is careful to forestall any stirrings of pride which such praise might evoke in you by seasoning it with pompous homilies and somewhat bitter criticisms. I will not attempt to guess what motive he might have had for changing his tone so suddenly and for entering with so much heat into a discussion in which he had, to begin with, seemed so disinterested. It only remains now to consider if his reasons are good and if the tone he has adopted is the most becoming. This is what I propose to do dispassionately, though with reluctance; but I must respond to the confidence you place in me, not in order to avenge your honour (for, once more, Monsieur, you have no need of it), but to defend the principles of an art which I love; lest foreigners might believe that the man of genius who has come to bring us a sublime new art has merely found prejudiced censors amongst men of letters; in order to bear out the admiration for your works which I have expressed publicly; perhaps also to soothe my injured vanity, for M. de la Harpe treated me somewhat roughly in a brief assault he made recently on your supporters.

M. de la Harpe has felt obliged, in his capacity as a journalist, to consider your works as marking an epoch in the history of the arts. Well and good; but he should, it seems to me, speak either as a historian or as a man of culture. If M. d'Alembert were publishing today, for the first time, his discoveries on the precession of the equinoxes or on the theory of fluids, M. de la Harpe, as a journalist, would do well to announce them, but I believe his readers would not require him to tell them what he thinks. One is never obliged to judge what one does not understand.

The objection will be raised, which is constantly being brought up, that, as the arts are made for the public, it is the natural judge; that the artists' finest productions must please the ignorant as well as the connoisseurs, and that everyone has the right to hold an opinion and to speak his mind. I must say that this seems to me perfectly fair; I would even add that there are sections of the arts, some of them technical, in which a man of intelligence can acquire a sound judgment, if his senses are well organized and he acquires the habit of observing and comparing. There are, in particular, certain basic principles, common to all the arts, which a man of letters, who has good taste, is better able to judge than the artists themselves. But if he departs from this sphere, if, not content to judge effects, he seeks their causes in artistic media, if he goes so far as to try to point the way which the artist must follow in order to achieve certain effects, if he sets himself up as a judge of style, who can apportion merit, etc., then he will fall into constant error or, when he is not mistaken, he will inevitably utter mere commonplaces, which will be no more instructive for the public than for the artists. This is what has happened to M. de la Harpe.

M. de la Harpe's entire criticism consists of paraphrasing the circular reproach levelled against you, Monsieur, that you lack melody and song, song and melody, and this because you avoid too many arias in the Italian style. This is a popular phrase with your adversaries, and M. de la Harpe merely repeats faithfully what has been written and said a hundred times; it has been answered as many times in jest, which is perhaps the only reasonable way of replying to it until such time as tempers have cooled sufficiently to make a serious and reasonable discussion possible.

One should begin by defining clearly what is meant by song and melody, what is the distinctive characteristic of the Italian aria, what are the effects produced by the symmetrical form of these arias and the effects arising from the development and movement of the song; one must ascertain if it is true that the finest of these arias owe their expression and their vigour to what is so vaguely called melody and up to what point this type of melody is compatible with marked rhythm, true accents and the contrasting movements which are required for forceful expression, etc. Perhaps one day this inquiry will be made; but M. de la Harpe is so little disposed to deal with such a question that he has not even deigned to acquaint himself with the meaning of the most familiar artistic terms, without which it is impossible to make oneself understood.

He constantly confuses song and melody, arias and formal songs; he calls all orchestral music harmony and accompaniment—a common mistake, it is true—but not to be forgiven in a man of culture who is discussing artistic principles with a *maestro*. He says that the monologue, 'Plus j'observe ces lieux', is a success largely by virtue of its accompaniment. He does not realize that the symphony played by the orchestra is the main subject, forms the real song and does not accompany anything, that it is a complete tableau which produces its entire effect independently of the song and the voice, and that, when the voice intervenes, this recitative is a mere accessory, a subordinate part which is not so much the accompaniment of the recitative as accompanied by it. What has led to so many futile comments being made on this monologue in public is that the effect has been sought in the song, as in the case of Lully, whereas you rightly felt, on the contrary, that the real expression could only come from the orchestra—in other words, a painting of an enchanted place, embellished by the murmur of the waters and the singing of birds, in which the characters do no more than relate what they see and feel.

A little further on, M. de la Harpe speaks of fragments of obbligato recitative which allegedly bear out the value of the technique of accompaniments. Is he referring, for example, to the moaning voices of the oboes, the heartrending cries of the violins, the mournful sounds of the horns and bassoons, which, in Agamemnon's monologue, depict the spiritual anguish of a father who thinks he hears the voice of his daughter at the place of sacrifice, who sees the torch of the Eumenides brandished above her head and suffers agonies of remorse? These passages of a sublime melody are accompanied by other sections of the orchestra and can hardly be said to accompany the voice, because they are almost always inaudible except when the voice is silent. These are not the fruits of technique but the work of genius.

M. de la Harpe sees song only in arias and melody only in vocal music; it has not occurred to him that the voice is merely another instrument with a character and properties of its own, that if part of a song is played by the violin or the flute it is none the less a song, that, as melody is no more than a pleasant sequence of sounds, it exists independently of the instrument which is used to communicate it to our ear. Almost all his reasonings are based on this misconception.

Now comes a remarkable passage. It may be, says M. de la Harpe, that M. Gluck is strong and fertile in the instrumental music but weak and poor in melody, which, however, is the happiest and rarest quality in music, like style in poetry, etc.

If one reads this half-phrase as carelessly as M. de la Harpe wrote it, that is without reflection and without having any precise ideas on music, one has the impression of understanding it and one can even find the germ of an idea in it. But a reader who is in any way informed finds to his surprise that in so few words there are four errors.

1. M. de la Harpe, as I have already remarked, regards melody as the opposite of instrumental music. He has only to consult a musician or read the article on melody in M. Rousseau's *Dictionary of Music* to learn that melody belongs to both the instrumental and the vocal parts.

2. He says that melody (vocal) is the happiest and rarest quality in music. How is it that this happy quality, which, according to M. de la Harpe, is so copiously used in Italian operas, does not prevent these operas from being the most boring of all spectacles? But, above all, how can it be so rare if it is so brilliantly displayed in a crowd of delightful arias by a crowd of great Italian composers quoted by M. de la Harpe, and in those of many other great masters whom he does not quote, whereas not one can be cited who has the power and fertility in instrumental music which he is prepared to concede to M. Gluck?

3. He gives us to understand that melody is to music what style is to poetry. He overlooks the fact that harmony is a much more distinctive part of musical style than melody and that, in referring to a piece of music as well written, musicans invariably speak of harmony and of the way in which the various parts are distributed.

4. But how could a man of letters, with so much understanding and taste as M. de la Harpe, go on to say that style is the rarest quality in poetry? It will not give me any pleasure to prove to him something that he knows better than I, that we do not lack poets who possess to a very high degree the qualities of precision, elegance, harmony and feeling, that is to say, the principal qualities of style, but that the genius who creates, the imagination that animates and fructifies, the original mind that gives everything a new and piquant form, the brain-power that shapes and executes vast and complex plans, the insight that penetrates, stirs and communicates, these are qualities somewhat rarer than talent in style. We have comedies written in a more melodious style than *Tartuffe*, but where is the genius that created *Tartuffe*?

M. de la Harpe seems to use the words 'aria', 'recitative', 'formal song' and 'melody' at random; he even employs them sometimes in a contradictory sense.

He says, speaking of the music of *Armide*: this eternal recitative has, of necessity, no effect, and he quotes as an example: 'Enfin il est en ma puissance'. If he means by that a simple recitative, then he has made a strange error, as this monologue is an obbligato recitative. If he is speaking of the obbligato recitative in general when he says that this recitative has, of necessity, no effect, then this is a new proposition for the partisans of Italian music, in which there are obbligato recitatives which produce the greatest possible effect and which, on the admission of the Italians themselves, are the most dramatic pieces of music in their operas. This, incidentally, should provide food for thought to those dabblers in systems, who can only see dramatic music in symmetrical and regular arias.

M. de la Harpe says a little further on that the verse sung by Armide, 'Je ne triomphe pas du plus vaillant de tous', is in no way different from the long sing-song which Armide's attendants have just delivered and with which it should have been in marked contrast. If this long sing-song were a fairly short aria concluding in a phrase from a lively duet, and if the verse of Armide were a simple recitative from a noble and serious song, which represents the most striking contrast one can devise in music, what would one make of this brand of criticism? Yet, this is the true situation.

Here is another and even more extraordinary mistake. He says that in the poem of *Armide* there is not a single aria suitable for a formal song, and by aria he appears to be referring to the words of an aria, which is again a novel way of expressing oneself. How can one believe, after this assertion, that *Armide* is in formal song almost from one end to the other, that there is hardly any recitative in the whole opera, that the parts of Hidraot, Hate, the Knights and the Attendants are almost entirely not merely in formal song but even in arias? There is certainly no other composer, be he Italian or French, who is not convinced of this. And to prove what I say, one only has to glance at the score or go to the Opéra or open one's ears.

As a result of the same confusion of ideas and terminology, he demands that the formal song should follow the recitative, as if all musicians, ancient and modern, Italian and French, have ever done anything else or could do anything else. He reproaches you finally with having substituted a declamation set to music for the formal song, you, Monsieur, who have striven to eliminate as far as possible this insipid, monotonous recitative, which slows down and stultifies all the dialogue in both Italian and French operas, in order to substitute the formal song almost everywhere, a characteristic which especially distinguishes your musical system from that of other composers.

As this is not a question of taste and as even the least experienced ear can easily distinguish between a formal song and one that is not, it is for M. de la Harpe to tell us how he managed to commit such mistakes and why he felt obliged to be dogmatic about the formal song when he does not even know what it is. It may be because he cannot distinguish between what is an aria in an opera and what is not, that M. de la Harpe prefers *Orpheé* to your other works on account of the arias, that he attributes its success in Italy to the arias, that he actually accuses you of having abandoned the plan for a truly lyrical drama interlarded with arias, as if you had put no more arias in your later operas. The fact is that there are only five arias in the Italian *Orphée*, which are not even in the Italian style; that it was only out of consideration for our ears that you added a sixth aria to the first act of the French *Orphée*, the only aria in the pure Italian style; that of all your operas *Orphée* has fewest arias and that there are ten in the first act of *Iphigénie* alone.

He says further that your *Orphée* was successful in France because, for the first time in our theatre, arias were heard which were full of expression and in keeping with the dramatic situations. Has M. de la Harpe forgotten that *Iphigénie* appeared before *Orphée*? Or could it be that for M. de la Harpe the impassioned and moving arias of Agamemnon, Clytemnestra, Iphigenia and Achilles, which have always earned such ovations, are not arias full of expression and in keeping with the dramatic situations? It is impossible to reply to him on this point before one knows what he wanted to say.

At the very least, a man of letters who knows Greek must know what is meant by the word 'melopoeia', which signified to the Greeks the art of composing song; it was, so to say, the poesy of song, but it was not song as such, as M. de la Harpe seems to believe. If he was not prepared to refer to Aristide Quintilien[8] to find out what the Greek melopée was, he had only to open the *Dictionary of Music.* He would not then have used the word 'melopée' of a declamation set to music, and he would not have spoken of the melopée of this character or the melopée of M. Gluck. Although the term 'epic' is given a less restricted meaning in relation to the epic poem than the term 'melopée' in relation to music, it would be somewhat strange to refer to the *Aeneid* or to the episode of Herminia in Jerusalem as Virgil's epic or Herminia's epic.

Such misconceptions by a man, who has not only a high degree of intelligence but also a very precise and well-trained intelligence, prove, it seems to me, that the words one employs most commonly in ordinary conversation, when one speaks on unimportant subjects, are those one most abuses; that precise language necessarily implies precise ideas; that, in order to make correct use of artistic terms which seem so simple, one must have a more detailed knowledge than is generally thought necessary. There is no practical art, the language of which does not require study if it is to be understood; one frequently thinks one understands when in fact one is merely guessing, and in general one guesses badly.

I will quote M. de la Harpe once again. In his *Journal* of the 15th of this month he wrote a report on the pictures in the Salon and spoke of them as a cultured man who only considers the parts of painting on which unfortunately the whole world can pass judgment. But in this article he uses only one artistic expression and he uses it in an unintelligible way. It is the word 'reflection'. Here is his sentence: 'You are enticed to follow the bark which, with an imperceptible movement, cleaves the motionless wave under the reflection of a beautiful evening.' A great painter was asked if he understood this sentence: 'No better than the author,' was his reply.

I feel, to be sure, no more inclined to reproach M. de la Harpe with not knowing what reflections in painting are than I do to give others credit for knowing. I could only wish that men of letters were a little less facile in talking about anything and everything, a facility that comes with the gift of writing, and that they would not apply to arts, which they have not studied, vague and general principles or ideas which they have borrowed without taking the trouble to examine their full context. Artists, who are more sensitive than they are to criticism, because they are less accustomed to it, often complain of the unenlightened strictures passed on their productions, and those who can write have remarked, sometimes with bitter irony, upon the blunders committed by men of letters who have written about the arts. M. Falconet,[9] in particular, has done so in a tone which, as a rule, is neither tactful nor moderate, but unfortunately his criticisms are all too often well-founded. It is true that the style in which he translates Pliny gives those whom he attacks a fine opportunity to take their revenge. But would it not be better if men of letters and artists were at one in exchanging their natural gifts? The knowledge and the ideas of the man of letters would perhaps widen the horizon of the artist, while the studies and works of the latter would provide the mind and imagination of the poet with new ideas and open up fresh vistas. I have observed that in the renaissance of the arts in Italy the greatest painters were friends of the most famous scholars and poets, that they stimulated, consulted and enlightened each other. Never had the arts more need of active interest on the part of men of letters, but only as seen from the particular viewpoint of their profession and as a means of bringing the artist back to the eternal principles of true beauty, which appear to be disappearing completely. Painting in particular is deteriorating in the most shocking fashion.

A number of factors oblige painters almost inevitably to sacrifice great artistic effect to professional expediency. Small, meticulous, stylized, highly polished pictures, cold reproductions of still life, portraits and miniatures have replaced those works of genius in which the great minds of antiquity, the great currents of history and all the human passions were represented on canvas. Our connoisseurs go for training to the school of picture-dealers and adopt its ridiculous jargon. When you speak to an artist about ideas, character and expression, he talks of blending, silvery tones and smooth tints. It seems that the same trend is creeping into music. It is not enough for you, Monsieur, to be moving, forceful and sublime; people want flowing lines, soft and graceful colours; they will only applaud woodland songs; finally they want to hear tragedy in ariettas, just as the Marquis de Mascarille[10] proposed to write the history of Rome in madrigals.

As you see, Monsieur, the way in which M. de la Harpe uses the elementary terms of your art to quarrel with you over your art, makes it impossible for me to discuss in detail with him a question which he treats so superficially; we would not be speaking the same language. But if he were prepared to define precisely what he means by song, by melody, by harmony, by arias, I would perhaps venture to try and prove to him that the delightful melody which he admires and which I also admire in the beautiful Italian arias, that those symmetrical forms, those periodic repetitions which give the arias a piquant and pleasant effect, that all these are incompatible with the expression and force needed to depict great inner emotions while at the same time lending truth, speed and unity to the dramatic action; that melody by itself has only very limited means of producing highly expressive effects; that it is through harmony and by a fruitful and varied combination of instruments that the Italians themselves produce those striking effects in their finest passionate arias, although they sacrifice part of the expression to the melody, because they never seek to achieve the effect of a dramatic whole, which is foreign to their type of spectacle.

I must confess that it is far beyond my capacity and my powers to discuss such a question; to muster all the evidence that is available, it may be necessary to combine, as you do, Monsieur, a study of the general principles of all the arts with the profound knowledge of the great artist. So, without encroaching further upon the art of music, I will take the liberty of putting to M. de la Harpe a few observations which imply no more knowledge than is common to all men of letters.

He believes that it is in the arias that the primary power of music resides. But the Greeks had moving and passionate music, which was susceptible of all forms of expression, had great vitality and produced effects which are confirmed by the marvels, however absurd some may be, that are credited to it. Yet these Greeks had no arias in their music. The beautiful obbligato recitatives which the Italians admire for their wealth of expression, the choruses which move the multitude so profoundly in *Iphigénie, Alceste* and *Armide*, the first sublime couplet of Pergolese's *Stabat*, the adagio which is so touching, despite the fact that it is only played on a pianoforte, these are not arias; those simple, crude songs which excite primitive peoples so powerfully to fight and rejoice, etc., the Alpine horn, which no Swiss far from home can hear without sinking into a profound melancholy, these are not Italian arias. There must, therefore, be a primary force in music, which can exercise a strong and agreeable influence on the souls of men without taking the form of an aria.

M. de la Harpe tells us that the arias—*hors d'œuvre* designed to give full play to an actress's throat—are the only things that sustain Italian opera, because lack of interest in the drama, the length of the performance and the insipid character of the recitative cannot hold audiences. If M. de la Harpe had seen Italian opera, he would know that the only thing that sustains it is the coming and going, eating, playing and chattering that goes on; it is like a concert which one attends in order to hear one or two pretty pieces and to judge the voices and talents of the singers. What makes any real interest impossible is the nature of the recitatives and arias, and, far from the drama being at fault, when Metastasio's operas were simply declaimed by bad actors they were listened to with interest in several theatres in Italy. It was Metastasio who wrote, well before Gluck's admirers, that Italian music was a slave in revolt against poetry, its legitimate sovereign, and that it should confine itself to concerts and ballet without becoming involved in questions of the Cothurnus.

M. de la Harpe is so enamoured of arias that he would like one or two in every scene of an opera. This, it seems to me, would be a great many arias, however beautiful they might be. Seaports are very useful but this does not mean one should emulate M. Caritidès[11] and build a whole kingdom of seaports.

As soon as one admits the song, says M. de la Harpe, one must admit it at its very best. He adds a little further on: when I go to see *Zaïre*, I expect to weep over the misfortunes of love and hear charming verses. There is something alluring about this phrase; but the comparison he draws between poetry and music should, it seems to me, have brought home to him the sophistry on which it is founded. Let us examine this comparison.

In a poem in which the aim is to arouse interest solely by means of the charm of the poetry, as in the ode for example, the poet can pour out all the wealth of his imagination and harmony; not only can his thoughts be couched in the most sonorous expressions, the most brilliant figures of speech and the most melodious verses, but the verses themselves—if written in a variety of metres and grouped in symmetrical, regular strophes which flatter the ear, relax the mind and highlight the ideas they contain—can be invested with a new kind of harmony.

But in a poem such as tragedy, where the poetry is merely an ornamental accessory, the artistry of which must make itself felt without becoming too apparent, because the primary aim is to arouse interest by means of the situations, the development of the characters and the portrayal of emotion, these poetic riches which are so lavishly displayed in the ode must be sacrificed to truth, to speed of action and to other dramatic conventions. M. de la Harpe knows that better than I. He knows that the epic and lyric style is not the style of tragedy; he knows that, while the poet can introduce more colourful images and a more obtrusive harmony at moments when there is less action, he must abandon these artistic expedients at moments where interest is high and where the soul must be deeply moved, because this deep emotion depends upon a species of illusion which any too apparent artistry would destroy.

It would, therefore, be a strange criticism to level against Sophocles that he did not write his tragedies in strophes like the *Odes* of Pindar, because these strophes give much more harmonious poetry than a succession of iambics; or that he did not employ the same poetry in his passionate scenes as in his choruses. One might well have said to him: If one admits poetry in drama, one must admit it at its very best.

Could one not also reproach Corneille for not having written the fifth act of *Rodogune* in the same style as *Berenice*, on the grounds that one goes to hear tragedy in order to hear charming verses? Now, there are remarkably few charming verses in that act of *Rodogune*, for most of them are sublime.

If the great Corneille, instead of turning his back on the stanzas which were in common usage and which he employed in a few monologues in his early tragedies, had, on the contrary, introduced them into the most vivacious dialogue and the most interesting scenes in the drama, if he had written them in the magical verse of Racine, I have no doubt that they would have produced the most striking effects, combining warmth, vigour and pathos with the beauty of symmetrical, regular, periodic forms and all the charms of melody. I do not doubt that the finest of these stanzas would have been applauded with perhaps even greater enthusiasm than ever greeted the finest scenes in *Cinna*, that Corneille would have been imitated by his successors, and that his stanzas would have been consecrated in our theatre. But there is also no doubt that the art of true tragedy would have gone by default. And if a man of genius had then appeared to compose tragedies in which he sacrificed these artificial beauties to truer, more virile, more vigorous beauties, I do not doubt again that men of culture, in order to justify the use of stanzas in tragedy and to underline the wonderful effects achieved, would have adduced the same reasons which are adduced today to prove that the Italian arietta is the most dramatic form one can give to music.

If no other poems existed in the world but the epics of Bojardo,[12] Ariosto and Tasso, the same arguments could still serve to prove that the octet is indispensable to the epic and one would have no difficulty in finding in *Roland* and *Jerusalem* octets which contain all the kinds of beauty of which poetry is capable.

I venture to suggest this to M. de la Harpe as a subject that might be worthy of his attention. I could develop it still further and apply it in more detail to all the arts, but this would take me much too far afield.

It only remains for me to reply to certain points in M. de la Harpe's criticism which I find particularly distasteful. A man of letters with such distinguished gifts can, without damaging his reputation, be mistaken about melody and formal song, but it is inexcusable that he should be deceived about what is owing to truth and genius. In his report on *Armide* he has departed too far from the truth, and, when one knows that he made his report on the first performance without having seen it, it is difficult to believe that his pen was guided by pure love of art. He prides himself on the strictest impartiality, yet this is how his impartiality finds expression. It seems that the chorus, 'Poursuivons jusq'au trépas', was well received. But can anyone believe that M. de la Harpe was seriously concerned to report accurately on the effect of this chorus which, both in rehearsals and in all the performances, aroused the most lively and universal enthusiasm? And can one interpret this approach otherwise than as an attempt to cover up a success which was disagreeable to him?

In the same article, to prove that your *Armide* cannot succeed, he says that it is a bad opera, that it developes in a way that is not suitable for music; in the next issue, being unable to dispute the success of *Armide*, he admits it as feebly as he possibly can and says that with such a poem as Quinault's it is very difficult not to attract the public. Is this impartiality and justice?

When, in order to give the music as small a share as possible in the success of the opera, he attributed it mainly to the perfect execution and to a rare combination of talents, is one to take M. de la Harpe seriously?

When, in order to deny you the honour of having been the first to conceive an opera plan that is both musical and dramatic, he says that in *Iphigénie* you followed a plan devised by Algarotti,[13] is he again showing impartiality in making an assertion that can so easily be disproved? For the plan of your *Iphigénie*, a truly dramatic plan, the execution of which does great honour to the poet, has nothing, absolutely nothing, in common with that of Algarotti, which I have before me and which is simply Racine's plan reduced and cut to the Italian form.

When, in order to denigrate your system and your works, he says that you seem to have set out to eliminate the song from the lyrical drama and that you appear to be convinced, as your supporters keep repeating, that the song is contrary to the nature of the dialogue, etc., how is one to describe such an imputation, since your plan, on the contrary, is to enliven the recitative by almost continual vocal phrases, since M. Rousseau finds that the song comes through your every pore, and since none of your supporters could possibly have said or written anything so absurd as has been so gratuitously ascribed to them?

These words of denigration and contempt which he employs for no other reason and with no other effect than to wound a man of genius, how can one reconcile them with the principles of an honest and balanced criticism? He reproaches you, Monsieur, with having made Armide a sorceress. In applying so improperly a word culled from his memory, did he attach any meaning to it? If Armide is an enchantress in Quinault's verses, could M. de la Harpe perhaps tell us by what artistic means you have turned her into a sorceress?

Is it a tone that is becoming to criticism to say that the part of Armide is a monotonous and fatiguing shriek almost from one end to the other?

Is it with any real awareness of what he is saying that M. de la Harpe reproaches you, Monsieur, with affecting to counterfeit nature? He knows his own language too well not to realize that to counterfeit means to burlesque, but it seems to me that until now no trace of burlesque has been found in your tragedies. He also seems to be afraid that imitations in music may be too near the truth. Let him be reassured. Tones and intervals in harmony, accompanied by violins, oboes and trumpets, will never be mistaken for the cries of a man in pain. It must be admitted that for some time strange things have been said and written about imitation and truth in the arts.

What a sad spectacle it is when the critic derives pleasure from seeking to disturb the artist at his work and persecute him in his success! And if this artist is acknowledged to be a man of genius, the creator of a new *genre*, who for several years has been intoxicating the entire nation with a pleasure which one has sometimes shared oneself, is it possible in these first moments when one should be filled with admiration and appreciation to think of disputing his triumph and dashing the laurel wreath from his brow just when the public has crowned him?

If this man of genius is a foreigner whose sole reason for coming among us was the desire to earn our applause and to bring us fresh pleasures, does he not deserve still more respect and appreciation? Finally, if this man of genius experiences all the contradictions which invariably pursue great and successful talents; if he is a prey to the petty persecutions and secret intrigues of a large cabal of virtuosos, strolling fiddlers, dilettantes, etc., etc., etc., is it for a man of letters to supply the enemies of talent with arms and lend his voice to the clamours of prejudice and jealousy?

After M. de la Harpe had decided to use the impressive words 'man of genius' in speaking of you, Monsieur, how could the first defamatory expression that entered his mind escape from his pen? Understanding, taste and even talent in all spheres are not rare, but when heaven presents the earth with a man of genius, can one receive him with too much respect? Men of letters frequently complain, and with justice, of the contempt and indifference that certain classes of the public display towards men of talent; is it for them to teach the public to treat genius with familiarity, or should they not rather set an example in the respect due to him?

If it were ever permitted to attack a man of genius openly in the midst of his success and to speak out against the applause of the public, it could only be out of zeal to prevent artistic principles from being corrupted, to enlighten a misguided public, to lead back to the truth an artist who has strayed. But when one does not even know the language of the art one wishes to defend, when one can only set one's own private feelings against those of the public and pit against the informed judgment of the most skilful connoisseurs mere vague, superficial ideas which have already been vainly repeated by others, what influence can one have on public opinion? What service can one render to an art one does not know?

M. de la Harpe had doubtless no intention of teaching you something new, Monsieur, when he told you that beautiful melody is beautiful, that the soul must be reached without offending the ear, and that one must try to combine beautiful songs with expression. No one would dispute these great truths. But when he adds that the most melodious song must be combined with the strongest expression, the symmetrical and periodic forms with the truth of dramatic action, as the Italian composers have done and still do, then he is stating something which he is in no position to prove or even to conceive.

If I were to say to a painter, 'I would like you to combine force with grace, perfection of design with the magic of colour,' he would almost certainly reply that he too would like to do it. But if I said to him, 'I seek in a picture the proud, bold, skilful touches of Michelangelo together with the pure, flowing, mellow strokes of Correggio, the truth and depth of expression of Dominicino, the graceful, piquant head of a Parmigiano, the effects of light, the fresh, glowing colours and the soft, harmonious transitions that enthral me in Titian's pictures, those great masses and strong contrasts of light and shade that give movement and grandeur to the compositions of Hannibal Carracci,' then my painter would perhaps say to me, as Apelles said to Megabises: 'Speak softly, lest the young boy who is mixing my colours should laugh at you.'

There are certain kinds of beauty which, by their very nature, are above the criteria of art. Is it not absurd, on looking at the figure of Laocoon as he utters his cries, his features convulsed, his muscles swollen by pain, to seek the grace and nobility, the elegance of form, the imposing calm which radiate from the Apollo Belvedere?

There are also qualities which are excluded by virtue of the imperfection of human nature; the greatest talent has its limitations and the greatest artists have always sacrificed certain parts of their art in favour of others which touched them more closely. But, although Raphael has not the brilliance of Guido or the colour of Titian, he is none the less the first of painters.

M. de la Harpe will be furious again at my enthusiasm on your behalf, Monsieur, but I am proud of it. As I have already said, enthusiasm is the only way to enjoy the arts. He who is merely just is cold, and it is better to wax enthusiastic over a man of genius than to be fanatical over a man of mediocre talent.

But my enthusiasm for a man of genius has never worked to the detriment of any of his rivals; he who truly loves the arts may show preference but not intolerance. I have always been a champion and sometimes a friend to composers who laid the foundations of good music among us; I have never belittled anyone.

A famous *maestro* who sets out to enrich our lyrical theatre with a product of his brilliant, facile and fertile genius will find no more sincere admirer and no more zealous champion than I; a reputation proven by twenty years of success has no need to be vindicated by our applause, and, whatever plan and method he may adopt for a species of melodrama which is very different from those he has been engaged upon so far, it is impossible that his music should not be full of beauty of the highest order and should not be applauded by all men of taste.

My admiration for you, Monsieur, does not also prevent me from finding shortcomings in your works. I do not believe that you have an all-seeing mind or an all-embracing genius. I too like symmetrical, regular arias, the duets and trios beautifully sung and in beautiful harmony; those you have introduced in your works have given me so much pleasure and have been so universally applauded that I sometimes felt the lack of them at certain moments when the situation and the feelings of the characters seemed to me to call for this kind of beauty. But, before I reproach you with this, I would like to ask you yourself what reasons you had for denying yourself such means of giving pleasure which come to you so easily? For if I were to speak to you of your art, it would be to ask for instruction and not to give it. It would be in order to ask you what means of expression pertain especially to melody and harmony, to vocal and to instrumental music, up to what point the accents of the recitative must conform to those of declamation. What particular instinct inspires you to write songs of a simple, religious character, which seem to transport us into the heart of a Greek temple and which fill us both with terror and with awe, as, for example, the chorus in the first act of *Alceste* and that in the third act of *Iphigénie*? And finally what mental power gives you the *sangfroid* necessary to embrace all the parts of a great drama at once and to subordinate them one to another, with the verve and enthusiasm which you bring to all this?

But you have something better to do than instruct us in our ignorance; continue to enthral us with fresh fruits of your labours. Resign yourself to criticism and even to satire; it is a price genius has always paid for human weakness. Be content with the glory of having created a new *genre* of dramatic music which will mark the beginning of a new epoch in the history of the arts, for I venture to predict that the revolution which you have effected in our lyrical theatre will spread to the other theatres in Europe, and all composers, according as they have more or less genius and sensibility, will advance more or less along the path you have opened up for them.

This revolution has been a long time in the making and during that time men of taste have been longing for it. It is true that, whereas the light was expected to come from the east, it has come from the north. This accident has somewhat disconcerted the prophets and has deprived you of several zealots, but in the end the public is just, and posterity, which cares little whether you were born in Prague or in Naples, will place you amongst the small, select band of creative geniuses.

Accept, Monsieur, the homage I pay you as a very feeble token of my admiration for your sublime talents and of my gratitude for the boundless pleasure which your works have so often given me.

[1] Lodovico Antonio Muratori (born Vignola/Modena 21st October 1672, died Modena 23rd January 1750) was librarian of the Ambrosian Library in Milan and later of the Duke of Modena; he finally became Provost at Santa Maria della Pomposa. He has been described as the 'father of Italian historical research'.

[2] Domenico Gravina (born Naples *circa* 1573, died Naples 29th August 1643) was Vicar-General of the Dominican Order and wrote an essay entitled 'De choro et cantu ecclesiastico'.

[3] Apostolo Zeno (born Venice 11th December 1668, died Venice 11th November 1750) was the most important Italian opera librettist before Metastasio. From 1718 to 1729 he was Court Poet in Vienna, then in his native Venice.

[4] Benedetto Marcello (born Venice 24th July 1686, died Brescia 25th July 1739) studied law, then became a Court and Government official. He established his reputation as 'principe della musica' by setting to music fifty psalms which his friend G. A. Giustiniani had translated into Italian. His book, *Teatro alla moda*, contains some trenchant criticisms of contemporary opera and is a valuable contribution to the history of opera.

[5] Conti. It is not clear whether J. B. Suard was referring here to the Abbate Antonio I. Conti (born Venice *circa* 1768, died *circa* 1749), friend of Marcello and Newton, who wrote a *Dissertazione sulla musica imitativa* (Venice, 1756), or to Conti de Cesena, who in 1774 submitted a *Dissertazio sopra il quesito: Dimostrare, che cosa fosse, e quanta parte avesse la musica* to the Academy of Mantua.

[6] Antonio Eximeno, S.J. (born Valencia 26th November 1729, died Rome 9th June 1808). After the suppression of the Order of Jesuits in Spain in 1767, he devoted himself entirely to music and published his famous book, *Dell' origine e delle regole della musica colla storia del suo progresso, decadenza e rinnovazione* (Rome, 1774), in which he attacked the traditional view that music and mathematics were closely related.

[7] Jean de la Bruyère (born Paris 16th August 1645, died Versailles 10th

May 1696), the famous French moralist. He started as a lawyer, then became Head of Treasury at Caen and was later attached to the Court at Chantilly. His most famous work is *Caractères de Theophraste, traduits du grec, avec les caractères ou les mœurs de ce siècle* (Paris 1688), which contains shrewd and witty observations on the Court of Louis XIV.

[8] ARISTIDES QUINTILIANUS, a Greek music historian of the post-Ciceronian period, whose work '*Περὶ μουσιχῆς*', according to Hermann Abert, is one of our main sources of information on ancient music.

[9] ETIENNE MAURICE FALCONET (born Vevey 1716, died Paris 4th January 1791), well-known French sculptor, amongst whose works were a statue of St Ambrose for the Church of the Invalides in Paris and an equestrian statue of Peter the Great in Petersburg. Amongst his published works was *Réflexions sur la sculpture* (Paris, 1768).

[10] Nothing further is known of MARQUIS DE MASCARILLE.

[11] Nothing further is known of MONSIEUR CARITIDÉS.

[12] MATTEO MARIA BOJARDO, COUNT OF SCANDIANO (born Scandiano *circa* 1434, died Reggio 20th December 1494), Italian poet whose *Orlando innamorato* (Scandiano, 1498) made him famous.

[13] FRANCESCO CONTE ALGAROTTI (born Venice 11th December 1712, died Pisa 3rd May, 1764), well-known Italian author who was invited to the Prussian Court in Berlin by Frederick II, was the embodiment of the' tasteful dilettantism of the time'. Important as a contribution to the development of music is his *Saggio sopra l'opera in musica* (1755), in which he called for the operatic reforms which Gluck carried through. It contains the text of a five-act opera, *Iphigénie en Aulide*.

[TO BARONESS ANNA VON FRIES.[1] *French*]

Madame,

I have been so plagued over music and I am so disgusted with it, that at present I would not write a single note for a louis. So you can imagine the extent of my devotion to you, Madame, since I could resolve to arrange for the harp the two songs which I have the honour to send you.[2] Never was a more terrible and more hotly-disputed battle fought than that over my opera *Armide*. The cabals against *Iphigénie, Orphée* and *Alceste* were by comparison mere petty encounters with minor forces. The Ambassador of Naples, in order to ensure that Piccinni's opera should be a great success, has been intriguing indefatigably against me both at Court and amongst the nobility. He has won over Marmontel, La Harpe and several academicians to write against my musical system and my way of composing. M. l'Abbé Arnaud, M. Suard and a few others have rallied to my defence and the quarrel became so heated that insults would have led to deeds, if mutual friends had not restored order amongst them. The *Journal de Paris*, which is sold daily, is full of it. This dispute is making the Editor a fortune, for he already has more than 2,500 subscribers in Paris. There, then, you have the revolution in French music carried out with the most blatant pomp. The enthusiasts tell me: Monsieur, you are fortunate to enjoy the honours of persecution; all great geniuses have experienced this. I would gladly send them to the devil with their fine speeches. The fact is that the opera which was said to have failed produced in seven performances 37,200 livres without reckoning the boxes rented for the year and the subscribers. Yesterday the eighth performance brought in 5,767 livres. Never has such a terrible crush nor such a sustained silence been known before. The pit was so crowded that one man, who had his hat on and was told by the attendant to remove it, replied: 'Come and remove it yourself, for I cannot use my arms.' That raised a laugh. I saw people coming out with their hair dishevelled and their clothes wringing wet, as if they had fallen into a river. Only a Frenchman would pay such a price for his pleasure. There are six points in the opera at which the public are forced to lose countenance and are carried away. Come, Madame, and see this tumult; it will amuse you as much as the opera itself. I am in despair that I cannot leave yet on account of the bad road: my wife is too frightened. I beg you to pay my compliments to the Baron and to Monsieur Gontard.[3] I remain with the most perfect esteem,

Madame,

Your very humble and very obedient servant,

Le Chevalier Gluck.

PS. My wife sends you a thousand tender regards.

Paris, 16 November 1777.

[1] Anna Baroness von Fries, *née* d'Escherny, was the wife of the Freiherr Johann von Fries.

[2] He is presumably referring to two odes by Klopstock, which Gluck had arranged for the harp. These arrangements have so far remained untraced.

[3] Johann Jakob Freiherr von Gontard administered not only the Viennese banking firm of Fries & Co. but also part of Gluck's personal fortune, amounting to 9,000 gulden and invested in a life annuity at 8 per cent. interest. He was born in Frankfurt-am-Main in 1739. In 1776 he became a member of the Lodge of Freemasons 'Zur gekrönten Hoffnung', to which Mozart also belonged. He died of senile decay in Vienna on 30th January 1819.

[FROM BERNARD SAURIN[1] TO GLUCK. *French*]
[before 28th December 1777]

Couplets
Sur l'air: Du haut en bas

Ton Art divin,
Puissant Maître de l'Harmonie,
Ton Art divin,
En miracles s'épuise en vain;
Plus tu triomphes, plus l'Envie
Montre de fureur & décric
Ton Art divin.

De tous les temps,
Ce fut aventure pareille
De tous les temps.
Laisse dire les mécréans;
Reine du cœur & de l'oreille,
Ta lyre sera la merveille
De tous les temps.

The text of the original couplet ran as follows:

Du haut en bas
Vous traitez vos amans, Climène,
Du haut en bas:
Pour moi, je ne m'en plaindrai pas:
Car j'aime assez qu'une inhumaine,
Quand je suis amoureux, me mène
Du haut en bas.

It was sung to the following tune:

[1] BERNARD SAURIN, who was born in Paris in 1706, was Secretary to the Duke of Orléans and a well-known dramatic poet. He died in his native City in 1781.

[FROM THE 'AMATEURS' TO GLUCK. *French*]

In our musical repertoire, Monsieur, we have a scene from *Armide* ('le perfide Renaud me fuit'). M. Cambini,[1] who is the author, begs us, for reasons of delicacy and out of respect for this piece which is so well treated in your opera, no longer to perform his scene.

You may rest assured, Monseiur, that we would share the honesty and delicacy of M. Cambini, if it were possible that his scene might harm yours or yours his. The two scenes in their respective places, one in the theatre, the other in the concert-hall, have different merits. We hope, Monsieur, that you will reply to this letter in such a way as to persuade M. Cambini to continue to enjoy the success of his work, which was known at our concert two years before you had made your opera.

[1] GIOVANNI GIUSEPPE CAMBINI (1746–1825) had composed the final scene of *Armide* ('Le perfide Renaud me fuit') two years before Gluck. On 27th January 1777 it was performed by Mlle du Chateau in the Concert des Amateurs and it was to be repeated in January 1778. Gluck answered this letter as follows:

[TO THE 'AMATEURS'. *French*]

[January 1778]

M. Gluck is very sensible of the honesty of Mm. lcs Amateurs and of M. Cambini; he has the honour to assure these gentlemen that he will have great pleasure in hearing the *Armide* scene by M. Cambini performed. It would be tyranny in music to profess that the 'Amateurs' should not be allowed to perform their productions. M. Gluck enters into no competition with anyone and he will always take pleasure in hearing better music than his own. One must have but one aim: the advancement of art.

[TO FRANZ KRUTHOFFER. *German*]

[In Kruthoffer's handwriting:
Replied Paris on 20th March, 1778]

Vienna, 2nd March 1778

Dearest friend!

Yesterday afternoon we arrived here, after we had endured much discomfort on this journey, the coach and wheels broken and stuck in the snow and every other form of misfortune. Moreover, I arrived here at the wrong time, for everyone is preparing for war,[1] which will be difficult to avert. I am sending you a letter to Mlle le Vasseur together with the ring, which I beg you to give soon to Mr Zoller,[2] so that he can put the piece in, and also our compliments to the same; when the ring has been cleaned and is in order, I pray you hand the same to Mlle le Vasseur together with the letter. Tomorrow I propose to go to Hoff to see what is happening there. Do not forget to send me plenty of news and a few scores from *Armide*,[3] if you have not already sent them. My head is still quite thick from the journey. I simply do not know what I am writing to you. Our respects to Herr von Blumendorff, to you and all our good friends. Remember us, as we you, with affection and think sometimes of your old servant.

Gluck.

PS. I beg you to see to the enclosed letters.
PS. I duly received your charming letter of the 17th and read it with much pleasure. You must not send my womenfolk any lace.

[1] The outbreak of the BAVARIAN WAR OF SUCCESSION between Prussia, allied with Saxony, and Austria had become inevitable when Frederick the Great took exception to the treaty concluded in January 1778 between the Emperor Joseph II and the Elector Karl Theodor of the Palatinate. In subsequent letters Gluck gives his friends in Paris detailed reports on the course of the campaign.
[2] Nothing further is known about the jeweller ZOLLER.
[3] The composer had been in touch with a new publisher in connection with *Armide*: Charles Mathon de la Cour, proprietor of the *Bureau du Journal de musique*. The engraving of the score was done by Mme Lobry, who had already engraved the *Orpheé* score in 1774 and the piano part in *L'Arbre enchanté* in 1775.

[FROM FRIEDRICH GOTTLIEB KLOPSTOCK TO GLUCK. *German*]

Hamburg, 16th March 1778

Brockmann[1] is bringing this letter to you. He is a man who can understand and feel what you sing to him.

You have certainly not yet forgotten and never will forget your dear little one,[2] nor will I. How would it be if once on your long journeys you went to Paris by way of Hamburg? We wanted to look after you properly with young and unspoiled attention, if you sang something . . . [illegible] with old wine. I hear that the *Hermannsschlacht* is to be produced in Vienna. Have you already progressed so far with the composition? A few words on this. But will the beautiful, splendid, delicious, beneficent war not cause this, like many other things, to stand still? The Kaiser[3] wins my heart more and more. He makes a tremendous mistake if he thinks the old man in Potsdam has grown too old.[4] If it were not that in war everything lies fallow, which is better than war, then I would repeat my request to you to remind the Kaiser that he did not keep the promise he made through me to the scholars. But now—

Your
Klopstock

[1] Johann Franz Hieronymus Brockmann was born in Graz on 30th September 1745. He became an itinerant comedian and belonged, *inter alia*, to the troupes of Joseph Bodenburg (1748–1788) and Joseph von Kurz-Bernadon (1715–1784). In 1771 Brockmann joined the theatre in Hamburg, which at that time was under the direction of Friedrich Ludwig Schröder (1744–1816) and where he became the leading actor in Germany, frequently compared with Garrick. On 6th April 1778 he arrived in Vienna on tour and on 30th April made his first appearance as Essex in the tragedy *Die Gunst der Fürsten*, by Christian Heinrich Schmid. From 1789 to 1791 he directed the Hofburgtheater in Vienna, where he died on 12th April 1812.

[2] Marianne Nanette Gluck.

[3] Joseph II.

[4] Friedrich II (the Great), King of Prussia, born on 24th January 1712, reigned from 1740 until his death on 17th August 1786.

[To de Vismes.[1] *French*]

From Vienna, 1st April 1778

Monsieur,

I received your kind letter with much pleasure, and I have been very appreciative of the marks of friendship and expressions of good-will which you show to me. I hope that some day an occasion may arise when I shall be able to show you all my appreciation. In the meantime I wish you every success in your new enterprise, which, my heart tells me, will not be denied you, for you have all the qualities necessary to make it succeed. It only remains for me to beg you to continue your friendship which is so dear to me and to accept the expressions of esteem and regard with which I have the honour to be

Monsieur
Your very humble and very obedient
Servant
Chevalier Gluck

PS. I beg you to give my respects to M. de Campan.[2]

[Address:]

From Vienna
To Monsieur
Monsieur de Vismes
Place de Victoires
à Paris

[1] Anne Pierre Jacques Vismes de Valgay was born in Paris in 1745. He was Sub-Director of the Treasury until 1778, when he acquired a

twelve-year concession for the Académie royale de musique. He was an enthusiastic Gluckist. He died at Coudebec in 1819.
[2] CAMPAN was valet de chambre de la Reine and had sponsored de Vismes's appointment.

[TO NICOLAS FRANÇOIS GUILLARD.[1] *French*]

Vienna, 17th June 1778

Your letters reach me very late, my friend. I received your latest yesterday; it took sixteen days. I thought that you were ill.

Do you wish me to reply as to the essential points? Gladly. In the first place, I will say that the changes you have made in your fourth act are to no purpose, because I have already finished the duet between Orestes and Pylades, and the final air of the act—'Divinité des grandes âmes!'—and I do not wish to alter anything in them. In what you call the fifth act, you must cut down the third strophe of the hymn, or else write a more interesting one; people would not understand the words, 'le spectre fier et sauvage', which, besides, scarcely make the situation any more moving. Your verses also must be of the same style, quatre à quatre; I myself have arranged the second strophe thus:

Dans les cieux et sur la terre
Tout est soumis à ta loi;
Tout ce que l'Erebe enserre
A ton nom pâlit d'effroi!

If then you wish to write a third strophe, it must go like the second; and an important thing that must not be forgotten is that the ceremony takes place while they are singing, and that the same air must suit the ceremony. I also want Thoas, the high priest, to enter in a fury, in the fourth scene, singing an air of invective; and every verse must be written without recitative, so as to be sung right up to the catastrophe. By this means the dénouement would be richer by a decisive emotion and warmth, which would penetrate the actors and chorus with an irresistible effect. So, as far as you approve my idea, hasten to send me your words; if not, I will keep to the words already written.

Now we come to the great air that ends the act during the sacrifices. Here I want an air in which the words explain the music at the same time as the situation. The sense must terminate at the end of each verse, and not be repeated either at the beginning or in the middle of the following verses. This is an essential condition for the verses; though it may be disregarded in the recitative, and so much the more happily as this mode of division is a certain means for distinguishing the lyric portion from the recitative, and for relieving the melody.

At the same time, for the words I ask of you, I want a verse of ten syllables, taking care to put a long and sonorous syllable wherever I indicate it:

se mai senti spirarti sul volto
lieve fiato que lento s'aggiri
di, son questi gli estremi sospiri
del mio fido che muore per me.

I would like the third verse to be cut by a monosyllable as in Italian, for example, 'vois nos peines, entends nos cris perçants'. Your last verse must be sombre and solemn, if you wish it to be congruous with my music.

After these four verses—or eight, if you wish, provided they are all in the same metre—will come the chorus, *Contemplez ces tristes apprêts*!' and this appears to me to suit the situation very well. I want the air here to have pretty nearly the same sense. After the chorus, the air will be resumed *da capo,* or else there will simply be the four verses you have written. I explain myself rather confusedly, for my head is excited with music; if you do not understand me, we will leave the thing till my arrival, and then it will be soon done; the rest, I think, we will leave as it is, cutting down the recitatives here and there, wherever they seem to be too long and mere repetitions. This will not damage the work, which ought, I think, to have an astonishing effect.

On the question of my establishment I will await your first letter with the proposals, before I give you my opinion. Meanwhile, arrange it so that the Queen only asks for me for an indefinite period, for a few years, to get me out of here in comfort. But let her do this without losing time, because I can no longer travel in winter. I would leave at the beginning of September. I must know a couple of months in advance so that I can sell my effects and arrange my affairs. Farewell, my very dear friend. I embrace you with all my heart, as also our acquaintances.

PS. I cannot find the Prologo.[2] In any case, the Abbé Pezzona[3] could have it sent from Parma. Mention it to our dear Abbé.

This is how I would like the piece to be divided into four acts:

Scene 1

Orestes and Pylades in chains; the whole scene rests upon and ends with the aria: *unis de la plus tendre enfance.*

Scene 2

Orestes, Pylades, the Minister, the five verses remain cut, for they are superfluous.

Scene 3

Orestes alone

Scene 4

Orestes, the Eumenides

Scene 5

Iphigenia alone with Orestes, without bringing Pylades back. This scene can become interesting in dialogue and the word 'Agamemnon', which Orestes repeats three times, is interesting. This will form a kind of duet between the two leading actors. The greater part of what they have to say can remain. That will give added variety to the piece, for Orestes and Pylades are too often together as it is and everything that he [Pylades] says in this scene is unimportant and forced. Orestes by himself is in a good position; Iphigenia almost tears the words from him by force. So it is not necessary for him to be held back by Pylades. Do this scene as quickly as possible; I would like the opera to be finished by the end of July.

Scene 6

The sacrifice scene, then the end of the act. So the opera can remain in four acts. But dividing it into five, the end of the second act is, in my view, bad, because the Eumenides appear to Orestes only in a dream and in his imagination. This destroys the idea that, on seeing Iphigenia, he thinks he sees his mother. He must still be immersed in his dream when he speaks the words: 'Ma mère! Ciel!' otherwise they would lose their effect. The act will be a little longer, but no matter. Everything in it is warmer.

[1] Nicolas François Guillard was born in Chartres in 1752. He joined the literary élite of Paris and wrote a number of pieces, which were soon forgotten. In 1779 he attended a performance of Gluck's *Iphigénie en Aulide*, about which he was so enthusiastic that he wrote his *Iphigénie en Tauride*. He died in 1814.

[2] *Prologo* had been produced in Parma on 22nd February 1767.

[3] Nothing further is known of Abbé Pezzona.

Interesting is the fact that Guillard had also negotiated with François Joseph Gossec in connection with his *Iphigénie*. When Gossec learned that Gluck had set Guillard's *Iphigénie* to music, he wrote to the latter as follows:

[François Joseph Gossec to N. F. Guillard. *French*]

[1778]

Monsieur,

All explanations concerning your *Iphigénie* become useless: you had destined this work for M. Gluck. This preference was legitimate; he has accepted; your expectation is fulfilled and we must think no more of it. I would be the more easily consoled, Monsieur, if this question had not for eight or ten years been the object of my desires and if the custom of this country and the law of honesty, which I profess, did not make it impossible that I should ever satisfy my inclination or rather my violent passion in this respect. I hoped that a skilful man of letters might undertake to deal with this subject. You have done so and it was not for me. That will in no way diminish the esteem I have for your talents, Monsieur; I confess that mine, which were stifled at birth, have not sufficient claim to confidence for them to be entrusted with a dramatic work of this importance.

Nevertheless, in renouncing it, M. Gluck thought me worthy to take it over (to some extent he owed me this reparation for having involuntarily taken for his *Iphigénie en Aulide* part of *Sabinus*, my first venture in this *genre*, in which he was kind enough to find things worthy of his attention). When M. Gluck decided not to undertake your work, M. le Bailli du Rollet promised it to me with the most complete and sincere assurance and with all possible authenticity. I was counting upon it, since you appeared to be in favour, Monsieur; during all this time he repeated his promise to me; during all this time M. Gluck for his part nourished my hopes by appearing markedly disinterested in the task and by his apparent resolve not to take on your work, frequently explaining to me the reasons why he had decided to decline. On the eve of his departure I was immediately after you in giving him fresh evidence of all my attachment and of my sincere regret at seeing him leave; well, Monsieur, he was cruel enough not to correct my mistake but protested yet again that he was not undertaking your *Iphigénie*. M. Gluck, for eight months, lulled me to sleep and, during all this time, I was a prey to a flattering dream; I did not expect, on waking, to find myself denied a boon which seemed to belong to me, relying upon his honesty and his tact. Such is the pleasure of sacrificing eight months of my time, eight months with so much coming and going, rejecting several good and reputable works, incurring the displeasure of several authors and other persons of the greatest distinction! However that may be, nothing will change my admiration for M. Gluck's great talents nor my esteem for yours, Monsieur; a lover of truth, I will always defend them against those who would wish to debase them before me. As to the alterations which I proposed to make in your *Iphigénie*, you could have attached less importance to them. A more detailed discussion with you would easily have rectified my error and the impression gained from a superficial and hasty reading. Nevertheless, my proposal was not without foundation, since M. Gluck himself demanded that this work be set in four acts, whereas it was only in three when it fell into my hands for half an hour; and assuredly half an hour is not enough to gain a perfect knowledge of so wide a subject. Perhaps it would have made a different impression on me if it had been arranged as M. Gluck proposed; it is quite possible that the same fault occurred to us both.

Accept my thanks, Monsieur, for your willingness to assign to me, in the dramatic part, a place immediately below M. Gluck. You flatter me and you are not sincere. I do not think as you do; I am too small to attain such a height. I cannot even hope to produce a work on the stage, so long as M. Gluck continues to hold it; *Sabinus* was eclipsed by him; *Iphigénie en Tauride* he took away from me; *Thésée*, fixed for next winter, will be postopned for two years by him. In two years, M. Piccinni or M. Gluck will relegate me to the third year, more especially as it is quite natural to leave to them the honours of the stage. In that time, my music will have an intolerable Gothic flavour and such few feeble sparks of goodness as it may possess will be sacrificed to prejudice. In the meantime my hair grows white, my hopes dwindle and my courage fails me. Everything merely disgusts me. Consequently, in order to be wise and prudent, to avoid strife and face up to prejudice, I think I must no longer work for the lyrical stage. So, Monsieur, I will not take advantage of the kind offers you have been good enough to make; I am most deeply obliged to you for them and, if it were possible that I might decide to attempt this folly once again and to take up this heavy plough once more, the succour of your talents, which you have so kindly offered, would lighten the load. Nothing would give me greater pleasure than to unite my talents with yours.

I have the honour to be with the greatest esteem and highest regard, Monsieur,

Your very humble and very obedient servant,

Gossec.

[Address:]
à Monsieur,
M. Guillard, rue des Petits-Champs St. Martin
Maison de Mrs. de St. Julien des Menestriers,
à Paris.

[To Franz Kruthoffer. *German*]

[In Kruthoffer's handwriting:
Replied Paris, 17th July 1778]

Vienna, 28th June 1778

Dearest friend,

You are most kind with your letters. I look forward to the courier only on account of you. Just continue to write me such long ones, for they cool my head, which at present is in a complete fever with two operas, *Iphigénie* and *Narcisse*, which are already in there. This is also one reason why I write to you so laconically, for I am sure you would not wish to hinder me in my work. You say I should not now come to Paris, but others write to me that I should not let the opportunity pass of presenting an opera before the Queen's accouchement;[1] whose advice shall I follow? I leave it to Providence and in the meantime will go on working. My very tender compliments to Mademoiselle le Vasseur. I never write to her because I wish to retain the title I treasure so much of 'foutu imbécile', which she has so kindly given me. My wife also sends her a thousand tender things. For the rest, always keep a little affection for us; my wife and I send you, H. v. Blumendorff and all friends a thousand compliments and I remain for all time,

Dearest friend,
Your most devoted servant
Gluck.

[Address:]
A Monsieur
Monsieur de Kruthoffer
chez S. Ex. Monsieur Le Comte de
Mercy Ambassadeur J. Roy. Apot.
à
Paris

[1] Marie Antoinette, after eight years of marriage, was expecting her first child, Marie Thérèse Charlotte, who was born on 19th December 1778 and died, as Duchess of Angoulême, in 1851.

[TO ABBÉ ARNAUD. *French*]

Vienna, 15th July 1778

You are quite right, Monsieur, I will not be able to finish my two operas in Vienna. I must get nearer to the poets, for we do not understand each other well from a distance. I reckon to leave here in the month of September, if Monsieur de Vismes can obtain the Empress's permission for me to go to Paris. Without it I could not leave. M. le Bailly [du Roullet] will tell you the reasons. So I will probably have need once more of your redoubtable arm to strike down my enemies this next winter; without you I have not the courage to risk another battle. Meanwhile muster your troops, cajole our allies, particularly Madame de Vaines,[1] to whom I beg you to present my respects as also to all her [sic] illustrious society. Has she still that beautiful Circassian head? I often see her in my mind's eye, when I am working and do not feel sufficiently inspired; she must contribute greatly to the success of my operas.

The opera at Bologna was very well patronized. The Duke and Duchess of Parma[2] and the Archduke and Archduchess of Milan[3]

went to see it. In general the Italians have called it the great Opera of Bologna. One of my friends who saw it presented in Vienna wrote to me that de Amici,[4] who played the part of Alceste, was in the nude, that the actor who played Admetos[5] was too old and that the ballets were all topsy-turvy; they danced right into the chorus, 'Pleure o patrie, o Thessalie!' so you can imagine what happened afterwards. My friend quotes an Italian proverb to compare the opera *Alceste* with the world: 'Il mondo va de se, e non casca, perchè non ha dove cascare.' I will add that the other day, when I was with the Prince von Kaunitz,[6] the envoy from Naples begged me to have sent to him all the operas which I have made in France; they are being asked of him in Naples, where people wish to have all that I have done. That is an anecdote which will not greatly please Monsieur l'Ambassadeur, God bless him. My wife pays you a thousand compliments and I remain, with the greatest admiration for your genius,

Monsieur,
Your very humble and very obedient servant
G. Gluck.

[1] MADAME DE VAINES was the wife of the Administrator of the State Domains, Jean de Vaines (1733–1803).
[2] FERDINAND VON BOURBON, Duke of Parma and Piacenza (1741–1802) married Maria Amalia, Archduchess of Austria (1746–1804) in 1769.
[3] FERDINAND KARL ANTON, Archduke of Austria (1754–1806), married Maria Beatrix d'Este, Duchess of Massa and Carrara (1750–1829) in 1771. He was Governor-General of Lombardy with his official residence at Milan.
[4] ANNA LUCIA DE AMICIS-BUONSOLLACCI was born in Naples about 1733. She was a pupil of the famous Vittoria Tesi-Trammontini. In 1762 she sang in the London Opera House under Johann Christian Bach and around 1766 in Naples. In 1772 she was in Milan, where she sang in Mozart's *Lucio Silla;* then she went to Venice. On 9th May 1778 she sang Gluck's *Alceste* in Bologna for the first time. She died in Naples in 1816.
[5] The programme for the performance of *Alceste* on 9th May 1778 (Library of Congress, ML.48. A5. v. 29) gives the cast as follows:

PERSONAGGI

ADMETO Re di Fera in Tessaglia . . Signor Giuseppe Tibaldi
ALCESTE sua Sposa . . . . Signora Anna de Amicis-Buonsolazzi
EUMELO } loro Figli
ASPASIA }
EVANDO Confidente d'Admeto . . Signor Francesco Cavalli, Virtuoso di Camera di S.A.R. l'Infante Duca di Parma

ISMENE Confidente d'Alceste .... Signora Giulia Moroni

Un Banditore
Un Nume Infernale
Gran Sacerdote d'Apollo
Apollo } ...... Signor Domenico Poggi

Oracolo.
Coro di Cortigiani, e Cittadini.
Coro di Damigelle d'Alceste.
Coro di Sacerdoti d'Apollo.
Coro di Numi Infernali.

La Scena si rappresenta in Fera.

La Poesia e del Sig. Configliere de' Calsabigi.

La Musica e del Sig. Cavaliere Gluk fra gli Arcadi Armonide Terpsicoreo.

CORISTI

Signor
Pictro Grazioli Direttore.

Signori	Signore	Signori
Gio. Battista Longarini.	Antonia Zaccarini.	Domenico Tibaldi.
Giuseppe Costa.	Teresa Ristorini.	Girol. Cortegiani.
Andrea Ristorini.	Lucia Durante.	Paolo Mandini.
Antonio Frascaroli.	Elisabetta Dalfùocco.	Gaetano Rizzardi.
Marco Lucchi.	Anna Lazzari.	Franc. Romagnoli.
Luigi Dorotei.	Maria Fioresi.	Giacomo Rossi.
Carlo Contucci.	Domenica Nannetti.	Petronio Sola.
Anastasio Massa.	Anna Tartarini.	Antonio Berti.
Giuseppe Garetti.	Anna Teresa Greca.	Tommaso Chermanini.
	Isabella Beni.	

Al Cembalo	Capo dell 'Orchestra
Signor Maestro Bernardino Ottani	Signor Cristoforo Babbi
Accad. Filar.	Accad. Filar.

LI BALLI

Sono d'invenzione, e direzione del Signor GIUSEPPE CANZIANI, ed eseguiti dalli seguenti.

PRIMI BALLERINI SERJ.

Signora Catterina Curz. Signor Giuseppe Canziani sudetto.

PRIMI GROTTESCHI.

Signora Gertrude Paccini Grisostomi. Signor Gregorio Grisostomi.

PRIMI BALLERINI SERJ FUORI DE' CONCERTI.

Signora Antonia Torri. Signor Michele Fabiani.

MEZZI CARATTIERI.

Signora Marianna Feracaccia. Signor Giuseppe Herdlitska.

Signora Anna Agostini.

Signor Giuseppe Bartolomei. Signor Eusebio Luzzi.

ALTRI BALLERINI.

Signora Teresa Boggi. Signor Antonio Papini.
Signora Gesualda Cocchi. Signor Giacomo Ostici.
Signora Maria Vicinelli. Signor Giorgio Ronzi.

[6] Presumably ERNST CHRISTOPH COUNT VON KAUNITZ, eldest son of the Chancellor, Wenzel Anton Prince von Kaunitz-Rietberg. He was born on 6th June 1737 and was Ambassador to the Court of Naples from 1765 to 1770. From 1773 onwards he was General-Hof baudirektor (Director-General of Court Building) in Vienna, where he died on 19th May 1797.

[TO FRANZ KRUTHOFFER. *German*]

[In Kruthoffer's handwriting:
Replied Paris, 16th August 1778]

Vienna, 29th July 1778

Dearest friend!

To me your reminders are commands, so I am sending to you the two letters you required, which I beg you to have delivered. Your charming letters always give us much pleasure, especially now that Mr Calin[1] has come down once more on my neck and is lodging with me. He sends his highest regards. He is now even more argumentative than before; we have also more to argue about with the present war, in which so far our forces have held the Prussians in all encounters. The Kaiser's presence produces an incomparable effect. Incidentally, I will take your advice concerning my Paris journey and also treat my work phlegmatically. I have undertaken two operas, because I did not want to displease either the Bailly [du Roullet] or the Baron Tschoudi,[2] for one or other of them would not have forgiven me. If, however, M. de Vismes does not succeed in obtaining the permission of the Empress [Maria Theresia], then I will stay at home and think, like Goldsmith's boy.[3] Send us plenty of news; our regards to you and all our good friends. I remain always yours.

[1] CARLO CALIN, like Franz Kruthoffer, had become friendly with Gluck in Paris. He is repeatedly mentioned in correspondence until 1781, and wrote the letter on 19th June 1781 on Gluck's behalf.

[2] JOHANN METZ LUDWIG THEODOR BARON VON TSCHUDI (born 25th August 1735) was the Paris envoy of the Archbishop of Liège. He wrote the libretto for Gluck's *Echo und Narcisse*, and died in Paris on 7th March 1784.

[3] The reference to OLIVER GOLDSMITH's novel, *The Vicar of Wakefield* (1766), shows that Gluck was familiar with it, presumably in one of the many German editions.

[TO FRANZ KRUTHOFFER. *German*]

[In Kruthoffer's handwriting:
Replied Paris, 19th September 1778]

Vienna, 29th August 1778

Dearest friend,

I am sorry that I cannot write you anything interesting on our war. There are frequent skirmishes and we have the upper hand almost all the time. A clear proof of this is that the Kaiser has promoted a number of officers on the spot, because they set such a good example to their subordinates. It is true, that General de Vins[1] was surprised by a Corps of Prince Heinrich[2] and lost some 1,000 men, but on the other hand Lieut.-Colonel Nauendorf[3] took from the King 243 waggons with victuals and thirteen supply waggons together with 300 horses, either capturing or destroying the convoy. It seems we do not want to strike, for his army has so much sickness and so many deserters that it will surely break up of itself. The King would like to join forces with his brother, but Loudon[4] stands between them. As soon as there is anything new, I will report it to you. Best regards to you and H. v. Blumendorff from my wife and from the bawler Calin. You should hear him now; he is bawling like a man possessed. Farewell, dearest friend. [turn over]

The news has just come in that the King has tried to force the Pass of Hohenelbe, where General Wallis[5] commands a corps of 15,000 men, to join forces with Prince Heinrich. He ordered General Anhalt[6] to attack him but he was thrown back, and the King must remain sitting in the mountains. General Wuntsch[7] has also attacked General Wurmser[8] with three cavalry regiments, and the latter has also flung him back with two regiments of Hussars and a battalion of Croats. The details will follow. Meanwhile, it is already agreed that before the end of the campaign the Prussian army will have to leave Bohemia; then it will be our turn to plunder in foreign lands. Adieu. I had to open the packet in order to send you this.

[1] JOSEPH NIKOLAUS FREIHERR VON VINS (1732–1798) later became G.I.C. Ordnance.

[2] PRINCE HEINRICH OF PRUSSIA (1726–1802) was a brother of King Frederick II of Prussia.

[3] FRIEDRICH AUGUST COUNT VON NAUENDORF (1749–1801) later became Lieutenant Field Marshal.

[4] ERNST GIDEON FREIHERR VON LOUDON (1717–1790) also became Lieutenant Field Marshal. When his body was displayed in the Müller Wachsfigurenkabinett in October 1790, W. A. Mozart was commissioned by Count Deym to write his famous Adagio and Allegro for a mechanical organ (K.V. 594).

[5] OLIVIER COUNT VON WALLIS (1742–1799) later became G.I.C. Ordnance.

[6] JOHANN ALBRECHT COUNT VON ANHALT (1735–1802) was a Prussian Major-General.

[7] JOHANN JAKOB VON WUNSCH (17??–1788) was a Prussian infantry General.

[8] Dagobert Count von Wurmser (1724–1797) later became General Field Marshal.

[From Franz Kruthoffer to Gluck. *French*]

M. l'Ambassadeur [Mercy-Argenteau] has entrusted me, Mr, with the honour of communicating with you on his behalf, to the effect that, having been informed of the proposals which M. de Vimes made to you concerning your new opera *Iphigénie en Tauride* and of the reply which you have just sent him on this subject, he believes that at this very moment, when, more than ever before, not only all the connoisseurs but a very large part of the public are paying just tribute to your talents and await this new work with impatience, you owe it to your reputation not to reject M. de Vimes's offers. His Excellency also authorizes me to point out that he hoped to obtain for you, if not the complete sum for which you asked, at least that of twelve thousand francs, and he believes that you can easily make good this small difference, as this sixth work must bring your pension to a thousand crowns.

As for the permission of H.M. the Emp. [Marie Antoinette], which you seem to need for your journey, His Excy^{l}. thinks that at this time of calamities and war it would not be becoming for the Queen to make a request to her august mother [Marie Theresia], the sole aim of which would be to add to her pleasure in this country, that this consideration would render any approach on this subject impossible, and that even Mr. de Vimes was not in a position to solicit such a favour from the Queen.

Moreover, His Excy^{l}. believes that such permission would be superfluous, since one could regard as a general permission the assurance which His M^{y} the Emperor gave last year to his august sister, to allow you to come to France as often as new works would enable you to contribute to his entertainment.

These, M., are the thoughts which H. Excy^{l}. has ordered me to communicate to you. I do so with all the more pleasure as I can take this opportunity of renewing my assurances of complete and sincere devotion to you. I am also to add many compliments on his behalf.

[Kruthoffer]

A. M. le Ch^{r}.
Gluck de
Paris le 4.7^{bre}
1778

[To Franz Kruthoffer. *French*]

Vienna, 26th September 1778

It was the day before yesterday, the 24th, Monsieur, that I received your letter of the 4th of this month, and I would not have it yet, if I had not sent my servant to ascertain if the Paris courier had arrived. This mishap compels me to beg you, Monsieur, to pay my very humble respects to His Exc. the Ambassador and tell him on my behalf that it is impossible for me to undertake any journey at this moment. I would require four weeks to get my travelling coach in order and arrange all my domestic affairs; there has been too much delay in letting me know; neither my wife nor I could endure the discomforts of such a long journey towards the end of October. I hope I will be able to return to Paris next spring, provided that Mr de Vismes does not wish to haggle with me, for he treats me like a man who lives on the streets of Paris. He cannot imagine how much one suffers on a journey of 700 miles. At my age I am too fond of my comfort; if it were not for my desire to see my friends again, I would not leave, [even] supposing I could earn the sum he offers me merely by making the journey. For the rest, I am extremely grateful for the kindness His Exc. the Ambassador has shown me on this occasion and for the interest he takes in all that concerns me, and I beg you to assure him of this on my behalf. Accept, Monsieur, the feelings of esteem and respect with which I have the honour to be

Your very humble, very obedient servant,
the Chevalier Gluck.

[turn over]
We have completed, thank God, one of the most glorious defensive campaigns without giving battle. The Prussians have lost at least thirty thousand men, their cavalry and guns ruined. Loudon is now in pursuit of Prince Henry, who is giving way before him, so that you will soon have the news that we are before Dresden.

from Vienna.

[Address:]
A Monsieur
Monsieur de Kruthoffer
Secretaire de Son Ex[ce] M.L. Ambasseur
Imp. et Royal. Apostl.
à
Paris au petit Luxembourg.

[TO FRANZ KRUTHOFFER. *German*]

[In Kruthoffer's handwriting:
Replied Paris, 19th October 1778]

Vienna, 30th September 1778

Dearest friend

I read your letter with much pleasure, but the *Mercure*[1] vexed me. I am now resolved not to come to Paris till Mr de Vismes has obtained an assurance from the Minister that justice will not be allowed to lay hands on me when I come to trim Marmontel's ears. Because the *Journal de Paris* has not been able to make him more modest, he needs a more violent medium and this will be the worst. We have excellent news. There is not a single Prussian left in Bohemia; immediately after the retreat of the King, Loudon kept close on Prince Heinrich's heels. He did not stand his ground but retired to Saxony in two columns; Loudon's advance-guard has also pushed forward. It is said, however, that in his withdrawal he left 1,900 prisoners, 3,000 deserters and twenty-three cannons. As you see, dearest friend, one can be satisfied with this campaign. It is with them as with my operas, first they are abused, then people find they are not so bad after all. Adieu, many compliments from me and mine to you, H. v. Plumendorff [sic], and all acquaintances. Mr Calin sends his respects. There is nothing to be done with him now; he quarrels and shouts like an incendiary.

[1] Gluck's remark refers to the 'Lettre de M. Marmontel à M. de la Harpe', which was printed on 15th September 1778 in the *Mercure de France*:

It came to me as no surprise, sir, that Prince Beloselski's essay on Italian music was not to everyone's taste. You see how the most polite and most moderate of M. Gluck's supporters mutilates this little work and with what skill he reduces it to nothing. Let us pass over the page where he has cut so skilfully and glance at a few of his critical passages.

'There is more than one point of resemblance between Vinci and Corneille', the Prince has said. 'Each was a creator in *genre*. The musician made the first comic opera, which is *Le Joueur*,[1] as the poet composed the first good comedy. Both have attained approximately the same heights in tragic ideas, the same warmth, the same fluency of style: the two operas *Artaxerce* and *Didon*[2] are sublime examples of this, as are *Le Cid* and *Cinna*'.[3]

Here is how this passage is reproduced: 'M. le Prince Beloselski says that Vinci is a creator like Corneille, because he made the first comic opera. It is hard to feel the justice of this comparison.'

Whose fault is it if it is not felt? This method of criticism is very easy; furthermore, it is very common, but the Censor finds his task more arduous when he quotes accurately.

The Prince said of Pergolesi that he was 'the most eloquent of composers', and he adds: 'There is nothing more simple than his melody, his methods, his motifs; nothing more harmonious than his accompaniments.'

The critic asks in which of his works Pergolesi was eloquent? 'The first couplet of the *Stabat*', he says, 'is one of the most moving and most sublime pieces of music, but pathos is not eloquence; and there is nothing so sure as eloquence in music.'

In the first place, is the first couplet all that is moving and sublime in the *Stabat*? Is not, for example, the line 'Vidit suum dulcem natum'? Does it not bring tears to one's eyes? Are there not also heartrending passages in the *Olimpiade* of Pergolesi,[4] such as the aria 'Se cerca, se dice'? One would like to know where eloquence is to be found if not in pathos?

I suppose that the Prince would have said: 'Pergolesi, of all the composers, is the one who possessed in the highest degree the art of communicating quickly and impressing forcibly upon the souls of others the profound feeling which fills him'. Would that not have been a truth which the whole of Europe has recognized, at least in the *Stabat*? Now, this definition of pathos in musical expression is precisely the one M. d'Alembert has given of eloquence; I have not changed a single word of it.

But Prince Beloselksi awarded the palm for eloquence to Pergolesi; and it is reserved for M. Gluck. He bestowed upon Vinci the title of 'creator' in dramatic music and compared him with Corneille; both this comparison and this title belong only to M. Gluck. The critic makes no secret of it; he makes a formal decision.

'M. Gluck', he says, 'will have the glory of having achieved in music what Corneille achieved in poetry: he conceived, he created the true lyrical tragedy. . . . His place is now assured amongst the small number of creative geniuses in the arts.'

And who assured him this high position? Who dispensed this glory? Two or three anonymous writers who repeat one another's words and echo one another's replies in the newspapers, in the gazettes, in the broadsheets? These are the voices of fame.

The poems of *Alceste, Iphigénie* and *Orphée* are doubtless tragic and have a more pressing appeal than those of *Hippolyte, Dardanus* and *Castor*,[5] but is this a new *genre*? M. Gluck's music, whether by its declamatory vehemence or by its forceful harmony or by several pieces of Italian song, is preferable to that of Rameau, although one finds in it a rougher and coarser strain; but can this reinforced French music be called creative? And between Dardanus's monologue in prison, his scene with Iphise, those of Teucer in the second and fifth acts, Theseus's prayer to Pluto, in the opera *Hippolyte*, Telaire's monologue, the funeral chorus, that of the demons, the tableau of the Elysian Fields, the beautiful scenes in the fourth and fifth acts of the opera *Castor*; between these passages, I say, and the most loudly-praised passages in M. Gluck's *Orphée, Iphigénie* and *Alceste* is there the same gap as between the tragedies *Hardi* and *Le Cid, Horace*[6] and *Cinna*? Is there even a sufficient distance between them for Rameau to be considered as of no account in theatrical music and for Gluck to be regarded as its inventor? This concerns the French and they are the judges in their own country.

But let us ask the Italians, the Spaniards, the English or the Germans themselves if in Metastasio's operas all the tragic pieces have not been rendered twenty times by composers, who are M. Gluck's masters, with more fidelity and emotion than he? There is not one of these nations which does not affirm having heard a hundred moving pieces which will always be beyond his reach.

To the ignorant everything is new, and we are ignorant in music. What seems to us an artistic prodigy may, therefore, be a mere common thing. Let us remember the travelling rat whom we resemble quite closely:

> Sitôt qu'il fut hors de sa case,
> Que le monde, dit-il, est grand et spacieux!

Voilà les Apennines et voiçi le Caucase.
La moindre taupinée était mont à ses yeux.

(No sooner was he out of his cage
Than 'The world,' said he, 'is large and spacious!'
There are the Apennines, here the Caucasus.
The smallest molehill was a mountain in his eyes.)

It is for the scholars, it is for the artists, it is for the public in an enlightened country to say: 'Such and such is a creator.' The geometricians said it of Newton,[7] the men of letters said it of Corneille, and the nation repeated it. But who has said it of M. Gluck? Two or three men, highly skilled no doubt in everything else, but still novices in music and who, like myself, have only heard it in the French theatres and the concert-halls of Paris.

That is why it is desirable that each one should make himself known by name in discussions on art, so that the name may determine the weight of the personal opinion. Anyone who, like myself, merely had instinct, would be permitted a personal feeling, but for himself and for himself alone. Anyone who, by habit and by comparison, had a rather more practised ear and more informed taste would be permitted to express his opinion with a little more assurance but always modestly. Anyone who had made some progress in the art and who had received some months of instruction, for example in music, would have his studies taken into account; and if he performed, reasonably well, a bass accompaniment, then he would be given the right to speak by virtue of his *savoir-faire*. Anyone who believed he had been endowed by nature with the gift of judging everything without having learned anything would be allowed to congratulate himself on possessing this rare gift from heaven; but if, in his enthusaism, he denied soul and intelligence to anyone who had the misfortune not to admire what he admires or to like what he does not like; if with one hand he sought to knock down the statues of the most famous artists and with the other to erect a great monument to the glory of someone whom he had chosen to idolize; his name would reveal if this fanaticism was sincere or feigned. Finally, anyone versed in the art and in the study of its models, who had taken instruction in the theatre and, for his edification, had listened to the popular voice in various countries, would be regarded with greater confidence but would never be given the right to make pronouncements in the absolute and trenchant tone of our self-styled connoisseurs. Thus each one would be put in his place and I would know at this moment what is the degree of authority of the critic to whom I am replying. To be sure, I invite no one to imitate Guillot the Sycophant,[8] but why not *write* one's proper name when one is not the wolf in sheep's clothing?

Prince Beloselski finds Piccinni admirable, particularly in conveying the sense of the words; and until now the whole of Europe has been of this view.

The anonymous Frenchman stands apart and would have us believe that the whole of Europe understands nothing of this.

'One can judge', he says 'from *Roland* whether M. Piccinni has sought with so much care the merits attributed to him. I am not speaking of his recitative.' (How excessively indulgent!) 'I am not speaking of the too pastoral character of several arias which were open to the most heroic expression.' (He should certainly have quoted them!) 'If one recalls', he adds, 'the aria of Medor, "Je la verrai: c'est assez pour ma flamme", one perceives that in this line, which the poet punctuates as follows: "Esclave, heureux de servir tant d'appas," the composer, in order to retain the symmetry of the musical phrase, was obliged to introduce a pause after the word "heureux" and to punctuate as follows: "Esclave heureux; de servir tant d'appas." Which no longer makes sense.'

The composer committed no fault: he wrote as an intelligent man with an abundance of taste. It is the critic who is mistaken and he will be the judge of it himself. The composer did not detach these words 'de servir tant d'appas'. He wrote 'Heureux de servir tant d'appas' as a continuous sequence and without any pause. The two words which he permitted himself to detach on one occasion, because they form a complete idea, are 'esclave heureux', and I would have been capable of detaching them myself, by giving the line as follows:

Esclave heureux, heureux de servir tant d'appas.

Now, this is not a fault; it is, in music, a graceful turn of style and it adds a new measure of force to the expression. There, then, is an obviously false criticism; and yet M. Gluck's supporters have not ceased to repeat it, ever since this aria of Roland's was heard on the piano and more than three months before it was sung on the stage.

'In Angelique's aria', adds the anonymous critic:

'Oui, je le dois: je suis Reine.
Du doux penchant qui m'entraîne,
Oui, je dois me garantir.

'One can also see how the second line,

'Du doux penchant qui m'entraîne,

closes, like the first, with a final pause which separates it from the next line and makes the words incomprehensible.'

The reply is simple: there is no 'final pause' after the second line; one has only to have an ear to realize that the accent of the voice is suspended at the comma; and M. Piccinni, who knows what a 'final pause' means in music, assures us that there is none.

'Everyone has observed' (so the critic continues) 'that in Roland's monologue "Ah! j'attendrai longtemps", the musician has depicted the calm of the night and the serenity of hope, while the poet wished to express the impatience of a frantic lover and the absence of the night.'

Everyone, I will say for my part, has found this monologue ravishing and most faithful in character, most sensitive and utterly in keeping with the situation: witness the renewed applause which interrupts it each time it is sung. But let us have done with these formal assertions and arguments and look at the monologue itself.

The musician wished to depict not 'the calm of the night' but the calm of hope; not 'the impatience of a frantic lover', for Roland is not that yet, but the impatience of a lover who is already happy in the presentiment of the happiness which has been promised him.

Let us now see if 'the poet's intention' was to make this monologue sweet and tender or to express, as the critic maintains, 'the impatience of a frantic lover'.

The nature of the poetry determines that of the music; and I ask what is the nature of Quinault's monologue? The reply will perhaps be that this depends on how it is declaimed; and it will be argued that Roland, as a frantic lover, must say:

> O nuit! favorisez mes désirs amoureux.
> Pressez l'astre du jour de descendre dans l'onde.
> Je ne troublerai plus, par mes cris douloureux,
> Votre tranquillité profonde.
> Le charmant objet de mes vœux
> N'attende que vous pour rendre heureux
> Le plus fidèle amant du monde.

I confess that if Quinault himself had told me that in such tender lines he wished to depict 'the impatience of a frantic lover', I would not have believed him. But he said quite the opposite. And to whom did he say it? To Lully, the confidant of his thoughts, who worked with him, under his very eyes. Open, sir, the score of the old Roland; at the beginning of the monologue, which is full of tenderness and voluptuousness, you will find a prelude which also expresses 'the serenity of hope', and at the beginning of the prelude Lully wrote one word, 'Tender', lest there should be any mistake. Now, let Messrs So-and-So shout all over Paris that this monologue is a complete contradiction from beginning to end and that it clearly proves that M. Piccinni is devoid of taste, talent and intelligence. One examines closely the style of a musician who wrote a French opera before learning French; one purports to discover three mistakes, and it turns out that the three mistakes are misapprehensions on the part of the critic. It is surely a somewhat uncommon way of praising an artist to show so clearly that one is powerless to comprehend him: a flatterer could not have done better.

'How comes it', the critic continues, speaking ironically of the Italian operas, 'that so many masterpieces make such superficial and fleeting impressions on the Italians themselves, that, after a small number of performances of the finest opera, this people, which is sensible to the charms of music, merely feels sated and bored?' And, assuming this to be a fact, he gives the following explanation. 'In all the arts, anything designed merely to produce an agreeable effect on the senses and to arouse in the soul only vague and superficial emotions, cannot fail to produce equally vague and superficial impressions, the effect of which comes very near to boredom.' Whereas 'works which make a lasting and ever-growing impression are those which captivate the mind by fine combinations, which elevate and expand one's ideas, which, by faithfully reproducing all the movements of the passions, excite in the soul touching and profound emotions, etc.' (like the music of M. Gluck).

That is certainly a fine, scholarly thesis; and were it properly applied, it would lead nowhere.

The fact that in Italy operas are changed every year and that in France operas which have succeeded are revived on the stage is due, one must realize clearly, to local differences. In Italy there is the luxury of abundance and in Paris the economy of poverty. Operas are changed like jewels, when riches provide the means; theatrical spectacles become worn just as clothes become worn, when one has no others to choose from.

Italy has crowds of composers: new ones are constantly being trained in her schools; either one must discourage them or hear them in succession; and if one allowed those who emerge to languish, the source both of talent and of pleasure would soon dry up. Curiosity combines with this political reason, and a music which is ever new, together with words already known and modified in a thousand ways by the genius of the composers, must have a powerful appeal to sensitive ears. This assault of the talents in one and the same arena constantly stimulates and arouses the spirit of rivalry in the athletes and the interest of the spectators. That is not all.

Delicate ears demand that music should have a perfect analogy with the voice which executes it: as soon as it is transposed, it is altered. The musicians, in composing, adapt the song to the organ for which the song is destined: they take account of its qualities, measure its range, select its finest sounds: all voices of the same kind do not possess the same degree of flexibility or of sensitivity; not all have the same tones, or some are not so full, so pure and so facile. Now, as a result of the rivalry amongst twenty theatres competing for the finest voices, the same voices are never heard in one place two years in succession. That is why, in changing instruments, one likes a change of music, and the change is inexpensive: a fresh cause of inconstancy. That is not yet all.

Every town in Italy has its theatre, but, apart from Naples and Venice, where they are open all the year round, there is opera for only three months; and it is the only public amusement. It runs six days a week; the whole town attends it every day; and when the season is over, the beautiful pieces which have been culled from it are sung at all the concerts; everyone knows them by heart. Would it be surprising if they became satiated?

Yet it is not true that music-lovers become satiated. Despite all the variations of taste in music, they still take a delight in the beautiful pieces from the operas of Leo,[9] Vinci, Pergolesi, Sassoni,[10] Galuppi and Jomelli: they are collected in pastiches, adapted for the piano, and people never grow tired of them.

The custom in Italy of changing opera every year does not, therefore, depend on the nature of the music; and if the critic is not satisfied with the reasons I have given, he only has to propose a test to M. Gluck, which, if successful, will make every musician in Italy sit at this composer's feet.

It is to arrange for Naples, Venice, Rome or, if you wish, London, Vienna or Madrid to see M. Gluck's operas two or three years in succession, 'those works, which produce a lasting and ever-growing effect and which one cannot tire of seeing'; and if, by the beginning of the second year, people are not overwhelmed by boredom, then the issue will have been settled.

But, the reply will be, the whole of Europe is a poor judge of music, and it is to Paris that one must look for the lasting effects of M. Gluck's music, which has been filling the theatre there for seven years.

Eh, Sir! we also saw the 'lasting' effects of music by Lully, by Campra,[11] by Destouche,[12] by Mondonville, and above all by Rameau. Forty years ago people did not tire of seeing again such works as *Les Talens Lyriques, Les Indes Galantes*[13], *Pygmalion*[14] and *Castor*. The last two operas in particular were constantly performed. There is no one of my age who has not heard them a hundred times and one never grew tired of them.

M. Gluck's admirers, who were then the admirers of Mondonville and Rameau and who wrote reams in praise of their excellent music, could well have said in favour of Rameau and Mondonville precisely what they now say in favour of Gluck: 'The Italians change their music every year; the French like to see again an opera which they have applauded; so Italian music is a superficial production of talent, and French music alone bears the stamp of genius.' Can it be that the champions of Mondonville have become infallible since they declared their enthusiastic support for M. Gluck? But, in order to put them more at their ease, let us forget the past and rest our case on the present.

The music of the *Colonie*,[15] of *La Bonne Fille*,[16] of *L'Ami de la Maison*,[17] of *Zemire et Azor*, of *Sylvain* bear no resemblance to the 'dramatic' music of M. Gluck: it is purely Italian music adapted to French words; for ten years this music has been filling and enriching one of the theatres in Paris: people are not yet tired of it. How can one explain this phenomenon? It is in a different style, one might say; but if this style of music 'only awakens vague and superficial emotions in the soul, it can only produce equally vague and superficial impressions'. Let the critic try to extricate himself from this labyrinth.

Until such time as he has adjusted his system to meet these facts, I will tell him the plain truth: it is that in France, like everywhere else, people enjoy what they have. As there is no school for composers, good composers are rare. Good poets are less so, but they scorn a difficult and unproductive medium, which was a source of torment to Metastasio and in which Quinault himself, the inimitable Quinault, was, throughout his life, the slave rather than the companion of Lully. That is why, deprived of new productions which we would like as much as any people in the world, we resign ourselves to our indigence and, sadly loyal, we endeavour to remain appreciative of our old pleasures. Happily, our ears are not so critical as those of the Italians concerning the analogy of music with the voice which executes it; and up to the present the French song has not presented those difficulties and those delicate nuances, which call for a certain vocal range or quality. Happily again, enjoyment of the theatre is not so subject to strain in Paris as in the towns of Italy: there are constant distractions, a great variety of theatres and an enormous number of spectators, with the result that no one sees a new opera in successive performances or often enough to grow tired of it. It is seldom produced more than twice a week; what one calls the public is constantly changing; and when one returns to it, the memory of it has almost faded. If, on the other hand, one sees it too often, one grows tired of it as everywhere else. Thus *Orphée,* one of those works which one should never tire of seeing, is nevertheless reduced to returns of from four or five hundred livres; and it is none the less highly esteemed for that.

Should the time come when our taste has so developed as to be more discriminating with regard to music, as it is with regard to jewellery, when the genius of the poets and musicians is as fertile as the industry of manufacturers, then we shall have new operas like new materials every year; and those of M. Gluck, like those of Lully, Campra, Rameau, Mondonville, etc., will be forgotten in their turn.

Let us imagine the contrary and suppose that the wellspring of good music were to dry up in Italy one day. Will the entrepreneurs not draw quite naturally upon their stocks and revive the old operas one after the other or incorporate them in pastiches? So the inconstancy of the Italians and the constancy of the French do not derive from their two kinds of music. And can one say in good faith, can one hope to persuade anyone that the French love M. Gluck's music so much that they prefer it to new works which they do not have? Would this not mean that people still crowd to hear it and wish for nothing new which is not by the same author? This is what emerges from the imagined distinction drawn by the anonymous critic between the lasting beauties of M. Gluck's operas and the fragile beauty of Italian music and of the opera *Roland*.

Roland, one of Quinault's weakest operas, was an outstanding success, despite the efforts of the most shameless clique and despite the care taken to denigrate it six months before in the cafés, the newspapers and the gazettes. For two months *Roland* attracted large crowds in spite of the distractions and fatigues of the Carnival, which do so much harm to the stage, and in competition with the fees of the actors, which is even more damaging to the work whose success it impairs. *Roland* is already known by heart by all who sing in Paris; it is a standard piano study for our young people, and in the theatre it was constantly applauded from beginning to end each time it was presented. What matter thereafter if, when the season reopened, the box-office returns from *Roland* dropped because the public were anxious to enjoy the first fine days of spring, were drawn to the country and walks in the open air, and were distracted by other accidental circumstances (which I will pass over in silence lest I should offend anyone)?

Which work has lasted longest in this theatre since Easter? *Armide, Alceste* and *Orphée* followed one another in languid succession. *Iphigénie,* one of our finest operas because it was made from the remains of one of our finest tragedies, Iphigenia, of which the pantomime alone would make an interesting and magnificent spectacle, had to be withdrawn. *Roland,* which after sixteen full houses lost its novel appeal, brought in good returns for the season, but they were nothing out of the ordinary: it was billed for the winter and, whatever one may say of it, will long remain a stand-by of the lyrical theatre.

Moreover, is one to judge the more or less lasting success of an art-form which has just become established by the returns of one given season? And when even a people, accustomed to a type of music the strength of which is its noise and which finds its expression in shouting, is less appreciative of the clear, pure harmony and natural, tender melody of Italian music, is it any the less the music par excellence which the whole of Europe admits it to be? Do habit, prejudice and bad taste, established for so long, disappear so easily? German music had gained a numerous and powerful following which clung, at least from vanity, to the object of its enthusiasm; was it to be suddenly dissuaded or dissipated? Was it not more likely to redouble its warmth and obstinacy at this moment of crisis? And in the midst of so many obstacles is it not astonishing that this new music, which was condemned so arrogantly as unworthy to take its place in the heroic theatre, should have become established in one day? The wise and impartial public, which asks only for enjoyment, welcomed it with delight and as a natural thing. This is enough: time will do the rest. When several works of the same kind have accustomed our ears to the charms of this music, then we shall see if it makes the same claims on us as on the rest of Europe, which has been enchanted by it for a century and which does not yet seem disposed to prefer M. Gluck's music.

We were asked to believe that the Italians themselves were 'sated, glutted, bored' with their music; and amongst those who had proscribed it the name of Father Martini has been quoted. I felt bound in my turn to quote him, and we saw whether he had ever intended to exclude Italian music from the theatre and substitute German music for it. But how is one to reconcile him with himself? As one reconciles the anger and tenderness of a father who is ready to punish his child when he is wayward but does not wish to banish him.

The Italian song displeases Father Martini, who finds it too sparkling and too mannered: it also displeases us. He blames the modern composers for having adhered too closely to the fancies of the singers and he congratulates M. Gluck on not having shown such deference, and he is quite right. But as everything in Italian music is not mannered and glossy, and as it has countless beauties of the simplest and most sublime kind, he does not confuse them with the false gems; and he demands at one and the same time that it be corrected and that it be preferred to any other music in the world. We shall see this in the same letter he wrote to a passionate devotee of M. Gluck, which has been hailed as a shattering blow to Italian music.

'In the past', says Father Martini, 'the same deference was not shown to the singers. Vinci, Bononcini, Scarlatti, Marcello, Porpora had succeeded, particularly in their lively and expressive recitative, merely by forceful modulation, in arousing extraordinary emotions to the point where members of the audience would grow pale and shed tears.'

There, to begin with, according to Father Martini, is the tragic music which was invented and flourishing in Italy a long time before M. Gluck.

'If in our time', he adds, 'this quality in vocal music were combined with the vivacity of modern instrumental music, oh! what a fine ensemble that would make! And what pleasure would result for the audience!'

So this wish of the good Father had not been fulfilled up to 17th February 1777, although M. Gluck had already composed his masterpieces: the man whom Father Martini sought to 'procure for Italian music all the advantages enjoyed by that of the Greeks', had, therefore, not yet been found, although one of our oracles had announced his coming.

Let us hear now what Father Martini has to say of the essential and distinctive character of Italian music, the music which he had denounced, if M. Gluck's supporters are to be believed:

'Amongst the advantages of our Italian music there are *three qualities which distingish it particularly from others,* namely, *the melody, the harmony and the modulations.* Italian melody today is more subtle than the French and more likely to stir the emotions, because the latter retains in great measure the style and taste of the melody which was in use in Italy more than a hundred years ago. And, in fact, how did the two great Saxon composers and masters, I mean George Frederick Handel[18] and Jean Adolphe Hasse, achieve such fame, if not as a result of *purifying their style in Italy* and *adapting it to the Italian genius*? (M. Gluck to note.)

'We knew what a reputation the former gained with the operas he composed in Rome, Florence and Naples, after *his taste had been formed in Italy.* We also know how successful were the large number of works composed by the second for the different theatres in Italy, after he had gone to Naples and had completed his education at the school of the celebrated Alexandre Scarlatti.'[19]

There we have two German composers, very different from M. Gluck, praised by Father Martini for having acquired the Italian style and taste in Italy, and this in a letter written to a great friend of M. Gluck.

'Allow me, sir', he continues, 'to explain to you a difficulty which I have been turning over for some time in my mind and which, by comparison with what is being done today, deserves very serious thought. I am referring to the immoderate use of dissonances. . . . I think that dissonances are and must always have been rough and unpleasing to the ear, because they are discordant by their very nature, and I cannot believe that they have changed their nature in our time and become agreeable. Dissonances are only suitable for expressing the most bitter feelings and the most violent and painful movements of the soul. How is it, then, that dissonance after dissonance is employed to express the most delicate and most tender spiritual emotions? This question has never ceased to trouble me and I submit it to your wise and profound judgment.'

It is thus that Father Martini takes leave of M. Gluck's admirer; and the good Father himself has said to M. le Comte Marcelli[20] that this article on dissonances was anything but favourable to the German composer. The compliment he paid him when the latter visited him and the praise he metes out to him when replying to one of his friends must, therefore, not be taken literally, and, in quoting them, it should not have been necessary to conceal what reduced them to their true value.

This, sir, is a very long letter, but it takes longer to unravel sophistry than to perpetrate it; and when one has no right to be trenchant, one can hardly be laconic. In my view, we should now leave the two varieties of music to contend for the public taste themselves, for it alone should be the arbiter and the true judge.

I have the honour to be, etc.

[1] The Library of Congress in Washington has a libretto of the work (ML50.2.G497): '*Il giocatore.* Intermezzo per musica. In tre atti. Da representarsi in Parigi, nell' Theatro, Opera, il 1752.—*Le joueur.* Intermede en musique en trois actes. Représenté (sic) à Paris, sur le Théâtre de l'Opéra en 1752.' On the last page, the Approbation, dated Versailles, August 20 1752. Cast: Serpilla—Anna Tonelli; Baccoco—Pietro Manelli. [cf. O.G.T.

Sonneck, *Catalogue of Opera Librettos printed before 1800*. Washington 1914].
[2] Leonardo Vinci's Opera *Artaserse* had its first performance in the Teatro delle Dame in Rome on 4th February 1730. His *Didone abbandonata* had been first performed in Rome four years earlier.
[3] *Le Cid* and *Cinna*, the well-known plays by P. Corneille, were first performed in Paris in 1636 and 1639 respectively.
[4] *Olympiade* by G. B. Pergolesi, which ranked as his best opera seria, was first performed in Rome on 8th (9th?) January 1735.
[5] J. Ph. Rameau's operas *Hyppolyte et Aricie* (1733), libretto by Simon Joseph de Pellegrin, *Dardanus* (1739), libretto by Charles Antoine Le Clerc de la Bruyère, and *Castor et Pollux* 1737, libretto by Pierre Joseph Justin (Gentil-) Bernard, were regularly performed in the Paris Opéra in the 18th century.
[6] *Horace*, one of P. Corneille's masterpieces, was dedicated to Cardinal Richelieu and first performed in 1639.
[7] SIR ISAAC NEWTON (born Woolsthorpe 5th January 1643, died Kensington 31st March 1727), was the founder of modern mathematical physics and physical astronomy. He discovered the law of gravity, invented the differential calculus, and published important theses on light-refraction and sound-radiation. His main work is the *Philosophia naturalis principia mathematica* [London 1687].
[8] GUILLOT LE SYCOPHANT is one of the characters in La Fontaine's fable *Le loup devenu berger* (III, 2).
[9] LEONARDO ORONZO SALVATORE DE LEO (born San Vieto degli Schiavi 5th August 1694, died Naples 31st October 1744) was one of the leading representatives of the Neapolitan school in opera buffa and religious music. In 1725 he joined the Court Orchestra and became conductor in 1744. Jommelli and Piccinni were amongst his pupils.
[10] *Sassoni* is JOHANN ADOLF HASSE (born Bergedorf near Hamburg 25th March 1699, died Venice 16th December 1783), in his time the leading representative of opera seria and known throughout Europe as 'il divino Sassone', for his fame had spread from Dresden, where, apart from a triumphal stay in Italy from 1731 to 1734, he was Court Conductor from 1730 to 1763.
[11] ANDRÉ CAMPRA (baptized Aix-en-Provence 4th December 1660, died Versailles 29th June 1744) was the most important composer of opera between Lully and Rameau. From 1694 to 1700 he was choirmaster at Nôtre Dame in Paris, then he took up opera and in 1723 became Royal Conductor and Master of Music.
[12] ANDRÉ CARDINAL DESTOUCHES (baptized Paris 6th April 1672, died Paris 3rd February 1749) was a pupil of Campra before he became Inspector General in 1713 and in 1728 Director of the Royal Academy of Music. He was one of the outstanding opera composers of his time and enjoyed the special favour of Louis XIV.
[13] *Les talents lyriques* or *Les fêtes d'Hebe*, a very successful operatic ballet by J. Ph. Rameau, was first performed in 1739 and, like the heroic ballet *Les Indes galantes*, which was first performed in 1735, it retained its popularity for a long time.
[14] *Pygmalion* is the well-known monodrama by J. J. Rousseau, which had its

première in Lyons in 1770 with music by Horace Coignet [1735–1821], who also introduced two musical numbers by Rousseau, and was later performed in Paris in 1775.

[15] *Colonie* is A. Sacchini's Opera *L'isola d'amore*.

[16] *La bonne fille* was a popular comic opera by N. Piccinni. It was first presented in Rome in 1760 and in Paris on 17th June 1771.

[17] *L'ami de la maison* by A. E. M. Grétry was first performed in Paris in 1771 and, like the operas *Zemire et Azor* (1771) and *Silvain* (1770), was still being produced in France in the early part of the 19th century.

[18] George Frederick Handel (born Halle/Saale 23rd February 1685, died London 14th April 1759).

[19] Pietro Alessandro Gasparo Scarlatti (born Palermo 2nd May 1660, died Naples 24th October 1725) was the leading exponent of the Neapolitan opera seria. He was a conductor in Rome and Naples. Among his pupils was Johann Adolf Hasse.

[20] Conte Marcelli is Benedetto Marcello.

J. B. Suard answered in the *Mercure de France* of 5th October 1778 as follows:

. . . . There are people who argue like travellers: the one who has taken a wrong turning moves farther and farther away from his destination with every step he takes.

One begins by discussing the question in hand; one finishes up by merely discussing one's opinions and one's phrases.

This is what would happen to me, were I to reply to all the points raised in M. Marmontel's letter. In truth, I would have made no reply at all, if it had merely been a question of defending my own opinions and my own taste. But reproaches have been made against me which I must rebut, for to keep silence would be to confirm them.

I love music. I am, as has been said of me, an 'enthusiast' for M. Gluck's operas; I regard him as the creator of the true system of dramatic music; to him I owe the most pleasurable moments and the sweetest emotions I have ever experienced in the theatre; I do not believe that a sincere love of the arts is possible without a deep sense of affection and gratitude towards those who enrich and perfect these arts; I have seen M. Gluck attacked immoderately and unjustly at a moment when, had he possessed even less genius and fame, he still deserved nothing but encouragement and applause; so I took up my pen to defend him. He had no need of my defence; the public avenged him much more effectively than my praises could ever do; but I was giving expression to a feeling which was dear to me and which seemed to me a duty.

For a long time M. Gluck had been enjoying his constant and frequent triumphs in peace, when M. Marmontel, in reviewing a brochure on music, thought fit to launch a fresh and somewhat uncalled-for attack on the merits of this composer. In order to prove that M. Gluck had not a very high reputation in Italy, he quoted a letter from Father Martini, which, although it praised M. Gluck, did so with some reservations. I felt obliged to quote an earlier letter, in which Father Martini praised M. Gluck even more forcefully and unreservedly, giving him the credit for having combined all that is finest in Italian music with all that is best in French and German music; the which he has never said and can never say of any Italian composer.

This was a simple question of fact. I endeavoured to give it a little more stress by making a few general observations on music which were designed to give birth to, I will not say new ideas but as least, interesting reflections on art. This, it seems to me, is the only way to make literary disputes more useful and more piquant.

I did not permit myself a single word in my reply which might, directly or indirectly, offend M. Marmontel. He did not feel obliged to show me the same consideration. He slightly ridiculed some of the phrases I employed. I am in no way offended; if I was wrong, then he was fully justified; if I was right, then I continue to be so.

In quoting M. le Prince Beloselski's *Essai*,[1] I spoke of his work with esteem and of his person with the greatest respect. I merely observed that he made too frequent use of vague, general expressions, figures of speech and comparisons borrowed from the other arts, which were hardly calculated to give a clear idea of the artists and the productions he was trying to describe; I thought this observation all the more useful as the misuse of figuratives or abstract expressions has become a habit with men of intelligence who, while they are skilful at arranging words, are not familiar with the alphabet of the arts, yet regard themselves as competent to judge anything and everything, because it pleases them to talk about anything, and they write on these arts, which they have not studied, with a confidence that one should not assume even when writing about subjects with which one is most familiar. M. le Prince Beloselski did not need to have recourse to this little trick of conscious ignorance in order to write in an interesting way on music, which he had studied in the home of music.

In taking some phrases from his *Essai* as examples, I transcribed the actual words quite faithfully, without drawing any inference and without reading more into them than was there; yet M. Marmontel accuses me of having 'mutilated' this essay, without, however, quoting or being able to quote any of the mutilated phrases.

I took exception to M. le Prince Beloselski's statement 'that Vinci[2] was a creator like Corneille'[3]; the author adds, it is true, that 'the musician wrote the first good tragedy', and that both have 'approximately the same high standard of tragic ideas, the same warmth and the same rapidity of style'. But, if I had quoted these reasons, I would have been obliged to add that Corneille has never been regarded as a 'creator' of comedy; that the *Menteur* is not a 'creation' but a comedy in the Spanish style; that it is possible to have 'a high standard of ideas and rapidity of style', without having 'created' anything, etc. I did not insist upon this, because I did not wish to embark upon a criticism of the *Essai*. And now that I am being confronted with these phrases, might I not ask those who quote them to tell me wherein lie the 'high standard and the rapidity of style' in Vinci's ariettas? All such words are easy to write and to read, and everyone believes he understands them, but it might perhaps be very embarrassing to apply them strictly to an aria from *Artaxerce* or *Didon*.

Once more, when one speaks of an art-form, one only makes oneself fully understood if one speaks the language of the art in question; comparisons and metaphors are only designed to make ideas more meaningful and more striking; but they must come to the aid of the proper word, not replace it.

On the same principle, I thought that to call Pergolesi[4] 'the most eloquent of composers' was not to express oneself with sufficient precision. I find the first couplet of the *Stabat* sublime and moving, but, I had added, 'to excite emotion is not the same as to be eloquent, and there is nothing so rare as eloquence in music'.

M. Marmontel protests that the first couplet of the *Stabat* is not the only one that is sublime and moving, which I have no desire to contest. He adds, 'Where then is eloquence to be found if not in the exciting of emotion?' Can one not reply: in Demosthenes,[5] who does not arouse emotion, in Bossuet,[6] who is hardly emotional, in several other writers, who have no intention of being so? On the other hand, are not the cries of Philocretes[7] in his cave moving without being eloquent? A simple word spoken by a suffering child, the incoherent speech of a maniac may move one to tears, but there is no eloquence. In fact, if, as M. Marmontel gives us to understand, 'moving' and 'eloquent' are synonymous, why did he not say that Pergolesi was 'the most moving of composers'? That would have been just as elegant and everyone would have understood it.

I do not believe, like M. le Prince Beloselski, that M. Piccinni was 'particularly gifted in expressing the meaning of words'. M. Marmontel says that 'until now the whole of Europe has held this view', and adds, in order to make me look ridiculous, that 'I wish to create the impression that the whole of Europe understands nothing of this'. I might ask where and when the whole of Europe said this. While I am waiting for this certificate from the whole of Europe to be produced in public, I must justify the criticism I made of three pieces in *Roland*, where I claimed that the sense of the music was hardly in accord with that of the words. This is the only point in the whole of this discussion which is close to my heart and which made me decide to reply, because I do not wish to be suspected of having lightly attacked a composer as famous as M. Piccinni, whose fine works I admire and love as sincerely as any of his most zealous supporters, though not in the same degree.

I have said that M. Piccinni, like the greatest masters in Italy, sometimes sacrificed the meaning and punctuation of a verbal phrase to symmetry and to the development of a musical phrase. I quoted as an example the air 'Je la verrai', and I said that 'this line, which the poet punctuated as follows:

"Esclave, heureux de servir tant d'appas",

the musician had punctuated thus: "Esclave heureux; de servir tant d'appas", which no longer makes sense.'

M. Marmontel replies that I am mistaken; that the 'composer did not detach these words, "de servir tant d'appas"', that he wrote 'heureux de servir tant d'appas', in one sequence and without pause.

As I had only quoted from memory, I was afraid, when I read such a positive assertion, that my memory or my ears might have deceived me. I procured the score and found written there what I had heard sung. 'Esclave heureux' is repeated three times in the aria. In each of these three places 'esclave' is always linked with 'heureux' by double crotchets; 'heureux' falls on a crotchet which forms the first beat of the measure and with the bass provides a perfect cadence; this constitutes a very appreciable pause: 'de servir tant d'appas' is then detached and is not written in immediate sequence.

This is not a question of taste or sentiment, but a question of fact; it is sufficient to know what one means by a 'pause' in a musical phrase. This is what I will try to explain clearly in taking up once again the second criticism I had made of Angelique's aria:

> Oui, je le dois; je suis Reine.
> Du doux penchant qui m'entraîne
> Oui, je dois me garantir.

I said that the second line ends with a pause, which separates it from the following line, to which it should be linked.

'The answer is simple', says M. Marmontel. 'There is no final pause after the second line; and M. Piccinni, who knows what a pause means in music, confirms that there is none.'

This is a very definite assertion and by a very impressive authority. And yet, believe it or not, I merely stated a simple truth which must be clear to anyone who understands musical terminology. I shall explain it as succinctly as I possibly can.

Musical discourse, like oratory, is divided into more or less prolonged phrases and portions of phrases, which are separated by more or less appreciable, more or less absolute intervals; these intervals are indicated by the nature, the value and the position of the note where they fall. Thus when a phrase in a song ends on the principal note of the scale of the aria, when this note is on the strong beat of the bar, when the bass, proceeding by way of the dominant to the tonic, stops on the tonal consonance, that is what composers call 'perfect cadence' and that is what constitutes a final pause. All these characteristics are indubitably present in the passage in question. The aria is in B flat; at the words 'du doux penchant qui m'entraîne' the song gives 'entraîne' three crotchets, the first of which is the *la*, forming part of the dominant seventh, and the two others are the B flat, a tonal note. The bass strikes the same note at the strong beat of the bar and all the instruments are in perfect harmony. Finally, to make assurance doubly sure, the phrase ends with a silence lasting half the bar, which separates it more markedly from the next phrase.

I crave the reader's forgiveness for entering into these technical details and I beg him not to believe that I wish to pose as a connoisseur or a scholar; I am merely a not very advanced student; my knowledge is derived solely from having read the works of the masters with sufficient application to enable me to understand the elements of the science. As I had to defend my criticism against a trenchant and positive assertion by M. de Marmontel, supported by the evidence of M. Piccinni, I could only meet such great authorities with reasons and famous names. Also what I have just said is not my doctrine; it is the simple doctrine, faithfully reproduced, of all the authors who have written on composition, of Rameau,[8] of J. J. Rousseau, even of P. Martini and several others, whose words I do not quote in order not to overload this essay with quotations which are of no value to men of learning and of still less value to those without learning. [*Vide* the various works by Rameau and particularly his *Code de Musique*; Ch. X Rousseau *Dictionn. de Mus.*, art. 'Cadence et Phrase'; M. Bemetzrieder 9, *Traité de Musique Théori-pratique*, p. 243; M. de Belesta 10, *Nouveau Système de Musique théori queet pratique*, p. 190; D. Eximeno, *Regole della Musica*; P. Martini, *Saggio fondamentale pratico di contrapunto*, parte prima, etc.] I consulted four composers on the same subject and all seemed astonished that such a question could have been raised; all offered to sign their names to their opinions; it emerges from this accumulated and unanimous evidence that the line 'Du doux penchant qui m'entraîne' clearly ends with a final pause, and so final that the aria itself could end on the same phrase of the song. The ear is a sufficient judge of this; but aural perception is open to dispute, and it is difficult to dispute clear and established principles which are accepted by all the masters in the art.

The question will now be asked how it comes about that so great a master as M. Piccinni contests these same principles. I have nothing to reply save that the question cannot have been posed to him as I had presented it or that he does not attach to the same words the same ideas as do the French composers; but if he took the trouble to read what I have just written, I am convinced that he would not affirm the contrary, unless he had evolved a new theory on this section of composition, which he should then be invited to publish.

There is a third criticism which still remains to be justified, that of Roland's monologue. I wrote that the musician had depicted 'the calm of the night and the serenity of hope'. M. Marmontel informs me that the musician did not set out to depict 'the calm of the night' but 'the calm of hope'. I ask M. Piccinni's pardon; it was M. de la Harpe who led me into error; they are his own words which I transcribed (*vide Le Journal de Littérature*, 5th February); and I quoted them with confidence, believing him to have discovered the composer's secret. It is for him to defend his phrase; as one cannot doubt his good intention, I am convinced that he will not be taken too much to task for this small incident.

As for me, I believe, like M. de la Harpe, that the musician depicted night and that he would have done better to depict the sun. And, when I recall the first four lines of the monologue, which clearly express the author's intention:

> Ah! J'attendrai toujours! La nuit est loin encore!
> Quoi, le soleil veut-il fuire toujours!
> Jalou de mon bonheur, il prolonge son cours
> Pour retarder la beauté que j'adore.

—In these lines I no more find 'the calm of hope' than I find 'the calm of the night'; I still see in them the impatience of a lover for whom the hours pass all too slowly; and when I think that this lover is the paladin Roland, who would fain draw out the sun's fire in order to bring forward the moment of a rendezvous and who is then plunged into a frenzy when he finds himself betrayed, I think one can call him 'a frantic lover'. Such are my views and my reasons, which I leave to whatever judgment may be passed on them; I have already spent too long on a frivolous discussion.

At this point I cannot refrain from making one observation on the redoutable influence exercised by the polemical spirit. On two musical phrases I made two critical remarks, which seem to me to be as apparent to the ear as they are obvious to the mind; M. Marmontel finds them 'self-evidently' false. He cites the authority of a great master, M. Piccinni; I can cite the authority of all the greatest masters who have written on composition and that of all the musicians I know. There must, on one side or the other, be some very strange illusion. It is for the reader to judge.

I will content myself now with recalling some of M. Marmontel's criticisms of my letter. I had said that the Italians, appreciative though they are of music, grew tired of the finest opera after a small number of performances and no longer wished to see it in the same theatre. This is a fact; I gave this explanation, which is based upon the principles common to all the arts: anything designed merely to flatter the senses and to produce vague and superficial impressions upon the soul cannot please for long, retains its appeal only by its variety and leaves the audience with no desire to see it again. This explanation may be trivial but it is clear and easy to apply to the Italian operas. M. Marmontel finds it bad: so be it. Are the explanations he gives of this phenomenon any more satsifying?

M. Marmontel believes that policy plays a great part in the inconstancy of the Italians with regard to music and to the distaste which they feel for even the finest opera when they have heard it five or six times, and that this 'policy' is to encourage the great composers who are emerging *en masse* in Italy. Italian policy has long been vaunted: people had not realized perhaps that it went quite so far.

M. Marmontel then says that 'for sensitive ears there is a powerful appeal in new music set to old words'. I can hardly believe that these 'sensitive ears' would find a very powerful appeal in hearing new music to the old words of the *Stabat*.

M. Marmontel adds that 'delicate ears require that music should have a perfect analogy with the voice which executes it' and that, as the voices are constantly changing in the Italian theatres, 'people like a change of music'. All this seems to me to prove irrefutably what I have been trying to say, that the Italians seek in music no more than aural pleasure.

M. Marmontel says again that, if our taste in music achieves perfection, 'we will look for new operas every year, like new materials'. This clearly reduces the effect of music to pure sensation; I would never have imagined that the success of works of genius could be merely a question of fashion and that the most moving and most endearing of all the arts could be compared to 'the industry of our manufacturers'.

M. Marmontel finally concludes from these various observations that it is from an abundanceof beautiful things that the Italians grow tired of beautiful things, and that it is through indigence that we never tire of applauding what we find beautiful.

It follows from this theory that the countless multitude of sonnets which abound in Italy must engender in the delicate ears of the Italians a revulsion towards the sonnets of Petrarch, and that, when Italy had more great painters than she has great musicians today, the new pictures must, of necessity, make them forget those of Michelangelo and Raphael.

Every year in Paris more tragedies are written than the comedians can or will perform; but, although we like novelty as much as any people in the world, I hope that our taste in poetry will never reach that stage of perfection at which we prefer what is new to what is beautiful, at which we forget the tragedies of Racine and Voltaire and wish to see on the French stage only those modern tragedies which are so highly praised by their authors and applauded by their friends.

M. Marmontel compares the success of M. Gluck's operas with that of our former operas at a time when we only knew our own music; he overlooks the fact that those who today applaud *Iphigénie* and *Orphée* have heard *Ermelinda*,[11] *Céphale*,[12] *Roland* and our best comic operas, all of which, according to him, 'are pure Italian music adapted to French words'.

M. Marmontel replies that *Iphigénie* had to be withdrawn this summer and that returns from the *Ophée* have been reduced to between 400 and 500 livres; this might happen to operas performed in summer for the hundredth or hundred and fiftieth time. Yet *Iphigénie* and *Orphée* are still filling the Opera House and returns have never been as low as 400 livres or even 700 livres. I am astonished that M. Marmontel should indulge in such forms of criticism.

I am no less astonished that he still insists that 'anyone discussing the arts should give his name'. He would like to know whether, like him, I merely have instinct or know how to accompany a bass, in order to judge what degree of authority I deserve.

Eh! Of what consequence is the name of someone who does not ask that his word be accepted as gospel, who does not dogmatize, who backs his opinions and discusses facts? What! the public must know if I am a scholar or an ignorant man in order to judge if I am right or wrong! And, as my readers will, of necessity, hold very divergent views of my *savoir faire*, each of them will, of necessity, hold a different view on the basic question from that of all the others! This is an entirely novel way of settling disputes.

If I had the puerile vanity, or, if you like, the humility to put my name to a few pages written in haste on a passing dispute concerning music, M. Marmontel might know that it is not merely in the concert-halls of Paris that I have heard Italian music, as he says, but that I have seen fine operas by Sacchini, by Bach,[13] etc., performed by highly skilled virtuosos in one of the great capitals of Europe; he would know that I have never been, as he suggests, an enthusiastic admirer of Rameau and Mondonville[14]; he might even remember that, in occasional discussions with him on Italian music and French music, it was not I who defended the operas of Rameau and Mondonville. But the public would be in no better position to judge us, and I would have the disadvantage of pitting my obscure name against the rightly famous name of M. Marmontel; that would be to fight with too unequal weapons.

In literature as at the Bar, it seems to me that, if the judges did not know the names of those pleading, the judgments passed would be none the worse. This I propose to consider more closely on another occasion. In the meantime, I take the liberty of saying to M. Marmontel, like Nicodemus[15]:

'My lord, if I am right, what matters it who I am?'

[1] Prince Alexander Beloselsky (born Petersburg 1757, died Petersburg 26th December 1809) was Russian Ambassador in Turin and Dresden. He was

a talented man of letters and his monograph *De la musique en Italie* was published in The Hague in 1778.

[2] LEONARDO VINCI (born Strongoli 1690, died Naples 27th May 1727) was one of the outstanding composers of the so-called Neapolitan School and, from 1725 onwards, conductor of the Royal Orchestra in Naples.

[3] PIERRE CORNEILLE (born Rouen 6th June 1606, died Paris 1st October 1684) was a lawyer and one of France's most famous dramatists. His comedy *Le Menteur*, which was first produced in 1625, was based on a plot from Juan d'Alcaron or Lope de Vega's *La verdad sospechosa.*

[4] GIOVANNI BATTISTA PERGOLESI (born Jesi 4th January 1710, died Pozzuoli 16th March 1736) achieved international fame with his opera *La serva padrona.* The Paris production in 1752 led to the famous 'Querelles des Buffons', the dispute between the champions of Italian and French Opera.

[5] DEMOSTHENES (born Demos Paeania 383 B.C., died Kalauria October 322 B.C.), the famous Greek orator, who distinguished himself in both law and politics.

[6] JACQUES BÉNIGNE BOSSUET, S. J. (born Dijon 27th September 1627, died Paris 12th April 1704) was a famous preacher and historian. In 1681 he became Bishop of Meaux and in 1698 first Almoner of the Duchess of Burgundy.

[7] PHILOCRETES was a famous archer during the Trojan War.

[8] JEAN PHILIPPE RAMEAU (baptized Dijon 25th September 1683, died Paris 12th September 1764) was known as a composer both of opera and of harpsichord music and also enjoyed a great reputation in the sphere of musical theory. In 1745 Louis XIV appointed him a 'Compositeur de Musique de la Chambre'.

[9] ANTON BEMETZRIEDER (born Alsace 1743 [1748?], died London *c.* 1817) was a Benedictine monk, who later became a student of mathematics and physics. He moved to Paris, where he became known as a writer on music and gave Diderot's daughter piano lessons. In 1781 he went to London.

[10] JEAN BAPTISTE DE BELLESTAT (born Burg Bellestat 18th April 1750, died Foix January 1816) was an engineer and mathematician.

[11] *Ermelinda, Princesse de Norvège*, an opera by ANDRÉ DANICAN PHILIDOR (1726–1795), which was first presented in Paris in 1767 and was again included in the repertoire ten years later.

[12] *Céphale et Procris ou l'Amour conjugal*, an opera by ANDRÉ ERNEST MODESTE GRÉTRY (1741–1813), which was first performed at Versailles on 30th December 1773.

[13] JOHANN CHRISTIAN BACH (baptized Leipzig 7th September 1735, died London 1st January 1782) was the youngest son of Johann Sebastian Bach.

[14] JEAN JOSEPH CASANEA DE MONDONVILLE (baptized Narbonne 25th December 1711, died Belleville near Paris 8th October 1772) was an operatic composer of standing and one of the first composers of piano sonatas with violin accompaniment. From 1744 onwards he was Surintendant of the Royal Orchestra at Versailles and from 1755 to 1762 Director of the 'Concert Spirituel'.

[15] NICODEMUS, a Pharisee and member of the High Council of Judaea, who embraced Christianity after Christ's death.

[TO FRANZ KRUTHOFFER. *German*]

Vienna, 1st November [1778]

Dearest friend!

The Empress has informed me that I may travel to Paris, because this could contribute to the Queen's amusement, especially if a Dauphin came to the world. So I have no further reason to delay. I beg you, therefore, to look round as soon as possible and procure for me a decent lodging. Perhaps you will find it with your friends, of whom you spoke last year. *Nota bene:* room, food, and bed-linen included. I plan to arrive about the 20th. Leave a note at the barrier addressed to me, so that I know where I can put up. I look forward with all my heart to embracing you soon. With God's help, we will have a good talk and divert ourselves. Adieu, dearest friend, till we meet again soon.

[LE BAILLY DU ROULLET TO FRANZ KRUTHOFFER. *French*]

in Paris this 11th November 1778

Yesterday evening, Monsieur, I received a letter from Mr. Gluck written on 31st October, in which he informs me that he will arrive in Paris towards the 20th of this month, so we will be embracing him in nine or ten days from now. He adds these words, which I copy exactly:

'Speak, I beg of you, to Mr. Kruthoffer so that he may find a suitable lodging with those people of whom he had spoken last year, and ask him to send the address to the stage-post where I must enter. I hope that he will find what I need by the 20th. . . .'

He does not inform me if he is arriving with Me Gluck, but I presume so, as I do not imagine that they can remain separated especially for so long a time.

The actors are negotiating with Mr de Vismes for the transfer of his concession. They are offering him twenty thousand francs a year during his twelve years' lease. He seems shaken, and he has promised to give them a prompt answer. As the certainty of M. Gluck's arrival might make Mr de Vismes more confused and his reply less favourable, I think we must keep completely silent about the early arrival of Mr. Gluck and I beg you to keep it secret from everyone. As he informs me that he wrote only as the courier was arriving, I presume that he may only have communicated his departure to me and in that case the actors may have de Vimes's reply before this news is divulged.

I have the honour to be very perfectly, Monsieur, your very humble and very obedient servant

Le Bailly du Roullet

[Address:]
A Monsieur
Monsieur Kruthoffer
secretaire de
Mr. Le Comte de Mercy
en son Hotel
rue Vaugirard
à Paris

[RECEIPT. *French*]

I have received in cash from Monsieur de Vismes the sum of two thousand livres for the expenses of my journey, in token of which this 22 February

1779 Chevalier Gluck.

2000

[CONTRACT WITH THE PUBLISHER CHARLES JOSEPH MATHON DE LA COUR.[1] *French*]

I, the undersigned, agree to having sold to Monsieur Mathon de la Cour my two scores, of *Iphigénie en Tauride* and of *Narcisse*, on the express condition that, if I do not give the opera *Narcisse* to the theatre, I will return to him in money or in his bills of exchange the value of the said opera, agreed between us to be two thousand livres, and that he will be able to claim no further compensation. At Paris this 5th May 1779

Chevalier Gluck.

[1] CHARLES JOSEPH MATHON DE LA COUR was the son of the author, Jacques Mathon (1712–1770), and was born in Lyons in 1738. From July 1764 onwards he edited the *Journal de Musique*, which continued until 1778 under Nicolas Framery and later E. de Framicourt as the *Journal de Musique historique, théorique et practique*. . . . From 1775 to 1778 Mathon edited the *Almanach musical*. He published the scores of *Armide* and *Iphigénie en Tauride*, as proprietor of the *Bureau du Journal de Musique, rue Montmartre vis-à-vis celle des Vieux Augustins*. As Mathon did not meet his contractual obligations, *Echo et Narcisse* appeared in 1781 with the firm of Deslauriens. Mathon was executed in 1793 as a counter-revolutionary.

[TO QUEEN MARIE ANTOINETTE. *French*]

[before 18th May 1779]

Madame!

In deigning to accept the homage which I venture to offer you, Your Majesty fulfils all my wishes. It was essential to my happiness to make public the fact that the operas which I have composed to contribute to the pleasures of a nation, of which Your Majesty is both ornament and joy, have merited the attention and gained the approbation of a sensitive and enlightened Princess, who loves and who protects all the arts, who, while applauding all forms of art, takes care not to confuse them, and who knows how to accord each the esteem it deserves.

I am with the most profound respect,
Your Majesty's
Very humble and very obedient servant
Le Chevalier Gluck.

The above letter was attached to the Score of *Iphigénie en Aulide* as a dedication.

[To Wolfgang Heribert Freiherr von Dalberg.[1] *German*]

High-born Freiherr!

I had the honour to receive Your Excellency's most honoured letter of 14th of last month: I had already read with much pleasure the poem *Cora* sent to me by Count von Seau,[2] and the news that the author of it gave the same a new worth. I was very anxious to be able to accept your gracious invitation to Mannheim, but as my affairs here have already detained me beyond the time fixed for them, as soon as they are completed I will have to start back to Vienna by the shortest route. With regard to setting the poem to music, it is important that I should first be fully informed of Count von Seau's wishes as to the execution of this piece, of the talents of the singers who are to take part and of the quality of their voices. On my way through Munich I will discuss these questions with the aforementioned Count, and armed with this knowledge it should then be an easy matter to decide, by letter and as the work progresses, upon the alterations and additions which you consider necessary. I regret only that circumstances deprived me of the benefit of a personal meeting with Your Excellency. In the meantime it would give me great pleasure if the fulfilment of your wishes brought me into closer touch with them and gave me more frequent opportunities to confirm the esteem for your achievements and the boundless respect with which I have the honour to be

Ever Your Excellency's
Most obedient and most devoted
Servant, Chevalier Gluck.

Paris on the 8th
June 1779

[1] Wolfgang Heribert Freiherr von Dalberg (born 13th November 1750, died 27th September 1806) was Intendant of the Mannheim National

Theatre. His *Cora* must have been based on J. F. Marmontel's *Les Incas ou la destruction de l'Empire de Perou*, which inspired Johann Gottlieb Naumann's opera, *Cora* (text by Gudmund Goran von Adlerbeth). Before Gluck declined, Dalberg had approached Mozart, who wrote to him on 24th November 1778 that he did not wish to compose it, and finally to Anton Schweitzer (1735–1787), who also declined to set it to music.

[2] JOSEPH ANTON COUNT VON SEEAU was Intendant of the Munich Opera from 1753 to 1799.

[TO MADAME DEPUIS.[1] *French*]

I had no doubt, Madame, when I presented you to M. de Vismes and he suggested that you should sing two days later in *Iphigénie en Tauride*, that you would be a success and that the public would press for you to be admitted to the Opéra. The event and the public have both ratified my opinion on the first point, and it seems to me that your admission should of necessity follow. Considering how very useful you would be there, I do not know for what reason you could be excluded, but I owe it to you to say and to make public that, in so far as voice, method, intelligence and sensibility are concerned, you lack nothing to merit and to obtain the most enthusiastic applause. I will add to this the especial esteem in which I hold your person and your character and with which I am,

Madame,
Your very humble and very obedient servant,
Signed, Chevalier Gluck.
Paris, this 6th October, 1779.

[1] Nothing further is known of MADAME DEPUIS, who sang the title rôle three times in *Iphigénie en Tauride* when it was revived in September 1779.

[TO FRANZ KRUTHOFFER. *German*]

[In Kruthoffer's handwriting:
Replied Paris on 16th November 1779]

Vienna, 31st October 1779

Dearest friend!

I am extremely obliged to you for all the trouble I cause you, but we are not yet dead, and who knows when one of us can do the other a favour in this world; but I alone am the debtor. I hope the other changes will also be made, but I beg you to urge Mr Matton to complete the score soon and to send me a copy at once, for I would like to present *Echo* here.[1] Send us as much news of the theatre as you can scrape together, for it amuses my wife, Mr Janson, who sends you his best regards, and me. Mr Calin wishes to be remembered to you and to H. v. Blumendorff. I beg you also to give him my regards as also to all good friends. My wife and I would like to thank Mr Marchand for the music he sent. The courier is leaving, so I am pressed. I remain ever your devoted friend and servant Gluck. PS. We have made the finest journey in the world.

[1] The performance of ECHO ET NARCISSE planned by Gluck in Vienna did not materialize.

[TO GERSIN.[1] *French*]

Vienna, 30th November 1779

Monsieur,

I am very sensible of the honour you pay me in sending me a plan of a tragedy for me to set to music. I find it well suited to the production of great effects, but you doubtless do not know that I will write no more operas and that my career has come to an end. My age and the disgust I experienced recently in Paris concerning my opera *Narcisse*[2] have robbed me for ever of any desire to write others. It would, however, be a pity if you did not finish your work, for you will surely find musicians of great merit in Paris who will be able to satisfy you in everything you desire. I have the honour to be with much esteem,

Monsieur,
Your very humble and very obedient Servant,
Gluck.

[1] The Vaudevillist GERSIN is held up to ridicule in Menegaut's *Martyriologie littéraire* (Paris 1816): 'M. Année et M. Gersin sont associés depuis longtemps pour les succès et pour les chutes.

En revenant sur son traversin
Aux admirables plans de son complice Année,
Il trace des couplets, cet immortel Gersin,
Qui ne vivent pas une année.'

[2] ECHO ET NARCISSE, Gluck's last opera, had its *première* in Paris on 24th September 1779,

[To Franz Kruthoffer. *German*]
[In Kruthoffer's handwriting:
Replied Paris on 13th and 16th December 1779]

Vienna, 30th November 1779

My dearest Kruthofferle!

You become more kind-hearted with every day that passes. My wife, Calin and I embrace you fondly, and we are always delighted to read your letters. Just remain as you are and send us all the theatre news. The Mathon affair I commend to your well-tried efficiency. I must see if I can succeed in finding you a position as Court Counsellor here, then things would hum.

I beg you to send me by courier: chest tablets[1] from Sr. Archbald, English doctor, two boxes at 24 sous each. You will take the necessary money from what I stand to receive either from Mathon or from the pension.[2] The tablets are to be had at the following address: le Brun, au dépôt général, Marchand Epicier, rue Dauphine aux armes d'Angleterre, Magazine de Provence et de Montpellier, Hôtel de Morny. Our best regards to H. v. Blumendorff. Adieu, dearest friend, I remain ever yours.

[1] 'Tablettes pectorales' are frequently mentioned in literature and take many different forms. Sometimes they consisted of ammonium chloride and licorice, at other times of marshmallow, sugar and tragacanth gum. This second recipe is given in the *Formules de Médicamens* (Paris, 1767, pp. 227 and 459) with the assurance that the pills relieve persistent coughing and with a reminder that each pill should be allowed to melt in the mouth. There is no reference, either here or in any of the biographical works of reference, to Archbald or Archibald. These eighteenth-century 'tablettes' were not pills in the modern sense but pastilles or morsuli, which were either produced cold from mucus or were boiled with sugar.

[2] In August 1774 Marie Antoinette had granted Gluck an annual PENSION of 6,000 livres and a payment of the same amount for each new work (*Mémoires secrètes*, VII, p. 209).

[Baron von Tschudi to Kruthoffer. *French*]

M. le Baron de Tschoudi [sic] has the honour to send Monsieur de Kruthoffer a revised copy of the opera *Echo et Narcisse*. He begs him to have it sent by the next courier to M. le Chevalier Gluck, and to join with him and M. le Bailli du Rolle [sic] in urging him to abide by these alterations, a task which will not cause him much difficulty and will ensure a favourable reception for his latest work at its second performance. Monsieur de Kruthoffer can also point out to him that, as the opera no longer begins with the aria 'Rien dans la nature',[1] there is nothing to prevent him from strengthening or altering the Overture, with which, I understand from M. de Kruthoffer, he is not satisfied. M. le Baron de Tschoudi begs him to acknowledge receipt of his packet and also has the honour to inform him that M. le Bailli du Rolle was very pleased with the alterations. He has the honour to send his greetings and to assure him of all his sentiments—

Paris 6th December 1779.

[1] Amor's ARIA 'Rien dans la nature' comes in the prologue in the new arrangement of the engraved score; it is preceded by the female chorus 'A l'ombre de ces bois épais', which originally formed the beginning of the third act.

[BARON VON TSCHUDI TO KRUTHOFFER. *French*]

Paris, 13th December 1779

Mr. de Tschoudi is most grateful to Monsieur Kruthoffer for the obliging note which he sent him. He has no doubt that Mr. Gluck's well-founded confidence in his friendship and his counsel will decide him to devote himself to the modest amount of work required by our corrections. He begs him to have the goodness to pass this letter to him as soon as possible. He also has the honour to inform him that rumours of a new direction under Mr Berton[1] are still circulating and that Mr de Caumartin[2] spoke to Tschoudi yesterday of the alterations in *Echo et Narcisse*. He enquired of him if this would present difficulties and was told in reply that only two rehearsals would be necessary and that it would not cost a sou; it seems, therefore, that a second performance is envisaged. I have had no reply from Mad. de la Ferté,[3] to whom I wrote begging her to join with us in our approach to M Gluck. Mr de Tschoudi begs Monsieur Kruthoffer to accept his sincere assurances of the highest esteem and of his attachment.

[1] The most likely successor to de Vismes, whose position was seriously threatened, was his predecessor, Berton.

[2] The Parisian merchant DE CAUMARTIN, 'prévôt des marchands', was involved in the administration of the Opéra. On the King's order, he had tried to settle the disputes between de Vismes and the singers (*Mémoires secrétes*, XIII, p. 315; 15th March 1779).

[3] MARIE-THÉRÈSE DE LA FERTÉ-IMBAULT (1715–1791) was a daughter of Mme Marie-Thérèse Geoffrin, *née* Rodet, who was one of the most brilliant women of the eighteenth century. Her daughter was crowned 'Queen of the Order of Lanturelus' (*Correspondance littéraire*, XI, p. 366–XIII, p. 258) and belonged to the circle around Friedrich Melchior Grimm (1723–1807) and the Marquis Marc Antoine Nicolay de Croismare, Baron von Lasson (1694–1772).

[TO FRANZ KRUTHOFFER. *German*]

[In Kruthoffer's handwriting:
Replied Paris, 17th January 1780]

Vienna, 31st December 1779

My wife, Calin and I wish you, dearest friend, and also Herr v. Blumendorff, everything imaginable for the New Year, and to all our good friends, but I cannot send your New Year present by this courier, for I have only just received your letters. It will not fail to reach you next month, however, because you deserve it for the way you collect and send us a true supply of news. I have given H. Bailly de Roullet the commission to have the 'Hymne à l'amour'[1] copied on small paper and to send it by the first courier without fail, because Mr Janson needs it for his 'Concert de benefice'. Look into this and see that it does not go awry, for it could land him in the soup. As regards the *Narcisse* of Baron Tschoudi, I am prepared to adjust[2] it, but I must at all costs have the score. Tell him to send me the written one by courier and I will return it corrected; I must see that the tones harmonize, which I cannot do without the score. Concerning M. Mathon, you must press for payment in every possible way, for I have transferred this debt to Baron Fries, at whose disposition it is in Paris. I would not for anything in the world have him harbouring suspicions about me, so I beg you to give your closest attention to this affair. Please tell Mr de Vismes that I thank him for his communication and will thank him in writing as soon as possible. Your news of the theatre is very remarkable. Please continue, for you do not know how grateful my wife is to you for this; you relate everything with a certain 'sale attico'. But I must not praise you too much; I will only say that I consider myself happy to be ever your true friend and servant. Adieu, cher ami! All in haste!

[1] The 'Hymne à l'amour' is the final chorus 'Le Dieu de Paphos et de Gnide' from *Echo et Narcisse*. It was the only piece in the opera that won universal applause and, when the work was revived on 8th August 1780, the public called for it da capo (*Mémoires secrètes*, XV, p. 258). Gluck required the hymn for a benefit concert by Janson, who shortly before, on 21st December 1779, had figured at the Vienna 'Tonkünstler Societät' as 'Kammervirtuose des Prinzen Conti' with a 'cello concerto. The main work of the evening was the oratorio *Die Israeliten in der Wüste*, by Maximilian Ulbricht (1752–1814).

[2] The failure of *Echo et Narcisse* was due largely to the poor libretto. 'The Chevalier's supporters blame the failure chiefly on the Baron de Tschudi's poem. It is true that it is not possible to read inferior words. The stilted, precious, nonsensical style of this poet is carried to an unprecedented degree,' say the *Mémoires secrètes* (XIV, p. 191), 30th September 1779. Baron von Tschudi therefore decided to make a drastic revision of the book and sought, through Kruthoffer, to obtain the composer's consent.

[To Jacob Freiherr von Goutard, 1779. *French*]

Gluck has the honour to advise M. de Goutard that here in Vienna no opera is sold in the French language, only *Alceste* and *Paris et Hélène* in Italian; your correspondent will easily obtain the operas he wishes in Paris: *Iphigénie en Aulide, Alceste* and *Orfée*, from M. Marchand, rue Grainelle-St-Honoré, *Iphigénie en Tauride* from M. Mathon at his shop, where he will also find *Armide*, perhaps the best of my works, which well deserves to belong to your friend's collection.

The same M. Mathon has the sole right to engrave *Echo et Narcisse*. He will know from him whether the opera will soon be on sale to the public.

[From Claude Joseph Dorat[1] to Gluck. *French*]

A. M. Gluck

Sending him an imitation in verse of Dryden's
Ode on the power of music.

Le Spartiste belliqueŭx
Respiroit les combats à la voix de Tyrtée;
Alexandre soumis dépendoit, dans ses vœux,
De l'Art savant de Timothée.
Ta chaleur, tes élans, tes traits vifs & profonds
Ont de cet Art dans toi reveillé la puissance;
Le froid méchanisme des sons
A fait place à leur eloquence.
Il nous faut des tableaux, & non pas des chansons.
Par la terreur tu consternes mon âme;
Tu l'amollis par la pitié;
L'amour à tes accens communique sa flamme;
Tu fais tonner la rage ou gemir l'amitié. . . .
La Musique est parfois sœur de la Poésie,
Et la scène lyrique, avec étonnement,
Voit enfin de nos jours, grâce à ton énergie,
L'auguste & sombre Tragédie,
Sans madrigaux notés, exprimer son tourment.
Trop foible pour te suivre en ta marche, hardie,
Loin de nous l'automate à ses calculs borné,
Qui sous les lois d'Euclide enchaîna Polymnie!
C'est dans un cœur passionné
Que tu puisas ton harmonie.
Bien sentir, c'est créer, crois-mio triomphe en paix,
Quand l'ignorance te déchire.
Eh! quels raisonnemens opposer au délire?
Le grand homme attaqué répond par ses succes,
Et l'envie est punie au moment qu'elle admire.
Poursuis; que sa fureur ajoute à ton repos.
Quand la gloire est au comble, il faut bien qu'on l'expie.
L'enthousiasme ou la haine des sots
Sont les deux malheurs du génie.

M. Dorat

[1] Claude Joseph Dorat (1734–1780), after abandoning a military career, had turned to poetry. He was very prolific but produced no important works.

Concerning the revision of *Echo et Narcisse*, Kruthoffer had in the meantime received the following letters from Baron von Tschudi:

[Baron von Tschudi to Kruthoffer. *French*]

Paris, rue St. Dominique. . . .
29th December 1779

The Baili du Roullet, Monsieur, with whom I am at present on intimate terms as a result of his frank and honest dealings with me and the necessity to work closely together against M. Gluck's enemies, has just informed me that in his latest letter he has urged my friend to make haste with his corrections. I ask you as a favour also to write to him and to insist upon the following points:

1. that he should write to M. de Caumartin and Mr de Vismes to say that he would like at all costs to have Mlle la Guerre for the revised production, which is not merely a repeat performance but in his case a new work, so that one takes whoever one wishes. La Beaumenyl(!)[1] cannot assert her contract rights, which, moreover, she forfeited by her unworthy behaviour. La Guerre knows the part, so it is for her to take it.

2. that the new arias which have been added should be given their full value as songs; I wrote the words expressly for that purpose. This part must be made into something brilliant and outstanding. In the original my words were written to be declaimed, and Gluck did not fail to conform to this, but here we have a song that requires development. Insist also that he takes the utmost care to revise his overture. Spare no effort, I beg and ask of you as a friend, Monsieur, to see that he does this work with taste and extreme care. The more his enemies howl for his blood, the greater the need to crush them with this final triumph. Abbé Arnaud and other cowardly friends will blush with shame at having abandoned us. You saw, Monsieur, how successful the repeat performance was, in spite of the second cast and the beginners.

I have the honour to be, with true attachment, Monsieur, your very humble and very obedient servant,

Le B[a]ron de Tschoudi.

[Address:]
A Monsieur
Monsieur Kruthoffer
Secretaire de l'ambassade
de Vienna, à l'hotel
S. Excell. Mons. l'ambassadeur
Boulevard au bout de
la rue Richelieu.

[1] Henriette Adelaide Villars (Beaumesnil) was born in Paris on 31st August 1758. She made her first stage appearance as an actress at the age of seven. Later she became a singer and was particularly successful in *Iphigénie en Aulide*. Although she had not a great voice, she was an extremely accom-

plished actress and was very musical. She was also the first 'Echo', a part which she had to hand over to La Guerre after only three performances (*Mémoires secrètes* XIII, p. 287). For health reasons, she retired from the stage on 1st May 1781 with a pension of 1,500 francs, and married a certain Philipp, who was in the service of the Duchess of Burgundy. She began composing, and wrote music for *Tibulle et Delie* (text by Fugelier) and the opera *Plain, c'est commander*. She died in 1803 in Paris.

[Baron von Tschudi to Kruthoffer. *French*]

Paris, 4th January 1780 in the evening.

I learn by letter from the Bailli, my dear Monsieur Kruthoffer, that, following his first letter, M. Gluck has decided to make all the changes immediately which we asked for in his opera *Echo*; as soon as he has received the three acts, he will write the music. I believe this piece of good news will please us, if you have not already heard it.

You see, dear *maestro*, that it will be easy for you to slip our ideas across to him gradually, gently and in a moderate way. The affair is in good hands; do not overlook anything. Your ideas on the part of *Echo* are very sound; it will be necessary, as death approaches, to quicken the action from time to time, and in some places too tragic passages will have to be dropped. The grief of a nymph is not like that of an Artemis; he must put in arias, which should be an easy matter, for I have given him three new ones.

As regards the part of Cynire, such is the insolence of Mr. le Gros, who always ruins it, and the inadequacy of his understudies, that I am almost convinced of the need to make it a baritone part for Arrivée or a tenor part for Moreau.[1] I find that there are many light passages in this work, so that a certain amount of shade would provide an attractive contrast. I put these ideas to you; spare no effort to induce our great *maestro* to make his work as perfect as he possibly can. I can already see that the theme will inspire him to perform miracles. Please accept, Monsieur, these fresh assurances of the devotion with which I have the honour to be you very humble servant

Le B[a]ron de Tschoudi.

[Address:]
A Monsieur
Monsieur Kruthoffer
Secretaire de l'embassade
de Vienne, chez son Excellence
Mr l'Ambassad[eu]r de LL Majest[é]s
impériales et royales
Boulevard Richelieu.

[1] The singer Moreau was not a tenor but a bass. He had sung the part of Thoas in *Iphigénie en Tauride*. Did von Tschudi make a mistake or had Moreau adapted the part? Cynire remained a tenor part, which, when the opera was re-presented, was transferred to the young singer, Lays (*Mémoires secrètes*, XVIII, p. 31).

[To Heribert Freiherr von Dalberg. *French*]

Vienna, 19th January 1780

Monsieur le Comte,

I have received the letter which you did me the honour to write to me. I read with pleasure the opera you were kind enough to send me, but, as I do not know any persons who might execute it, I could not agree to compose the music. As soon as I have finished the opera I am arranging here, of which I had the honour of speaking with you, it will give me pleasure to communicate with you and we will have a further discussion.

I have the honour to be, with greatest respect,

Monsieur le Comte,

Your very humble and very obedient servant,

Christoph Gluck.

[To Franz Kruthoffer. *German*]

Vienna, 31st January 1780

Dearest friend!

I am obliged to you for your news of the theatre. Do but continue to ply me with it. I send you enclosed the song you asked for;[1] go on working with me. I will not write to H. v. Comartin [Caumartin]. If they want me to make alterations, then they must ask me for them. I am quite indifferent to applause or criticism in Paris. As far as the Marmontel gang are concerned, I can only refer them to the *Dunciade* of Mr. Palissot;[2] there they will find what their General is worth—he has answered for me and his answer will last for ever.

As regards the Mathon affair, I pray you write to him yourself again and ask whether he is prepared to pay or not, otherwise it will be his own fault if he becomes unhappy, and you can then let things take their course. Many greetings from my wife, from Janson and Calin, to you and the whole house and all good friends. Do not take it amiss that I write such a short letter; I am not at all well. But I am and remain ever your true friend and servant

Gluck.

[1] Whether the song in question was one of Klopstock's odes or one of the two ariettas 'Amour en ces lieux——' and 'Quand la beauté lance——' (Hopkinson, Nos. 60 and 61) is not known.

[2] Charles Palissot de Montenoy (1730–1814) was a well-known opponent of Jean Jacques Rousseau, Voltaire and the Encyclopaedists. The title of his work was taken from Alexander Pope's *Dunciad*.

[To Grand Duke Carl August von Sachsen-Weimar.[1] *German*]

Most Serene Duke,
Most Gracious Herr!

At the time I received Your Serene Highness's gracious letter, I had fallen victim to a mortal sickness. Your letter was filled with so many tender and moving expressions [of sympathy], that it contributed greatly to my recovery, and, when I was again in a position to communicate my most profound gratitude to Your Highness, the newspapers told me that Your Serene Highness had set out on a journey. As I have now learnt, however, of your happy return, I can no longer delay in telling Your Highness that never can music combined with the finest poetry have made such a powerful impression upon any man's heart as this most treasured letter upon mine.

I have now become very old and have lavished upon the French nation most of my spiritual powers, notwithstanding which I still feel an inner urge in me to accomplish something for my nation, and I am filled with a burning desire to be able to hum something German to Your Serene Highness before my end, and at the same time to express to you my gratitude and indebtedness for your gracious feelings for me. Until then I beg Your Serene Highness to accept my deepest respect, with which I will ever remain,

Most Serene Duke,
Your Serene Highness's
Most humble
Gluck mp.

Vienna 10 February 1780

[1] Karl August Grand Duke of Sachsen-Weimar was born on 3rd September 1757, became Grand Duke in 1815 and died on 11th June 1828.

[To Franz Kruthoffer. *German*]

[In Kruthoffer's handwriting:
Replied Paris, 17th March 1780]

Vienna, 2nd March 1780

Dearest friend!

Hardly has the courier arrived when I must immediately reply, because the other is despatched again. I am glad that the little song I sent you gives you pleasure; the Klopstock *Odes*[1] will also follow in good time. This letter consists entirely of commissions, for which

I beg your forgiveness in advance. Firstly, please to tell Baron Tshudi that, if he wants me to arrange his opera, he must send me the score by the next courier, for the words he sends me I have sent him myself. If I once start on something else, the old stuff is left lying. Secondly, ask Mr de la Parte[2] for the poem, which belongs to Mr Millicent,[3] and act as if I had sent it to you from Vienna, and give it to him instead of mine. Thirdly, enquire of Mr de la Parte where the nuns live who make the little candles to burn in the lamp—they cost 24 sous a box—and send them to me by courier. You will earn a miniature painting from Mme. Gluck, who sends her kindest regards. That is all for now. Do not forget Mathon. Adieu, dearest friend. Our regards to H. v. Blumendorff and all our good friends. I would like the opera *Atys*[4] to be well received, so that I am left in peace.

[1] Gluck's music for the Klopstock ODES first appeared in the *Göttinger Musenalmanach*: in 1774 *Wir und Sie* and *Schlachtgesang*; in 1775 *Der Jüngling* (original version) and *Die frühen Gräber*. In 1785 the well-known Artaria edition appeared (Hopkinson, 46A). In the same year the ode *Die frühen Gräber* appeared in a revised version in the *Musenalmanach*, edited by Johann Heinrich Voss.

[2] ABBÉ JOSEPH DE LA PORTE, S.J. (1713–1779) was the editor of the *Almanach des Spectacles de Paris*, which appeared from 1750 onwards. Gluck's commission came too late, for the Abbé had already died on 19th December 1779.

[3] JEAN GABRIEL MARIE MILLICENT (1747–1833) was the author of the beautiful poem on the 1776 *Alceste*: 'L'œil humide des pleurs que tu m'as fait verser, O Gluck! j'écris ces vers, enfans de mon délire. . . .'

[4] Niccolo Piccinni's opera ATYS (libretto by J. F. Marmontel from a text by Philippe Quinault) had a successful *première* on 22nd February 1780. The *Mémoires secrètes* of 12th March 1780 contain the following remark: 'The Chevalier Gluck . . . complains of the lack of esteem shown for his works by presenting them with mediocre actors; he appears reluctant to work henceforth for our Opéra. The success of *Atys* will not help to bring him back to us. . . .'

[TO CHARLES PALISSOT. *French*]

Vienna, 18th March 1780

I can no longer refrain, Monsieur, from expressing to you the supreme pleasure I feel in reading your works, and I am greatly obliged to Monsieur le Comte de Brancas for having brought to my knowledge one of the greatest geniuses of France. If during my sojourn in Paris I had been acquainted with your comedy *Les*

Philosophes[1] and with your *Dunciade*, oh, what good use I could have made of them against the invective of the Marmontels and their colleagues. If I ever return to Paris, your works will serve me as an aegis against those insects of Parnassus. Monsieur Janson, the bearer of this letter, is as enchanted as I am by your genius and is very desirous of making your acquaintance. I did not wish him to leave this country without taking this letter with him and the occasion will be reckoned amongst the most agreeable of his life. I beg you never to doubt the esteem you have inspired in me. I am, with 'perfacto' perfect respect

Monsieur
Your very humble and very obedient
Servant Gluck.

[Address:]
A Monsieur
Monsieur Palissot
en sa maison,
à Paris.

[1] Palissot's comedy *Les Philosophes* had appeared in Paris in 1760.

[To Franz Kruthoffer. *German*]
[In Kruthoffer's handwriting:
Replied Paris, 16th April 1780]

Vienna, 31st March 1780

Dearest friend,

I am obliged to you for the little lights [candles] and for the news. This makes it much easier for me to forget Paris, for I know everything that goes on there. Just carry on with your letters; a letter always travels with the courier. I can well do without Mr. de la Blancherie's gazette[1] and you must send me no more. If you wish to have your expenses paid, then make a neat and tidy job of collecting from my creditors. I have finally received the score of *Echo* and everything will be finished by the end of April.[2] That I myself, however, should again come to Paris, nothing will come of this so long as the words Piccinnist and Gluckist are still used, for, thank God, I am now healthy again and have no wish to spew any more gall in Paris. It is difficult; the courier has barely arrived before he is off again. Adieu, dearest friend! Our regards to H. v. Blumendorff, who wrote me an incomparably handsome tribute which I have not yet been able to answer, and to all good friends.

Your most devoted
Gluck.

[Address:]
A Monsieur
Monsieur Kruthoffer
chez S.E.M. Amb. Imp. Royal . . .
à Paris

[1] The Parisian writer DE LA BLANCHERIE, who had adopted the title of 'Agent général de la correspondance pour les sciences et les arts', had been publishing a periodical, *Nouvelles de la république des lettres et des arts*, since early 1779 (*Mémoires secrètes*, XIII, p. 275, and XIV, p. 287)

[2] The passage in the letter, 'Everything will be finished by the end of April', proves that the version of the work in the engraved score was Gluck's own work and that Tiersot's view to the contrary is not tenable. The letters quoted here provide the 'preuves positives' which Tiersot sought in vain!

[TO FRANZ KRUTHOFFER. *German*]

Vienna, 29th April 1780

Dearest friend!

It is truly a wretched business; barely has one time to read the letters through before the answer has to be ready; one must perforce be laconic. I am not likely to be talked into becoming once more an object of criticism or praise by the French nation, for they are as changeable as fire. If it should happen, then it would have to be very comfortable, for idleness is now my sole pleasure.

Wait a little longer until the time set by Mr Mathon for payment. It is as well that he has not yet had the score engraved, because, under the new arrangement, the work will not come out so well. Besides, when one buys something, one must know whether it will turn out 'a conto' or not, and the agreement must be kept.[1]

It is true that, because Mr Mathon has failed to pay, I have had to send quittances to M. Rilliet[2] in order to satisfy Baron Fries, for whom I had intended the 1,000 livres, in order to discharge a certain debt.

The affair of the portrait made me truly angry. The French seek every excuse to plague themselves or others. The portrait could not be put in the bracelet, because it was too big, and it was too small to hang up;[3] the copy we have had made takes its place. It would have been a pity if the painting had merely remained in a box. It is now in good hands and many people will find pleasure in seeing it in a place where the original is loved by the public. In this affair I am like the lamb in the fable. Madame Gluck sends her fondest wishes; our regards to all good friends. I need no more packages; it is all nothing but poetry. Your pleasant letters are enough for me. Adieu, dearest friend, farewell.

[Address:]

A Monsieur
Monsieur de Kruthoffer
chez S. Ex. M. L'Ambassadeur Imp. et Roy.
à
Paris

[1] Gluck had the same unhappy experience with the publisher MATHON DE LA COUR as previously with Le Marchand. Work on the engraving of the *Echo* score had not yet started; apparently, after the setback suffered by the opera, Mathon tried to withdraw from his contract. Somehow or other he must have succeeded, in fact, for the score appeared in 1781 'chez des Lauriers M[archan]d des papiers, rue St. Honoré à côté de celle des Prouvaires'. Baron von Tschudi mentions this in his *Mémoire* of August 1781, in which he suggests to the Minister Amelot that the work should be produced again: '. . . the score having been engraved and selling at Deslauriers', near the rue des Prouvères, the public is thereby reminded of the importance one must attach to this work'. Tschudi's efforts were not in vain: the opera was once more included in the programme on 31st August 1781 and at last received the recognition it deserved (*Mémoires secrètes*, XVIII, p. 31). As the Opera House was burnt down on 8th June—during a performance of Gluck's *Orphée*—the production took place in the small hall of the Menus-plaisirs du Roi.

[2] RILLIET was presumably a Parisian banker; nothing further is known of him.

[3] No trace has been found of this portrait.

[TO FRIEDRICH GOTTLIEB KLOPSTOCK. *German*]

Vienna, 10th May 1780

This is to inform you, dearest friend, that Herr Schroter was given a very good reception here both by the Court and by the public. And he deserves it, for he is truly a quite unusual and very natural actor. I do not doubt that he will be very satisfied with Vienna.

You are constantly reproaching me for not having sent you any explanation as to how *Alceste* should be produced. I would have done it long ago, if I had found it practicable. As regards the songs, it is easy for a person who has feeling; all that is needed is to follow the dictates of the heart. About the accompaniment, where the instruments require so many directions, nothing can be done unless I am there in person; some notes must be drawn out, others pushed out, some at half-volume, others louder or softer, not to mention the movement. A little slower or faster destroys a whole piece, so I believe, dearest friend, you will find it much easier to make the Germans familiar with your new orthography[1] than I will to produce an opera by my method, particularly in your district, where the art of composition takes first place and imagination is despised and abused, which is why most of your musicians wish only to be masons but not architects.

Although you have not composed anything on the death of my dear departed one, my wish has nevertheless been fulfilled, for your *Dead Clarissa*[2] bears so close a resemblance to my girl that, for all your great mind, you could not have produced anything better. This is now my favourite ode and very few hear it without being moved to tears. You do not know why I have taken so long over the *Hermannsschlacht*—because I want to make this the last of my musical works. Until now I have not been able to stop, because the French gentlemen had kept me so busy. But, although the *Hermannsschlacht* will now be my last work, you must believe that it will not be the least important of my productions, for I had collected the main material for it before age weakened my thinking powers.

Fare thee well! I remain ever your devoted admirer

Gluck.

[Address:]

A

Monsieur Klopstock

à

Hamburg.

[1] Klopstock's new ORTHOGRAPHY is explained in his correspondence with Professor Tetens in Kiel, and L. Muggenthaler: 'Orthographiereformbestrebungen und ihre Bedeutung für die Gegenwart' [Dittes: *Pädagogium*, VII, 1885].

[2] Gluck's music for the ode *Die tote Clarissa* is not extant.

[TO FRANZ KRUTHOFFER. *German*]

[In Kruthoffer's handwriting:
Replied Paris, 17th June, 1780]

Vienna, 30th May 1780

Dearest friend!

I beg you to forgive me if I pester you so with Mr Mathon. You can tell him at once he is to have the opera *Narcisse* engraved; as it is corrected, the music becomes no better but the piece is much more regular. Opera has suffered a heavy loss in Mr Berton;[1] I shall miss him. I wish someone would appear some time who would take my place and could please the public with his music, so that I would be left in peace, for I still cannot forget all the chatter I have had to listen to, from friends and foes, about *Narcisse*, or the pills I have swallowed; these French gentlemen cannot yet distinguish between a musical eclogue and an epic poem.[2] I am sending the corrections for *Narcisse* to the Bailly du Roullet; please forward them to him. My best regards to Mr Rousseau[3] and all good friends. I will not fail to report to M. Abbé Pezzana, if anything should happen concerning *Iphigénie*. I am glad the songs I wrote pleased the Ambassador. My regards to H. v. Blumendorff and Janson, to whom I have written, but I addressed the letter to Faubourg St. Germain, because I do not know where he lives. Tell him to seek out the letter and answer it and send me his address. We are all well, and my whole society and all his good friends, as also Mme Gluck and I, send him best regards. Adieu, dearest friend. Write to me soon with some news. I am ever your

Gluck.

[1] Pierre Montan Berton died suddenly on 14th May 1780 after a performance of Rameau's *Castor et Pollux* (*Mémoires secrètes*, XV, p. 156); barely two months earlier, on 17th March, he had taken over the direction of the Académie de Musique following the resignation of de Vismes. He was succeeded by the composer Antoine Dauvergne (1713–1797), with Gossec as Assistant Director.

[2] '. . . one must not imagine that this is a pastoral: it is true tragedy', was the opinion in Paris of *Echo et Narcisse*, whereas Gluck claimed that the work was generally regarded as a musical eclogue.

[3] The reference is to the young tenor J. Rousseau (1761–1800), who joined the Opéra in 1780 as successor to Le Gros.

[To Franz Kruthoffer. *German*]

[In Kruthoffer's handwriting;
Replied Paris, 14th July 1780]

Vienna, 30th June 1780

Dearest friend!

I am most grateful for the trouble you take in looking after my affairs. Your last letter was greatly appreciated here; you must write more often and give us Viennese more of your wit and your brilliant mind, so that we can more often admire it. If the stupid arguments in Paris over music and spectacles were to go out of fashion, I might perhaps decide once again to come to Paris and whistle something to you again, but I no longer trust them. A child that has been burnt shuns fire. It might well happen, however, to please my friends, of whom you are one of the oldest. Many regards to all our acquaintances and friends. I am ever your

Gluck.

[To Franz Kruthoffer. *German*]

[In Kruthoffer's handwriting:
Replied Paris, 18th August 1780]

Vienna, 30th July 1780

Bravo, dearest friend! Your letter earned more applause here than all my operas in Paris; if you do not become a Hofrat [Privy Counsellor], you deserve to be one; yet who knows what can become of you with your talents: *accidit in puncto quod non contingit in anno.* I regret that with the new arrangement I cannot have a little talk with you,[1] for barely do I get the letters before I must send the answer, so much so that I hardly have time to acknowledge receipt of same, which is why I remain so laconic. My wife, who sends you her best regards, cannot understand why you have changed your mind in connection with my return to Paris, you who before were always so opposed to it. She asks you to explain, but I remain, now as ever, my most lovable friend's

completely obedient servant and friend

Gluck.

PS. I am also gradually beginning to become English again.[2]

[Address:]

A Monsieur
Monsieur de Kruthoffer
chez S.E.M. le Comte de Mercy
Ambassadeur Imp. et Roy.
à
Paris

[1] The first performance of Echo et Narcisse in the new two-act version on 8th August 1780 was also a failure: the takings fell from nearly 2,000 to less than 700 livres. After the ninth repeat performance the work was dropped from the programme.

[2] Gluck's remark refers to the war between France, Spain and America on the one hand and England on the other, which followed on the American Declaration of Independence in 1776 and ended with the Peace of Versailles on 3rd November 1783.

[FROM FRANÇOIS FRANCOEUR[1] TO GLUCK. *French*]

From Paris, 4th August 1780

You have had sufficient proof of my zeal to be persuaded of my friendship for you and of my admiration for your talents, you are not unaware even of the many enemies I have made by this devotion to you, and you know also that the fine performance of the orchestra in your works derives not only from the merits of the performers but also from the pains and the care taken by he who conducts them. Well, Mr, despite the great success of your operas and the justice that you have always shown to this same orchestra which is wholly devoted to you, M. le Bailli du Rollet has no confidence in me for the new production of *Echo et Narcisse*; he cavils with me over the movements and demands that all those you have given should be changed; as I believe (having obtained them from you) that I am fully entitled to retain them, I must not yield; moreover, I think that in this respect my knowledge is superior to his and, furthermore, my reputation depends in part on the success of the work, and the interest I take in it is at least as keen as his.

I have discovered that M. le Bailli had been warned against me by the late M. Berton, who for some time had ceased to like me. . . . As a result of his ill-founded warning, I have just learned that he wrote to the Committee advising them against allowing me to conduct your work. He even carried his hostility to the point of threatening not to give it, if I were wielding the baton. As I would be in despair if the public were deprived, because of me, of the pleasure of seeing one of your works again, I felt bound to give way without regard for my reputation, which M. le Bailli appears to compromise somewhat lightly, and despite my friendship for you, which made me reproach myself for leaving the conducting of your work in other hands. So it is to you, Mr, that I turn, begging you to settle this quarrel. I hope that one word from you will destroy the derogatory impressions that M. le Bailli has created concerning me, and, as my enemies can have no doubt of the confidence you have shown in me thus far, such an admission on your part will close their mouths and bring happiness to one who has the honour to be with the most respectful devotion, etc.

I beg you to convey my respects to Mme your wife and to honour me with a word of reply as soon as possible.

[Address:]

A M. le Chevalier Gluck, compositeur de Leurs Majestés
Imperiales et Royales, près le théâtre françois
à
Vienne en Autriche

[1] FRANÇOIS FRANCOEUR was born in Paris on 28th September 1698. He joined the Opéra House orchestra as a violinist in 1710, graduated to chamber musician, composer of chamber music, inspector of Opera and finally in 1760 to Senior Intendant of Music. Together with François Rebel, with whom he had a lifelong friendship, he composed ten operas and two books of violin sonatas before he died in Paris on 7th August 1787.

[GLUCK TO FRANÇOIS FRANCOEUR. *French*]

Vienna, 20th August 1780

Monsieur,

I am very disturbed by the dispute that has arisen between you and M. le Bailli du Roullet over one of my works. Can I never be free of the theatrical troubles of the Paris Opéra, either at first or second hand? I read a few days ago a small French gazette in which I am alleged to have said that I was opposed to Mlle Beaumenil playing the role of Echo in the same opera. I am no longer surprised that I have found so many enemies in Paris, since so many lies are fabricated about me. All this greatly weakens my former resolve to return to Paris, for I hate all these disquieting suggestions like the plague. Forgive me, I beg of you, Monsieur, if I decide to leave it to the Directors of the Opera House to settle your complaint against M. Bailly [du Roullet], especially as I am not myself in Paris. If I were the master, you would have no reason to complain of anyone, for I have always attached great value to your musical talent and to your constant friendship, which you have demonstrated towards me on several occasions. I hope that you will receive justice without delay and that peace will soon be restored. I have the honour to be, with the highest esteem,

Monsieur,
Your very humble and very obedient
Servant Gluck.

I pray you to make my compliments
to the gentlemen of the orchestra.
[Address:]
de Vienne
A Monsieur
Monsieur Francoeur Maître de Musique
de l'Opéra rue Neuve St. Eustache
près l'Hôtel de Carignan
à Paris

[TO FRANZ KRUTHOFFER. *German*]

[In Kruthoffer's handwriting:
Replied Paris, 16th September 1780]

Vienna, 30th August 1780

Dearest friend!

If you continue to write letters like the last two, I will make a collection of them and have them printed by subscription, which will bring me in more than the operas I have sold to Mathon. I beg you from the bottom of my heart, have him, if not hanged, at least put to street-sweeping, if he does not pay promptly. Joking apart, your letters do you much honour, and everyone would like to make your acquaintance. Mr Riedl,[1] Calin, myself and our friends always await the courier impatiently, for the fluency of your letters is a delight to us. You are surely right in thinking that my journey to Paris will not take place yet, because I have not yet been able to find a sponser through whom I could be summoned to the Court. My wife sends her best regards and will follow your advice faithfully, should it come to our travelling from here. Then we shall eat, drink and make merry with you, dearest friend, and our other good friends. Remember me to H. v. Blumendorff and Janson. I can think of nothing more to write to him than that I am fond of him and wish him a contented life. I remain ever your most devoted friend and servant

Gluck.

[Address:]
A Monsieur
Monsieur de Kruthoffer
chez S. Ex. Mr L'Ambassadeur
Imp. Roy. Apost.
à
Paris

[1] Friedrich Justus Riedel (1742–1785), the well-known author and 'depraved Klotzian' (i.e. supporter of the well-known opponent of G. E. Lessing), was one of Gluck's friends. He went to Vienna in 1772, when he was appointed Professor at the Academy of Arts and Privy Councillor. He corresponded, amongst others, with Klopstock and Weiland and, apart from the periodical *Literarische Monate* (1776 onwards), published a book, *Über die Musik des Ritters Gluck* (Vienna, 1776).

[To Franz Kruthoffer. *German*]

[In Kruthoffer's handwriting:
Replied Paris, 13th October, 1780]

Vienna, 30th September 1780

Dearest friend!

I received your letter today and must reply *stante pede*, if I am not to miss the courier again. The Emperor is in Bohemia, which is why the parcels arrived so late. I am greatly obliged to you for the news I get from you, apart from that concerning Mathon. I thought that, as he had been given so much time to pay, he could be distrained, for he deserves no further consideration. As regards the opera *Echo*,

I had not imagined that the Directors of the Opera House would treat it so contemptuously, because the profit is theirs.[1] As I now realize that they are not well-disposed, *nothing* will come of my return to Paris, for I will not become involved in any more quarrels. But we will meet, dearest friend, on some other pretext. Shortage of time does not permit me to answer the enclosed letters. Please give my regards to your whole family and to our other friends. Many kind regards to you from Mme Gluck. I remain ever your most devoted

Gluck.

[Address:]

A Monsieur
Monsieur de Kruthoffer
Chez S.E. Mr L'Ambassadeur Imp. R.
Apost.
à
Paris

[1] The BENEFIT PERFORMANCES on behalf of the singers in March 1780—*Iphigénie en Aulide* and *Armide* were each performed twice—yielded 40,420 livres, on which *Mémoires secrètes* (XV, p. 85, of 17th March 1780) commented: 'an enormous benefit, without precedent in the lyrical theatre'.

[TO FRANZ KRUTHOFFER. *German*]

Vienna, 31st October 1780

Dearest friend!

I deeply regret your indisposition. If you were here, you would immediately shake off your fever, for I have a good friend who cures such fevers infallibly within a few days.[1] I am obliged to you for the news, although most of it was already known to us here. I hope to communicate a piece of news to you within two months,[2] which will give you great pleasure. When you next see Baron Tschoudj [*sic*], please ask him if he received my letter. I wrote to him with the following address: à M. le Baron de Tschoudj Envoyé du Prince Évêque de Liège. I was not able to add the name of the street where he lives,[3] because I do not know it. Please do the best you can to make Mathon pay and, when you receive the money, give M. Corrances[4] a louis for the Rousseau subscription, of which I make you a present in advance. My wife sends her kindest regards to you and to H. v. Blumendorff, Rousseau, Thierri,[5] Roland[6] and all good friends. I remain ever, dearest friend,

Your most devoted servant

Gluck

I have a headache and cannot write clearly.

[Address:]

À Monsieur
Monsieur de Kruthoffer
Chez S. Excellence Mr L'Ambassadeur
Imp. et Roy. Apost.
à
Paris

[1] The doctor, Professor DR. JOSEPH FREIHERR VON QUARIN (1733–1814) was 'Royal Imperial Government Councillor for Health in Lower Austria and "Physikus" of the hospital of the Brothers of Charity', a famous physician who became Rector of the University in 1797.

[2] The NEWS was an invitation Gluck had received to produce four operas in Naples. The project was cancelled following the death of the Empress Maria Theresia (29th November 1780).

[3] BARON VON TSCHUDI lived in the rue St Dominique.

[4] OLIVIER DE CORANCEY (1743–1810) was the editor of the *Journal de Paris*. He was a faithful supporter of Gluck and an intimate friend of J. J. Rousseau. In 1796 he published *Poésies suivies d'une Notice sur Gluck et Rousseau*.

[5] THIERRY was Louis XVI's first Valet de Chambre. In the beginning of September 1792, during the so-called prison murders, he was executed.

[6] ROLLAN was one of Gluck's admirers who in 1776 subscribed towards a bust of Gluck by Jean Antoine Houdon (*Mémoires secrètes*, IX, p. 192).

[TO FRANZ KRUTHOFFER. *German*]

[In Kruthoffer's handwriting:
Replied Paris, 21st December 1780]

Vienna, 29th November 1780

Dearest friend

The confusion and compassion which have beset me and all inhabitants here in the sad circumstances of Maria Theresia's demise prevent me from answering your letter in detail, although it is of great interest to me. One thing only will I tell you, because of the flea sitting in your ear, namely that I am to go to Naples to make four operas there. I did not wish to divulge it to you till I knew whether my conditions would be accepted or not. A droll occurrence for the anti-Gluckists in Paris. With that I embrace you with my whole heart

Gluck.

[To Franz Kruthoffer. *German*]

[In Kruthoffer's handwriting:
Replied Paris, 20th January 1781]

Vienna, 3rd January 1781

Your letters, dearest friend, are so tasty and amusing that they make us forget Linguiet[1] and his *Annals*. All those to whom I show them have a burning desire to meet you. You are acquiring more fame here with your letters than I with my operas in Paris. Madame Gluck is enchanted with you. She sends you her kindest regards and asks at the same time if you can give her any information about a certain doctor medicinae from here, who calls himself Mesmer,[2] whether he is in Paris and how much credit he has gained by his magnetic cures. The death of the Empress has led to my Neapolitan journey being postponed. We are opening the theatres again on the 21st. My return to Paris will hardly materialize. You are right: a man of mature years can no longer associate with the rabble, yet I would like to see my friends again. Greet them all fondly from me, Janson, Rousseau, Moreau,[3] Thierry, etc., and put H.v. Blumendorff at the head of the list. Get Mathon firmly by the ears, so that we can finish with him once and for all. If the book on strategy is not very big, please send me a copy. Farewell. I give you a kiss on your left eye and remain ever your

Gluck.

[1] Simon Nicolas Henri Linguet (born 1736 in Rheims) wielded such a sharp pen that he was compelled to leave France in 1776. In April 1777 the first of his sensational *Annales politiques, civiles et littéraires du XVIIIe siècle* appeared, and continued through nineteen volumes until 1792. In 1794, after returning to Paris, he was executed.

[2] Dr. Franz Anton Mesmer (1733–1815), the well-known founder of the doctrine of so-called animal magnetism, had transferred his activities from Vienna to Paris. He was a great lover of music and was on friendly terms with the Mozart family.

[3] Jean Michel Moreau le Jeune (1741–1814), an excellent painter and copper-engraver, is the Moreau referred to here, not the opera-singer of the same name.

[To Franz Kruthoffer. *German*]

Vienna, 31st January 1781

PS. There is no word here of changing a post, as the Parisians are thinking.[1]

Dearest friend.

Mr. Blumendorff[2] sends me your packet with the advice that, if I wished to forward anything to Paris, I should send it at once, because the courier is already about to leave again. So how is it possible to write you a complete letter, as I barely have time to read yours? You must be patient until some order has been restored to the couriers' movements, when I shall be able to give you news of what is happening here with us, for until now one has heard nothing but gossip. I will wait for something reliable, which will be more agreeable to you than all the chatter. This much is certain, that the Emperor works so astonishingly that all *praesidia* together can barely keep pace with him. I await Mr. Maureau's[3] drawings by the next courier. Please to remember Madame Gluck and myself to Mademoiselle le Vasseur and to explain to her yourself why the couriers prevent me from writing to her. We are both certain of your noble heart and true friendship, nor must you ever doubt the same of us. I am surprised that M. le Bailly has not replied to my letter. My respects to Baron de Tschoudy; I cannot answer him, because I have not yet had time to read and examine the poetry[4] he sent me. Adieu, dearest friend. I remain ever yours.

[Address:]

À Monsieur
Monsieur de Kruthoffer
chez Son Excellence Mr. L'Amb. Imp. et Royal
à
Paris

[1] The rumours which circulated after Maria Theresia's death that Ambassador Mercy-Argenteau was to be recalled were without foundation. He was not transferred to Brussels until 1790.

[2] The Blumendorff mentioned here was the brother of Franz von Blumendorff, Head of Chancery in the Paris Embassy, and lived in Vienna.

[3] Gluck was waiting for the stage designs by Jean Michel Moreau le Jeune for the Vienna production of *Iphigénie en Tauride*.

[4] The poetry which Baron von Tschudi had sent to Gluck was presumably 'Les Danaïdes' (*Hypermnestra*), which the author, Raniero di Calzabigi (1714–1795), had sent to Gluck in 1778 and which Baron von Tschudi had revised. Gluck intended to set the work to music but, owing to a breakdown in his health, was unable to finish it. On his recommendation, the Académie

de Musique commissioned Gluck's pupil ANTONIO SALIERI to do it in 1783—without the knowledge and against the wishes of Calzabigi, who was justly angry. The work was performed for the first time under Gluck's name on 26th April 1784 in Paris and was a great success. Only after the twelfth performance was the truth made known—namely, that Salieri was the sole composer of the opera and that Gluck's share in it had been confined to occasional advice. [Cramer's *Magazin der Musik*, II, pp. 417 *seq*.].

[TO FRANZ KRUTHOFFER. *German*]

[In Kruthoffer's handwriting:
Replied Paris, 18th April 1781]

Vienna, 28th March 1781

PS. Had almost forgotten to thank you for the constant trouble I cause you; I hope soon to show my gratitude.

Dearest friend!

Although I cannot always answer your welcome letters because of the irregular arrival and departure of the couriers, I hope you will never forget me as a friend but continue to regale me with your correspondence. I have read your very successful translation with much pleasure and congratulate you on it; perhaps it will help me to make your talent known here in Vienna, for this is a much better way of persuasion than mere speeches. Give M. Moreau a few dozen kisses for me; he has enchanted me with his drawings. I am not feeling well;[1] March keeps me indoors, but as soon as I am out and about again, I will present you to the High Chamberlain and pass on to you the applause which you will inevitably receive. If I can obtain anything agreeable from him, it will be all the more agreeable to me. Mde. Gluck sends her best regards to you and begs you to send her a few boxes of small night-candles. Try to make Mathon pay, so that we can pay for them too. Tell the Bailly du Roullet he is to come to Vienna to cure me with his entertaining conversation, for I am suffering much from melancholy. I beg you also to give my best regards to Mademoiselle le Vasseur and to H. v. Blumendorff. Farewell, dearest friend! Love me a little.

[Address:]

À Monsieur
Monsieur de Krutthoffer
chez S. Ex. M. L'Ambassadeur Imp. et. Roy.
à
Paris

[1] In 1781 Gluck was in poor health. During the rehearsals of *Echo et Narcisse* in Paris in 1779 he had suffered a slight stroke (*Journal de Paris*, No. 209 of 5th September 1779). Early in June 1781 followed a more serious stroke, the after-effects of which Gluck suffered for a long time.

[2] The High Chamberlain was Franz Xaver PRINCE OF ORSINI AND ROSENBERG (1723–1796).

[TO FRANZ KRUTHOFFER. *German*]

[In Kruthoffer's handwriting:
Replied Paris, 30th May 1781]

Vienna, 1st May 1781

Dearest friend!

I can give you no news yet of my restored health; I must have patience till the good weather comes, when I hope to convalesce again in my garden;[1] I have spent a long time in a state of constant inaction, but the *Iphigénie en Tauride,* which is to be presented very soon, will bring me back into action and set my blood flowing. I am deeply obliged, however, to you and all my friends who took such an active interest in my health. If they intend to present all my operas *ad nauseaum,* will the whole world not find them intolerable in the long run? This is the only and the best way to establish Italian music in Paris, so let us congratulate those French gentlemen. I thank God that I am quit of them. From the Bailly's letters I have noticed that he does not feel too well, for, like myself, he writes with a trembling hand; I could do with his company. Mme Gluck, who sends you her best regards, is disappointed that you have not sent her the night-lights; do not, for heaven's sake, forget them. Our regards to all our friends. I embrace you most fondly

Gluck.

[1] In 1776 Gluck had bought a house from Baron von Sandor at Rennweg No. 22, not far from the St Marxer Linie. He exchanged it in September 1781—probably for the country house at Perchtoldsdorf—with a doctor, Johann Nepomuk Ritter von Humbourg (1731–1795).

[TO LOUIS PETIT DE BACHAUMONT.[1] *French*]

[Vienna, 11th May 1781]

Do not believe the rumours which are going round about my early return to Paris; unless superior orders take me there, I will not go to this city till the French are agreed as to the kind of music they want. This fickle people, after receiving me in the most flattering manner, seems to have lost all taste for my operas, which are no longer attended by the same crowds as before; and today we have the Lord Bountiful's attention being drawn; he seems intent upon returning to his Pont-neufs;[2] one must let him do as he pleases.

[1] LOUIS PETIT DE BACHAUMONT was born in Paris in 1690. He frequented Madame Doublet's literary salon and in 1777 his *Mémoires secrètes pour servir à l'histoire de la république des lettres* began to appear. He died in May 1771.

[2] PONT-NEUFS—a familiar eighteenth-century expression for prostitutes who haunted Pont-neuf, and also used occasionally of light songs.

[CARLO CALIN TO FRANZ KRUTHOFFER. *German*]

Highly honourable Herr, best friend.

Is one really to believe that the Chevalier Gluck felt obliged to write to you through me? And yet there is not the slightest doubt of it. The fate that always governs our lives attacked his hand some weeks ago, so that we have reason to deplore this occurrence and to wish that the forces which assailed him through a stroke on the right side will be checked by the baths he has been taking; it is our fondest wish to ask the Almighty to grant our entreaties and avert what He in His Omnipotence has decided. The hopes of men spring eternal and no effort will be spared to do what is humanly possible. Bitter as this letter sounds, future news may be joyful. What also hurts the Chevalier in his difficult circumstances is that he has received no news from his good friends in Paris for some time. From you, best friend, he hoped for something by the courier, but as His Majesty the Emperor's journey has gone awry, that too has been lost and we do not know where we are. His good friend the Ballie de Rollete [sic], who never failed to answer, has made him wonder anxiously if he had not perhaps paid his debt to Nature. All in all, it is depressing for someone who himself seemed to be on the point of death. To give the Chevalier some comfort, I pray you, best friend, to let us know, as soon as you receive this, the state of your health and the reason why the Ballie has not replied. He will be expecting letters by your hand every day, and, for my sake as well, give him an account of the developments in the Opera House which people in Paris are discussing. The war news is beginning to fall off here; if you have any more secret and more reliable [information] as to what is happening in America, this might help, but it must not be bad news. There will be no better evidence how a little sympathy can give new strength to the Chevalier's paralysed arm than if you carry on a lively correspondence with him, for he has no one else left.

And now, farewell. Continue to love your friend who honours you and give his respects also to your good friend, Hr. v. Plumendorf. This is all your servant can say, that he closes with all respect as a

Most devoted friend
Carlo Calin.

Vienna, 19th June 1781

[To Grand Duke Carl August von Sachsen-Weimar. *German*]

Most Serene Duke
Gracious Herr!

It has pleased Your Serene Highness in a letter of the 8th of this month to give me a proof of your favour and most gracious sympathy. I express my most heartfelt and humble thanks for this high favour.

The paralysis of my right hand, which still persists, makes it impossible for me to express my most humble thanks to Your Serene Highness in my own hand, but I hope that the Baden bath which I am now using for the second time will gradually relieve this affliction, at least in part.

I am truly sorry that this same illness makes it impossible for me to carry out Your Serene Highness's gracious wishes with regard to the young musician,[1] for, notwithstanding that, thanks be to God! my unhappy affliction has had no ill effect upon my powers of understanding, my present state still does not permit of any effort such as would be required for an affair of this kind. Should Your Serene Highness wish, nevertheless, to send this young man here, I am sure that his stay will not be without real value, for in the presence of the Czar opera[2] will be presented from which he can learn more in a short time than from prolonged studies. In so far as my condition permits, I will serve him with joy and endeavour to be of use at least with good advice and arranging good contacts.

Awaiting Your Serene Highness's further gracious orders, I am, with humble devotion,

Serene Duke
Gracious Herr
Your Serene Highness's
Most humble servant
Gluck mp.

Vienna, 21st August
1781

[1] Duke Karl August had, presumably at Goethe's suggestion, written to Gluck on behalf of Philipp Christoph Kayser (1755–1823), who was to study in Vienna.

[2] On the occasion of a visit by the Czar Paul of Russia Gluck's *Alceste* was performed at the end of November 1781. See note 2, letter of 30th November 1781.

[To Franz Kruthoffer. *German*]

[In Kruthoffer's handwriting:
Replied Paris, 16th December 1781]

Dearest friend!

I have read the two letters you sent me with the greatest pleasure, particularly as I thought from your long silence that you had quite forgotten me. I have again escaped from the clutches of death before I had previously recovered from my first illness. An inflammation of the lung accompanied by a fever completely robbed me of the little strength I had left. I am now a feeble convalescent again. I must tell you that on the 23rd *Iphigénie* was presented here with the greatest applause;[1] M. Moreau's designs did much to contribute to the warm reception. I am sending the pictures back to you, although I wished to keep them and this sacrifice does not come easy to me; only for you could I decide to accept this privation. Pay him many compliments on behalf of all the public here; when I am once more in a position to be out and about, I will not fail to try to obtain something from the Emperor for him. The whole of Vienna, myself included, rejoice at the birth of the Dauphin,[2] not on account of those French but on account of the Queen. I advised against dealing so gently with the scoundrel Mathon, who should be forced to abide by his bills, for his claims have always been made out on the basis of his own accounts; he should rather be obliged to make some redress for his long-delayed payment. My wife sends you her best regards, Calin wishes to be remembered, and I embrace you, dearest friend, with all my heart.

Vienna, 2nd November 1781

[Address:]

à Monsieur
Monsieur de Kruthoffer
chez son Excellence M. l'Ambassadeur Imp. et Roy. Apo.
à Paris

[1] As background to the Viennese performances of Gluck's operas, W. A. Mozart's letters to his father provide some fascinating details. On 29th August 1781 he had this to say about the engagement of Signora Bernasconi in London: 'I think . . . that Gluck, to enable him to present his French operas in German, has also contributed . . . and, so that she does not take the 500 ducats for nothing, the Emperor was persuaded, with much difficulty, to have *Iphigénie* and *Alceste* presented by Gluck.—The former German, the second foreign. . . .' There is another reference in the letter

of 12th September, and on 24th October he writes: 'Yesterday was the first performance of *Iphigénie*, but I was not there. For anyone who wished to enter the parterre had to be there at 4 o'clock—but I was at almost all the rehearsals. . . .' The performance, in which Antonia Bernasconi played the title rôle, Valentin Adamberger the part of Orestes, and Ludwig Fischer the part of King Thoas, was an enormous and enduring success (cf. Cramer's *Magazin der Musik*, I, p.353).

[2] Marie Antoinette's first son, LOUIS JOSEPH XAVIER FRANÇOIS, was born on 22nd October 1781. He died on 4th June 1789.

[TO FRANZ KRUTHOFFER. *German*]

[In Kruthoffer's handwriting:
Replied Paris, 3rd February 1782]

Dearest friend!

I read your letter with the greatest pleasure, especially as it gave me so much news of the war and the theatre. I regret the loss of gallant General Koch[1] and wish the news of his complete recovery had proved to be true. The applause given to the German *Iphigénie* has a better foundation, for the Grand Duke of Russia[2] was so delighted by it that he came with the Prince [Ferdinand] of Württemberg the other day to visit me and expressed a great desire to make my better acquaintance. This created a great sensation here, and the place where I have my lodgings was quite full of people all talking about it. He also heard the foreign *Alceste* and was particularly impressed by the aria which comes at the end of the revised act, and more especially by the words 'Me déchire le cœur'[2]—a particularly appropriate lesson for M. Marmontel, for he [the Grand Duke] paid me the compliment of saying that, while he had heard a great deal of music, none had so touched his heart as mine. I am sending you the German translation[3] as requested. I hope you received the letter and the drawings by M. Moreau, which I sent you by a French courier; if not, please advise me at once. Do not send me any more newspapers from M. de la Blancherie, for it is not worth the trouble of reading them. I also wish to hear no more of Mr Mathon. Do with him as you think fit, for I can rely upon your insight and honesty. Madame Gluck sends her best regards and I remain ever your

Most humble servant

Gluck.

Vienna, 30th November 1781

[1] JOHANN BAPTIST FREIHERR VON KOCH, Lieutenant-General in the Imperial Army, who had distinguished himself in the Seven Years' War, had travelled to France in 1777 for health reasons and died in Paris in the autumn of 1781.

[2] Grand Duke PAUL PETROWITCH (1754–1801), who was crowned Czar Paul I in 1796, had embarked on a prolonged tour abroad on 30th September 1781 with his wife, Maria Feodorovna, Princess Sophia Dorothea Auguste Louise of Württemberg (1759–??). On 21st November they arrived in Vienna as Duke and Duchess von Norden. In their honour a series of brilliant festivities was organized. On Sunday, the 25th, they heard Gluck's Italian *Alceste* in the Schlosstheater at Schönbrunn and two days later *Iphigénie en Tauris* in the National theater in Vienna. Accompanied by his brother-in-law, the young Prince Ferdinand of Württemberg (born 1763), the Grand Duke visited Gluck the following day (Wednesday, 28th November) and the composer was overcome with pride and joy.

The Grand Duke's visit to Vienna is also mentioned in Mozart's letters to his father: 'The Grand Duke of Russia is not coming until November', he writes, 29th August 1781, then on 24th November: 'Now the grand-ducal great bear is here—Tomorrow is *Alceste*/foreign/at Schönbrunn, followed by an open ball—' After the performance there was a great masked ball, to which several thousand people were invited, and the climax was a magnificent banquet (report in *Wiener Zeitung*, 1781, No. 95).—'Yesterday, or to be more precise last night, was the great fête at Schönbrunn, which was a resounding success. Nearly 4,000 masks, everyone supped, and all the rooms without exception were thrown open. Apart from this, the opera *Alceste* was presented with marked success—' writes Josef II to his brother Leopold on 26th November. A detailed description of the visit of the Grand Duke and Grand Duchess to Vienna and of the musical performances arranged for the occasion is given in C. F. Pohl's biography of *Haydn* (vol. 2, pp. 183 *seq.*). '. . . To make the acquaintance of famous persons is . . . a feature of their thirst for knowledge. . . . Good music and a fine spectacle . . . give them pleasure. . . . The Grand Duchess plays the piano very well . . .' wrote the Emperor Josef to his brother Leopold in January 1782. They met all the important musicians in Vienna, called not only on Gluck but also on the aged Court Poet Pietro Metastasio (died 12th April 1782), and Maria Feodorovna was present at the contest between Mozart and Clementi on 24th December. Joseph Haydn's 'Russian Quartets' (opus, 33, Hoboken III/37–42), which Artaria brought out in January 1782, are dedicated to the Grand Duke. The departure from Vienna took place on 4th January 1782. In October, on their way back to Russia, the royal couple spent a further fortnight in the imperial capital.

[3] The German translation which Kruthoffer received was the book entitled: *Iphigénie en Tauris. Ein tragisches Singspiel in vier Aufzügen. Aus dem Französischen des Herrn Guillard. Die Musik ist vom Ritter Gluck. Aufgeführt auf dem K. K. Nationaltheater. Wien, beym Logenmeister, 1781.* This German translation was by the Viennese poet Johann Baptist von Alxinger (1775–1797). Gluck had made substantial changes in the music, as can be seen from his sketch-books in the Municipal Library at Leipzig and from the score in the Austrian National Library in Vienna.

[To Franz Kruthoffer. *German*]

[In Kruthoffer's handwriting:
Replied Paris, 3rd February 1782]

Vienna, 30th December 1781

Dearest friend!

I beg you to carry out the following commission for me: to hand the enclosed letter together with the portrait[1] in the tin box to the Bailly du Roullet, but please to open it first and have it stretched on a frame before you deliver it, because when stretched it makes a better showing. Ask him from me if he would be good enough to hand the letter and the portrait to Madame de la Ferte.[2] Should he, however, be out of Paris, then I beg you to undertake this for me. I cannot answer your letter this time, because the room is full of people, so I close with the assurance that I remain ever your

Most humble servant
and friend Gluck.

[1] The portrait in question was presumably a copy of the oil painting which Joseph Silfrede Duplessis (1735–1802) completed in Paris in 1775 and which is now in the Kunsthistorisches Museum in Vienna. In 1783 Gluck had another copy made for Johann Friedrich Reichardt.

[2] The husband of Madame de la Ferté was a keen collector of pictures who, according to the records left by the painter Joseph Vernet, acquired 27,000 livres worth of paintings between 1776 and 1784.

[To Valentin.[1] *French*]

From Vienna, 17th April 1782

Monsieur,

Your obliging letter gave me great pleasure and I must thank you for it.

It is very flattering to me and I see in it the imprint of an ardent genius, eager to learn, as well as the essential qualities of a good heart an and excellent character, which do you much honour.

If the state of my health permitted it and if I could still undertake something relating to dramatic art, I could think of nothing more pressing than to accept the offer you have just made me, and I am convinced that we would be both well pleased.

I have been ill for several months following an apoplectic stroke, which came upon me last year. My head is weakened and my right arm is paralysed. I am incapable of doing the least work which is continuous; I am not allowed, and still less am I able, to apply myself in any way. So you see, Monsieur, that I cannot lend myself to your request, which does you so much credit and me so much honour. It is against my wishes but it is impossible to do otherwise.

You are young, Monsieur, and you are full of goodwill; work, and I have no doubt you will make progress, gain advancement and achieve success.

Determination and courage in your studies, reflection and a sense of unity in a work as a whole, and above all the seeking of truth in expression: all these, allied to the rules of art, will take you far. The simplicity of nature and the force of emotion must be your guides more than all else. He who departs from them invariably slips into absurd incongruities which condemn him to mediocrity.

These are my masters; they must be yours. In this school and with the natural and acquired qualities which are necessary, one finds the right road.

Several stray from it by failing to observe these rules of conduct while following an everyday routine.

Sound them, these masters, consult them, question them. They are gentle with those who seek them. They listen to you; they will reply; they will lead you.

Adieu, Monsieur.

Pray accept these few pieces of advice given to you by an invalid, who is no longer good for anything else, and rest assured of the feeling of esteem which you deserve, which you have inspired in me, and with which I have the honour, Monsieur, to be

Your very humble and very obedient servant
Le Chevalier Gluck.

[Address:]
À Monsieur Valentin,
Directeur de la musique de Monsr. le duc d'Aiguillon,
par Bordeaux, Aiguillon en Guyenne.

[1] VALENTIN, Director of Music at Aiguillon, was the author of a 'hiérodrame', which was based on Voltaire's *Samson* and produced at a "Concert spirituel" in 1782.

[TO FRANZ KRUTHOFFER. *German*]

[In Kruthoffer's handwriting:
Replied Paris, 12th March 1783]

Dearest friend!

If until now I have not conducted a regular correspondence with you, the reason is that in present conditions one never knows if a courier is leaving or arriving. I would also like to save you the postage money. On the other hand, I have felt a slight sense of grievance against you, because you pursue my affairs with such indifference, you who have so much skill in carrying out everything that comes your way. Perhaps the new Peace with England will make you more active again. As a test I will burden you with a few commissions and when you receive the money you will deduct the expenses together with the interest. My wife, who sends you her most polite respects, begs you to buy some fine rouge, two small pots for brunette and two small ones for blonde faces, 4 pieces in all, further, 4 pounds of brown 'Poudre de maréchal á la Canelle', further some night-candles such as you have already sent us, finally a [round] box of the white sugar-cakes, which, when one puts them in one's mouth, bite and make one quite cool. It is not necessary to send everything at once but only one of each kind and the remainder bit by bit. Forgive me if I burden you with fresh commissions; when one is in need, one seeks out one's old friends again. On the other hand, I do not ask your help for nothing, as I have already decided to include you in my will for your efforts on my behalf.[1] One thing more: I beg you to speak to Monsieur le Gros on behalf of my wife and to announce a certain Mr Fischer,[2] who has an incomparable bass voice, with which he can give a good account of himself at his concerts. He proposes to travel from here to Paris at Lent. Be good enough to let me know whether he [Le Gros] will make use of him and what reply he has given. My regards to Herr von Blumendorff and to all other good friends. Perhaps we shall meet again this year,[3] if my wife does not rule it out. I remain as ever

dearest friend!

Your most humble servant

Gluck.

Vienna, 22nd February 1783

[1] Gluck did not remember Franz Kruthoffer in his will.

[2] LUDWIG FISCHER (1745–1825), who had an exceptional bass voice, was invited to Vienna in 1780 by the Emperor Joseph. 'Displeased by certain innovations in the theatre', he left for Paris in 1783. On his performances there, Cramer's *Magazin der Musik* (I, p. 839) reported as follows: 'Paris in May 1783: In this "Concert spirituel" Herr Fischer, a singer from Vienna, was also heard. His voice is pure, beautiful and of an extraordinary range. His style of singing is very good; he will always earn more applause when he chooses arias which are suited to his voice.' Fischer's voice ranged from

bottom C to treble A (Reichardt: *Musikalische Monatsschrift*, 1792, p. 67); he was the outstanding German bass singer of his time. Mozart, who mentions him frequently in his letters, wrote the part of Osmin in the *Entführung aus dem Serail* for him and the two beautiful concert arias, K.432 (1783) and K.512 (1787). Later, Fischer went to Berlin, where he remained with the State Opera until 1815.

[3] Gluck's journey to Paris had already been planned for October 1782: '. . . the Chevalier Gluck, who has completely recovered from his illness, has decided to set out for France and should arrive in Paris in the month of October', the *Mémoires sècretes* (XXI, 72) reported on 24th August, but this is denied in Cramer's *Magazin*, I, 238.

[TO FRANZ KRUTHOFFER. *German*]

[In Kruthoffer's handwriting:
Replied Paris, 19th April 1783]

Dearest friend!

The night-lights and the pastilles duly arrived, and my wife, who sends her kindest regards, thanks you most warmly for them. The rouge can only cost 12 fl. and the hair-powder 15 fl. You will be good enough to take the money for all these from Mathon's payment; my wife requires the powder brown and the rouge not pale. I hope to thank you personally for all the inconvenience I am causing you, for I am really thinking of coming once more to enjoy the company of my friends, but not to expose myself by fresh work to the critique of those Marmontels and de la Harpes. Please to see to the enclosed packet; it came to me from you, so I am forwarding it to you again. I have the honour, to be,

Dearest friend!
Your most humble servant
Gluck.

Vienna, 28th March 1783

[TO FRANZ KRUTHOFFER. *German*]

[In Kruthoffer's handwriting:
Replied Paris, 16th August 1783]

Vienna, 9th July 1783

Dearest friend!

My Secretary's illness prevented me from replying to you earlier and reporting at once that my wife, who sends her kindest regards, duly received the hair-powder. She also hopes to receive in due course rouge which is suitable for a brunette. It would be presumptuous on my part to mention Mathon's debt again; you yourself will make the best arrangement you can. But I must now trouble you for a fresh favour. Herr Rilliet has cashed my nine months' pension, but the rate of exchange is so low here that I beg you to take over this money from him—he has already been informed of this—and send it to me bit by bit *in natura* by the guardsman who travels from there monthly, otherwise I would lose all too much, for the louis d'or here is worth only 8 [florins] and some fifty xr.[1] Forgive me my secatura. Why has heaven destined you to be my friend? You know that you are seldom left alone, particularly when one possesses so many fine qualities as you.

I remain ever
Your most humble servant
and friend Gluck.

[Address:]
à Monsieur
Monsieur de Kruthoffer
chez son Excellence Monsieur
l'Ambass. Imperial
à
Paris

[1] Internal corruption in France a few years before the Revolution had led to serious monetary devaluation. As a careful 'pater familias', Gluck tried to offset the effects of the devaluation by having his pension transferred '*in natura*', i.e. in cash, as the rate of exchange in the Viennese banks was very low and would have meant serious losses. Gluck's pension for three-quarters of a year was 4,500 pounds = 225 gold louis. According to the rate of exchange at that time, this would only have represented 1,912½ florins.

[To Franz Kruthoffer. *German*]

Vienna, 4th August 1783

Dearest friend!

Your letter duly arrived but the promised rouge has not come with the 'Noble Garde' who arrived here, nor has any packet addressed to me reached the Customs, so I beg you to enquire what can have gone wrong. Lest we should incur any further embarrassment over the despatch of the money, the best plan will surely be for you to deliver it to Herr v. Blumendorff addressed to me.[1] As regards the Mathon affair,[2] I deeply deplore the fact that even bills of exchange no longer carry any weight with the French gentlemen. My idea would be to take a 'doctor'[3] and to pay, in order to have done with the matter once and for all. I have acquired such a dislike of the French that I no longer feel any desire to see them in Paris. Perhaps I will travel through to reach London, where I have been invited to produce the foreign operas I have already completed. I remain with all respect

Dearest friend!
Your most humble servant
Gluck.

PS. My wife sends you her kindest regards.
[Address:]
à Monsieur
Monsieur de Kruthoffer
chez son Excellence Mr l'Ambassadeur
Imper. et Roy.
à
Paris

[1] A brother, resident in Vienna, of Franz von Blumendorf, Head of Chancery in the Paris Embassy.
[2] The 'Mathon affair', which had been going on since 1779, had not yet been settled. Gluck's annoyance at the publisher's failure to pay his debts became directed against the whole French people. He refused to contemplate another visit to Paris, but another and hitherto unknown plan now emerges: an invitation to London to produce the foreign operas he has already completed. The offer appears to have come from Robert Mac O'Reilly, the Director of Italian Opera at the King's Theatre, who later also invited Mozart to go to London for the first six months of 1791 and write two new operas. The fact that Gluck seriously thought of accepting this invitation to London, which he had only visited once before in his early years, shows how much vitality the seventy-year-old composer still possessed. This was in the summer of 1783, when Reichardt paid him a memorable visit and found the 'old and extremely dignified man' still mentally alert. The following year, however, Gluck had another stroke and, although he partially recovered, thanks to the devoted care and attention of his wife, there was no question of continuing the correspondence with his friends in Paris.
[3] i.e. call in a lawyer.

[To Johann Friedrich Reichardt.[1] *German*]

Vienna, 11th November 1783

Dearest friend!

A few days after your departure I suffered an attack of rheumatism in the head and of catarrh, which still torments me and is the reason why you perhaps received the portrait you asked for before you received my reply to your very agreeable letter. I wish for nothing so much as to be able to carry out your plan next spring, and to be able to spend some time in pleasant converse with you and Klopstock. My wife, who sends you her kindest regards, is of the same mind as myself, although we differed over your portrait, for she wanted me to meet the cost on this occasion, but I maintained that one must not purchase the applause of a scholar and musician by means of gifts; so I prefer to appear unmannerly rather than base. Adieu, dearest friend.

Your most sincere servant
Gluck.

[1] JOHANN FRIEDRICH REICHARDT was born on 25th November 1752 in Königsberg in Prussia. From 1771 to 1774 he toured Germany and Austria. In 1775 he became Kapellmeister at the Court of Frederick the Great. In 1782 he travelled to Italy and in 1785 to Paris and London. In 1791 he was given three years' leave of absence, which he spent in London, Copenhagen and Stockholm. In 1794 he was dismissed for having revolutionary sympathies. He retired to his country estate at Giebichenstein near Halle, where he became Inspector of Saltworks in 1796. The years 1802 to 1803 he again spent in Paris. In 1805–1806 he edited the *Berlinische musikalische Zeitung*: in 1806 he fled to Königsberg. In 1808 he became Jerome Napoleon's Kapellmeister in Cassel, then travelled to Vienna to persuade Beethoven to move to Cassel. He spent the remainder of his life at Giebichenstein, where he died on 27th June 1814. As a composer he found an admirer in Goethe, but his many works are now forgotten. His writings, on the other hand, which show him to have been a sensitive and highly-cultured man, are amongst the most vigorous and attractive contributions ever made to musical literature (cf. K. M. Schletterer: *J. F. Reichardt*, 1864; C. Lange: *J. F. Reichardt*, 1902; W. Pauli: *J. F. Reichardt*, 1903).

Reichardt reported as follows on a visit to Gluck (*Allgemeine Musikalische Zeitung*, October 1813): 'The most profitable part of Reichardt's stay in Vienna was his personal visit to Gluck, who received him at his country house, a mile from the city, with great kindness and friendliness. Reichardt's visit having been announced, he was invited to spend the afternoon and evening. When he arrived, he was met by an imposing figure in a grey coat embroidered in silver, in full toilet, accompanied by his domestic staff. The young Kapellmeister, who arrived in travelling clothes, was received with more dignity and splendour than he had expected. They sat down to luncheon, which was served very attractively but at which the hero, weakened by apoplexy and under strict supervision by his careful wife, had to be idler than seemed agreeable to him. None the less, the conversation became and remained cheerful and varied. The lady of the house, who has much understanding and is well informed on many things, and a family priest who looked after Gluck's correspondence and accounts—Gluck was always very active on the stock market, in order to invest and increase his considerable fortune—played an active part in the conversation. There was much talk at first of Klopstock and the Margrave of Baden, at whose house the two great poets and artists came to know, love and honour one another. Reichardt, who had known Klopstock intimately since early youth and had remained in close touch with him, and who had stayed with the Margrave of Baden while travelling to Italy with Lavater, was able to take a very lively part in the conversation. He was also given a promise that after the meal he would hear something from the *Hermannsschlacht* and some compositions to Klopstock's *Odes*, although Gluck's wife anxiously protested. As soon as coffee had been taken, followed by a brief walk, Gluck did, in fact, sit down at the piano and, in a weak, rough voice and with palsied tongue, accompanying himself with an occasional chord, he sang several of those original compositions, to Reichardt's great delight, who also received the *maestro*'s permission to write down an *Ode* to his dictation. Several times between the songs from the *Hermannsschlacht* Gluck imitated the sound of horns and the cries of the warriors behind their shields; once he broke off to say that he must invent an instrument of his own to sing to.

'It is difficult to give a clear picture of those songs and the exposition that went before. They seemed almost entirely declamatory, very seldom merely melodious. It is certainly an irreparable loss that the artist did not write them down; this would certainly have been the surest way to appreciate the true genius of this great man, for he was not on such occasions bound by any conventions of the modern stage and singers but gave free rein to his great genius, deeply imbued by the same spirit of the great poet. Had it not been that love filled the traveller with a longing to see his fiancée, he would certainly have taken advantage of the noble artist's friendly offer to remain longer with him and would have tried to the best of his ability to put these songs on paper; that the hero himself, weakened by age and sickness, might do so was out of the question, and the Viennese atmosphere seemed too carefree for that.

'Hanging in the room was the beautiful, life-size oil painting by Duplessis of Paris, which shows the artist brimful of vitality, heaven in his eyes and love and goodness on his lips. Reichardt had no sooner expressed a wish to possess a good and faithful copy of the beautiful painting than Gluck readily promised him one. Several months later it arrived in Berlin, most welcome and with an obliging letter from the great artist, since when it has been the finest ornament in our artist's country house.

'In the evening and morning hours Gluck entertained his guest alone in his study with an account of his stay and his work in Paris. He knew Paris and the Parisians through and through and spoke with real irony of how, after experiencing their narrow-mindedness and presumption, he had treated and used them in his own grand manner.—Many more such details from the life of this great artist must remain unpublished till the completed autobiography appears.

'Reichardt had to promise him to see and hear his operas in Paris as soon as possible, because some good traditions have still survived from his former direction. Gluck was satisfied with Reichardt's judgment of him and several splendid pieces from *Alceste* in the art magazine and took it as a good sign that, without having heard them on the stage, he [Reichardt] had properly understood and judged them. He promised to give him an introduction to his best friend and poet, the Bailly du Roullet, and to provide him with many other good introductions, as soon as he required them, to ensure that, while in Paris, he was able to hear all the operas which Gluck had staged there; and, even after a period of several years, he kept his word and his friends have fulfilled his wishes in all respects to the best of their powers.

'In the evening, during a lively conversation, Gluck had promised to travel to Vienna with Reichardt the following morning and to take luncheon with him, to which he proposed to invite the poet Schroder and the very worthy Kapellmeister Krause from Stockholm, thus arranging a small and stimulating artists' meal. This idea seemed to frighten the solicitous lady of the house no little, and, as her husband felt greatly affected by the unusually lively events of the previous day, which had included a walk and a drive in the carriage, she took care to frustrate the plan. The two artists parted with feeling, the traveller being most painfully moved, as he could hardly hope ever to see his splendid host again.'

[TO THE BAILLI du ROULLET. *French*]

Vienna, this 26 April 1784

I pray you, my friend, to have printed in the *Journal de Paris* a statement which I must make and which I make here and now, to the effect that the music of the *Danaïdes* is entirely the work of M. Salieri[1] and that I had no part in it except to give advice which he was kind enough to take from me and which my esteem for him and his lack of experience inspired me to give.

Chevalier Gluck.

[1] ANTONIO SALIERI was born at Legnano on 18th August 1750. In 1765 he became a pupil at St Mark's in Venice. In 1776 he went to Vienna with Florian Leopold Gassmann. In 1770 his first opera, *Le donne letterate*, was produced and won Gluck's approval. In 1774 after Gassmann's death, he became a composer of chamber music and Director of Italian Opera. From 1784 to 1787 he was in Paris, where Gluck, who did much to advance his career, helped him with introductions. From 1788 to 1790 he succeeded Bonno as Court Kapellmeister in Vienna. Then he was suspended by the Opera House authorities and continued only as Director of the Court Singers and as Court Composer. In 1824 he retired. He died on 7th May 1825 in Vienna [cf. J. Mosel: *A. Salieri*, 1827; A. v. Hermann: *A. Salieri*, 1897].

The opera in question was produced on 5th January 1784 under the title *Hypermnestre* and soon after under the title *Les Danaïdes, tragédie en cinq actes, paroles de M^xxx* [the libretto was by Baron Tschudi, the librettist of *Echo et Narcisse*, based on a book by Raniero di Calzabigi and revised by du Roullet], *musique de M. M. le Chevalier Gluck et Salieri, maître de musique de S. M. l'Empereur et des spectacles de la cour de Vienne*. Only after the next performance was Gluck's name omitted from the announcements [cf. Ad. Jullien: *La Cour et l'Opéra sous Louis XVI*, p. 183]. The work had 127 performances and ran until 7th January 1828.

[To Valadier.[1] *French*]

Monsieur,

Very flattered as I am by your obliging letter, Monsieur, I am at the same time mortified that my state of health and my circumstances do not permit me to respond to your plea and accede to your wishes.

I am absolutely incapable of undertaking any work whatsoever which requires application and, as regards entrusting it to someone else under my direction, this is always a most uncertain and ticklish affair, which is subject to a thousand hazards, the more so as he whom I might have had in mind is heavily committed with other works and could not even accept this commission.

Your piece is rich in tableaux and in stagecraft and, as for the few slight alterations which might be advisable, we would require to be near to each other in order to reach an understanding—it not being possible to perform this task from a distance, as can readily be appreciated. Since *Cora* is your first dramatic work, I assure you that you have made a happy beginning, and, if you continue to use your talents along those lines, as I advise, you can look forward to the most marked success.

I thank you, Monsieur, for the gracious feelings you express towards me and for the good opinion you have of me; hoping, as indeed I feel sure, that you will find some composer who (by his good music) will uphold the beauty of your opera, which I herewith return.

I have the honour to be with
highest esteem
Monsieur
Your very humble and very obedient servant
Chevalier Gluck.

From Vienna, 1st May 1785

[1] Nothing appears to be known of Valadier's private life. His *Cora* libretto had been awarded a prize by the Académie Royale in open competition in 1783. It was later set to music by Méhul. The opera had its *première* on 15th February 1791 but met with such a poor reception that it was taken off after the fifth performance.

[Life Certificate. *French*]

We, Emmanuel Louis Marquis des Noailles,[1] Maréchal des Camps et Armées du Roi, Chevalier des Ordres Royaux, Militaires et Hospitaliers de St. Lazare et de Notre-Dame de Mont-Carmel, Gouverneur de Vannes et Aurai, premier Gentilhomme de la Chambre de Monsieur, Frère du Roi, Ambassadeur Extraordinaire de France près de Sa Majesté l'Empereur, Roi de Hongrie et de Bohème, do certify to all whom it may concern that Christophe Gluck, born the second July one thousand seven hundred and fourteen, composer and Director of Music of H.I.M. residing in this city, rue de Carinthie, paroisse S-Etienne—is at present alive, having appeared today before us in order to obtain the present life certificate, which he has signed with us. In token of which we have surrendered to him this document, countersigned by one of our secretaries and sealed in the margin with our coat-of-arms.

Made in Vienna in our Hotel, the eighth October one thousand seven hundred and eighty-five.

Le Mrs. Noailles m.p.
Par son Excellence
La Quiante m.p.
gratis, Christophe Gluck m.p.

[Outside:]

Certified authentic in Paris twenty-ninth October one thousand seven hundred and eighty-five.

S. Rillet m.p.

[1] EMANUEL MARIE LOUIS MARQUIS DE NOAILLES was born in Paris in 1743. He entered on a diplomatic career and in 1762 was Governor of Vannes, in 1768 Minister Plenipotentiary in Germany, then Ambassador in Holland, and in 1776 in London, from whence he notified his Government of the alliance with the United States. From 1783 to 1792 he was Ambassador in Vienna; then he returned to France and during the Revolution he was imprisoned. After his release he retired from public life. In 1784 he was made a Field-Marshal. He died in Paris in 1822.

[FROM KARL HANKE TO GLUCK. *German*]

Great, Noble, Excellent Man!

That I thus address myself to YOU on the occasion of the production of my first major musical effort calls, I hope, for no apology to YOU.—Those unforgettable days, which I had the good fortune to spend in YOUR near vicinity, thanks to my late patron, the worthy Albert Count of Hodiz zu Rosswalde, and to a kind introduction from His Serene Highness, the present ruling Prince Johann Karl von Dietrichstein, Imperial Master of the Horse, etc., are still alive in my memory!—Those days during which I came to admire YOUR all-embracing talents and so fully enjoyed YOUR soulful harmonies and thought what that youth in the September month of the German *Merkur* of the year 1776 had felt so keenly and so deeply! Those days that will always be memorable to me, in which I listened at YOUR piano with amazement and filled with an emotion never felt before to YOU, the inimitable!, and then to YOUR excellent and now departed niece.—YOU it was who laid and strengthened the unshakeable foundations of my pronouned leaning towards the divine art of music.—If a worthy thought ever flowed and should ever flow from my pen, then it is YOUR WORK and to YOU I will owe it.

Should YOU detect in this first effort at least a few glowing sparks of that fire, without which any work of art and any poetry must remain lifeless and ineffectual, then this, together with the applause I have already won from one of the most perceptive publics of our fatherland both for this operetta and for the songs in the *Marriage of Figaro*, would inspire me to still further efforts in the course I am pursuing. That this is no empty boast is clear from my earlier works, such as *Dr Faustus Leibguertel*, a comic opera in 2 acts after Rousseau and Mylius by my friend, Dr D'Arien of Hamburg, whose talents have long been recognised both in dramatic and in musical poetry and more recently in the aforementioned songs for the *Marriage of Figaro*, and such as a GREAT ROMANTIC OPERA *Xaphire*, which the latter also undertook to adapt to my design. In this way I will continue to strive to be ever more worthy of the honour of being a pupil of the greatest musician in Germany and worthy of the applause of connoisseurs with taste and perception.

YOU, however, GREAT MAN! may YOU long continue to be the ornament and pride of Germany and her music. I beg YOU always to look upon me with YOUR inestimable and friendly benevolence and to recall often and with love one who never thinks of YOU without reverence

YOUR
eternally most humble
Karl Hanke

Written at
Hamburg, 27th February 1786
[Address:]
An Herrn Ritter Gluk zu Wien

[1] KARL HANKE (1754–1835) was from 1775 to 1779 Kapellmeister of Count Hoditz-Rosswalde and married the singer Stormkin (died 1789), with whom he appeared in various theatres. In 1786 he was Court Kapellmeister in Schleswig, in 1792 he went to Flensburg as Cantor and Director of Music and finally he became Director of Music at Hamburg, where he remained until his death. His operetta *Robert und Hannchen* was first produced in Warsaw in 1781 and was presented in Vienna in 1786.

[LAST WILL. *German*]

As nothing is more certain than death, but the hour of it is uncertain, I, the undersigned, being of sound mind, have made my last will and testament, as follows:

1. I commend my soul to the infinite mercy of God, but my body shall be consigned to the earth in accordance with Christian-Catholic custom.

2. I bequeath 25 florins for 50 high Masses.

3. I bequeath to the Poorhouse 1 florin, to the general hospital 1 florin, to the civic hospital 1 florin, to the Elementary School Fund 1, altogether 4 florins.

4. To each of the domestics still in my service at the time of my death I bequeath a year's wages.

5. I leave it entirely to the discretion of my sole heiress whether she chooses to give anything to my relatives[1] or not; and

6. As it is fundamental to any will that a sole heir be appointed, I hearwith name as my sole and universal heiress my beloved wife and consort, M. Anna v. Gluck *née* Bergin, and in order that no doubt may arise concerning the silver and jewellery, as to whether it be the property of myself or my wife, it shall therefore belong to the goods I endow. Furthermore, should this my last will not be accepted as a testament, then I wish it to serve as a codicil or the like. Finally I name my highly-esteemed cousin, Joseph von Holbein,[2] Imperial Privy Councillor, as Executor of this my testament and bequeath to him a snuffbox as a memento. In witness and confirmation whereof I append my name and seal and those of outside witnesses.

Made this 2nd April 1786
in Vienna Christoph v. Gluck.

[Outside:]

Kristoph von Gluck
Antonius Riedl, Notary and advocate[3] at Court of Exchange as oral witness
Joseph von Baltech,[4] (likewise)
Joseph von Strohlendorf[5] as oral witness
Joseph de Rosa[6] (likewise)

[1] Gluck's relatives were: Christoph Anton, born 1716, Maria Anna Rosina, born 1718, married name Hedler, died 1760 (1761?), Franz Anton Ludwig, born 1720, died *circa* 1799 as Chief Forester in Prague, Franz Karl, born 1722, gamekeeper in Baumgarten (Lower Austria), Anna Elisabeth, born 1725, Heinrich Joseph, born 1727, Felix Matthes, born 1732, and Franz Johann Alexander, born 1734, died 1795, who was a weighing official in the Corn Exchange in Vienna and lived at 306 Erdberggasse.

[2] Joseph Holbein von Holbeinsberg was a Director of Lotteries.

[3] Antonius Riedl lived at 534 Gundlhof.

[4] Nothing is known of Joseph Baltech.

[5] Joseph von Strohlendorf (1765–1855), a well-known Viennese character who had become closely associated with the theatre and could be found daily at the Café Daum.

[6] Joseph Rosa (correct name Roos) (1726–1805) was Director of the Imperial Picture Gallery, lived in the Schloss Belvedere and was a friend of the Mozart family.

[DEED OF SALE WITH ANTONIA FREIFRAU VON GUDENUS. *German*]

Whereas I, the undersigned, have today duly received in cash, and have duly acknowledged receipt of, the sum of 6,200 fl., say six thousand two hundred gulden, from the High- and Well-born Freifrau Antonia Freiin von Gudenus *née* Freiin von Kronburg through her attorney Herr Johann David Schmid, this being in payment for the purchase from me of the house and garden at Partholdstorf in the Knappenstrasse number 175, recorded in the Monserat land register, together with the furniture and fittings therein, as laid down in contracts of purchase and sale of 9th June 1787; I do herewith solemnly declare that I have no hesitation in giving the Freyherrliche Frau possession of the aforementioned dwelling, but on the other hand do promise without further written communication, to indemnify the relevant land-register in every respect, in witness whereof I and the witnesses named below, though these last without prejudice or damage, have appended our signatures. Vienna, 9th June,

787

Christopf v. Gluck
Joseph v. Strohlendorf
summoned as witness
Johann David Schmid
as oral witness.

[TO JOHANN CHRISTOPH VOGEL.[1] *French*]

Vienna, 3rd August 1787

Monsieur,

I have received through M. Salieri a copy of your first opera, the *Golden Fleece*,[2] which you wished to do me the honour of dedicating to me. My eyes no longer permit me to read; M. Salieri gave me the pleasure of listening on the harpsichord to this music which I find worthy of the praises it has evoked in Paris. It is the dramatic talent which shines above all other qualities and it is on this that I congratulate you with all my heart. It is a talent that is all the more rare because it derives not from experience but from nature. The same M. Salieri has also told me all that he had heard in praise of your second work;[3] may it add to your reputation as much as I would wish and make you the most famous of artists. It is with these sentiments that I pray you to believe me.

Your, etc.

Signed, Gluck.

[1] JOHANN CHRISTOPH VOGEL was born in Nürnberg on 17th March 1756. In 1776 he went to Paris and became an admirer of Gluck. As a result of dissolute living, he died an early death on 26th June 1788 in Paris. Apart from his two operas, a number of instrumental works were published.
[2] His first opera *La Toison d'Or* (libretto by Philippe Desriaux), after lying dormant for ten years in the Opera House archives, was produced on 5th September 1786. In February 1787 it appeared in print.
[3] His second opera *Demoophon* (libretto by Desriaux, based on Metastasio), as the composer had died, was not produced until 22nd September 1789 after the work of the same name by Luigi Cherubini, which was presented on 1st November 1788.

SUPPLEMENT

[I. NANETTE GLUCK: DECLARATION FOR FR. G. KLOPSTOCK]

I, the undersigned, sorceress of the Holy Roman Empire as also of the Unholy Gallic Empire, do hereby declare and testify that I have promised and do promise Klopstock that as soon as I, arch-sorceress, have returned to the arch-city of the arch-house called Vienna and have spent there three days and three nights consecutively to recover breath from my journey, that I will despatch to him at once, without delay, and without further procrastination: 1. the aria in which Orpheus calls after Euridice,[1] 2. the aria in which Alceste calls after her children;[2] and that under each of these arias I will set down a few words which shall contain, inasmuch as words can contain, the manner and method, nature and essence, and, as it were, the finer points of my magical discourse on music, so that the aforesaid Klopstock for his part can send back these my words together with the arias to his niece in Hamburg, who, he alleges, is also a victim of sorcery.

Made in Rastatt on 17th March 1775

Nanette Gluck.

[1] The aria 'Che faro senza Euridice'.
[2] The aria 'Ah per questo gia'.

[II. NANETTE GLUCK TO ABBÉ ARNAULD. *French*]

You will be surprised to receive a letter from your little Chinese girl, but, as Papa has been indisposed and had to be bled, he asked me to write to you and tell you that he is very anxious to hear from you and to know if you are well pleased with the performance of Orpheus. . . .

Marianne Gluck

Papa and Mama send a thousand fond regards.

This letter remained unanswered. This is clear from Gluck's letter to Abbé Arnauld of 12th May 1775. [cf. p. 61].

[III. Marianne Gluck to F. A. de Lasalle.[1] *French*]

Monsieur,

Your heart, ever open to friendship for my husband, Gluck, will not refuse to share the grief in which I have just been plunged by his death. Impelled by duty and by feeling to inform you of his death, allow me, Monsieur, to unburden myself to you of the pain that weighs so heavily upon me, by describing in detail the final disaster that befell my beloved husband.—On Wednesday, the fourteenth of this month, while we were driving in the carriage between midday and one o'clock, he was seized at my side by an attack of 'apoplexie sereuse'. He was bled and appeared to recover completely; but on Thursday a second attack robbed him of all power of speech and sight and paralysed his left side. The same day, 15 of this month, at a quarter past seven, he expired. It is from a heart filled with grief and tears that I now thank you, Monsieur, in his name for all the marks of affection that you displayed to him, assuring you for my own part of the deep gratitude I owe you.

Convinced as I am of your probity, Monsieur, I venture to beg you to set the seal upon it and to be good enough to give me your advice. The favours which France and Her Majesty the Queen in particular heaped upon my late husband will always be deeply engraved upon my heart and I will carry the memory of them to the tomb, as he has done. For that reason I hesitate to throw myself at Her Majesty's feet to entreat her to let the effects of the favour with which she honoured the husband fall upon the wife. Have the goodness, therefore, Monsieur, to help me with your advice and to direct my actions in the most grievous circumstances in which it has pleased heaven to place me. Could one reproach the grief-stricken widow of Gluck for going to the source of his fame, for asking the French to give substance to the hopes which she had attached to their generosity? The trickery of which we have several times been the victims forces me to take this cruel, hard step. I hope to receive from you, Monsieur, some enlightment on this point. I hope you will condescend, Monsieur, to express your feelings to me openly and sincerely. You will thereby multiply the reasons for the esteem and gratitude which for a long time past have been felt by

Your very humble and very
obedient servant
ve. Gluck *née* de Bergen.

Monsieur
Vienne ce 18 9bre 1787
Allow me, Monsieur, to convey to Madame de la Sale my deepest respects.

[1] The addressee was presumably the philosopher François Antoine de Lasalle (1754–1829).

[IV. Marianne Gluck to Johann Friedrich Reichardt (?). *German*]

High and nobly born
Especially most honoured Herr Kappelmeister

Hard as it is for me to think of the death of a husband whom I so deeply loved, it is a comfort for me to speak with his friends. Dearest Herr Kappelmeister, Gluck, the man you esteemed so highly, is no more. Death took him from me on the 15th of this month after two attacks of apoplexy and plunged me in grief and melancholy. The friendship which you have always shown towards us is assurance enough for me of your share in my loss.

I thank you once more for your friendship in the name of my late husband and am with highest esteem

Your High and Nobly Born's
humble servant
von Gluck *née* von
Bergen

Vienna 20th November 1787

[V. Marianne Gluck to J. F. Reichardt. *German*]

Highly and Nobly Born
Especially esteemed Herr Kappelmeister

Your comforting letter bears all the imprint of your feeling and your friendship. Thanks to you, respected friend, and warm thanks to your wife for all the beautiful and agreeable things you write to me. May you be rewarded by Almighty God, with whom my Gluck now is.

Much as I would like, worthy man, much as I would like to meet your wishes concerning the compositions of my late husband, I regret I cannot. Only the following am I able to send you. Gluck was born on the 3rd July 1714. The history of his childhood, youth and adolescence is quite unknown to me; moreover, it would lie heavily upon my heart to revive an image which was so dear to me, the image of his years of manhood, whose subject is no longer with us.

I pray you, estimable Herr Kappelmeister, to convey my appreciation to your wife and to believe that I remain with highest respect

Highly and Nobly Born
Herr Kappelmeister
Your
Grateful Servant
Von Gluck *née*
de Pergin [*sic*]

Vienna 29th X^bris^ 1787

[VI. Antonio Salieri to Franz Kruthoffer. *French*]

[In Kruthoffer's hand:
Replied 23 February 1788
enclosing a letter from Mr Lasalle
and another from Mlle Le V[asseur] to M^d^ Gluck]

This 4th January 1788 Vienna

Monsieur,

Madame Gluck, highly sensible of your good heart and of the trouble you are still willing to take in the affair of Mons. Mathon, has asked me to thank you a thousand times on her behalf, Monsieur, and to inform you that she was about to order the procuration for which you asked in this connection but that her lawyer has impressed upon her the necessity for a formula, without which, he has said, something indispensable to the laws of the country might be omitted, so giving rise to fresh chicanery.

She therefore begs you, Monsieur, to have the goodness to send either to her or to me the formula required by the advocate, on which the procuration will then be drawn up and in the meantime she asks you to excuse the double inconvenience.

Having carried out my commission, I also have the honour to present my compliments and to be

Monsieur
Your very humble and
very obedient servant
Ant. Salieri

[Address:]
A Monsieur
Monsieur de Kruthoffer
Secretaire de S.E.
Comte Mercy Ambassadeur
de S.M. l'Impereur
Paris

[VII. ANTONIO SALIERI TO FRANZ KRUTHOFFER. *French*]

8th March 1789, Vienna

Monsieur,

It was destined, it seems, that the affair of Mons. Gluck should not end as we have for so long wished.

Last year, when you had the goodness to send me, at the request of Mons. l'advocat de Haim, the model of the procuration, I first called upon Mad. Gluck to take the testament of Mons. Gluck which Mons. de Haim[1] had asked for, and also to have a copy of it forwarded to you in Paris with the procuration, something he considered necessary to remove all obstacles. The testament was still in the hands of the advocate in charge of the affairs of the heir, Mad. Gluck; this advocate falls ill; Mons. de Haim asks me for the model of the procuration and agrees to speak himself to the sick advocate which proved to be a friend of his. I beg him to advise me as soon as everything has been arranged; he promises. Several months pass without my hearing anything further. Finally, Monsieur, when your last letter obliged me to speak once more about this affair to Mad. Gluck, who had changed her advocate and prevented Mons. de Haim from acting, I received the testament from her. But when I then thought that in this way I would also obtain the procuration, Mons. de Haim could no longer find the model and said that without this formula he could do nothing more that would be valid in Paris.

When Mad. Gluck heard that you would have to be asked once more to send the model of the procuration to Vienna, she told me to ask you, on the contrary, to take no further trouble in an affair which was begun badly by Mons. Gluck himself and for which, as the expenses involved after so long a period would most probably leave only an insignificant sum remaining, she could no longer allow you to be further inconvenienced. She thanks you a thousand times, Monsieur, and hopes to be able to show the gratitude she feels for the trouble you have taken in the past and for your goodwill.

I thank you also, Monsieur, for the news you have sent me of the new Italian opera. I wish those who are launching it all possible success, but I find it hard to believe that Italian *opera buffa* as presented in Italy could survive long in Paris;

the themes, the plan, the tempo and the language of all these operas are in bad taste, very often dishonest and in consequence quite anti-Parisian.

I do not give up hope of returning to Paris for the third time at some future date with a new work[2] which I have already commenced for the Opéra theatre. I hope to be able to fulfil my wish, in order to have once again the opportunity to tell you in person how proud I am to be

Monsieur
Your very humble
and very obedient
Servant
Salieri

[1] FORTUNAT JOSEPH VON HAIMHOFEN, Notarius Publicus and advocate at the Court of Exchange in Vienna, Untere Breuner Str. 1155.

[2] The two operas produced in Paris were *Les Danaïdes* and *Tararc* (libretto by P. A. Caron de Beaumarchais), which had its *première* on 8th June 1787 and ran for 131 performances up to 1826. Salieri's third opera was produced at the Théâtre de Monsieur on 15th March 1790: *La grotta di Trofonio* (libretto by G. B. Casti) with two arias by Luigi Cherubini which had already been performed in Vienna in 1785. Other operas by Salieri were presented in Paris in subsequent years: on 20th May 1791 *La Scuola de' gelosi* (libretto by C. Mazzola), which had its *première* in Venice in 1778, and on 29th May 1792 in the Théâtre Feydeau *La locandiera scaltra* (libretto by D. Poggi, based on a work by C. Goldoni) with contributions by Cherubini. This opera had already been performed at the Burgtheater in Vienna in 1773.

[VIII. ANTONIO SALIERI TO FRANZ KRUTHOFFER. *French*]

Vienna, 25th July 1789

Monsieur,

Madame Gluck, whose health compels her to make only short journeys, asked me, on passing through Pressburg, to forward to you in Paris the attached procuration, drawn up on the model which you, Monsieur, were kind enough to send a second time.

She was ashamed that she had failed to realize or perhaps forgotten after so long a time the expenses you have incurred on behalf of the late M. Gluck and hopes either that the affair in question may be settled as soon as possible or that you will suggest some other way by which she can meet her obligation to you.

I have also been charged to thank you and Monsieur de Blumendorff for the flattering reception you gave to her recommendation with regard to Monsieur de Strohlendorf, and she wishes to have an early opportunity of reciprocating so much honesty.

With Madame Gluck's compliments, Monsieur, I beg you to accept and to transmit to Monsieur de Blumendorff the respectful homage of one who has the honour to be

Monsieur
Your very humble
and obedient
Servant
Salieri

APPENDIXES

THE SOURCES

IMBA = Internationales Musiker-Brief-Archiv, Berlin

Letter	*Autograph*	*Printed Source(s)*	*Source used*
8/14 Jan. 1749	Württemberg State Archives, Stuttgart	E. H. Müller; *Angelo und Pietro Mingotti*, Dresden 1917. p. 93	Facsimile IMBA
3 Dec. 1748	Württemberg State Archives, Stuttgart	E. H. Müller; *Angelo und Pietro Mingotti*, Dresden 1917. p. 90	Autograph
3 Sept. 1750	Stadtarchiv, Vienna	*Jahrbuch des Vereins für Geschichte der Stadt Wien*, 1953, vol. X, 1953. p. 237	Autograph
June 1763	Unknown	S. Favart: *Memoires et Correspondence littéraire* II, 114	Favart
16 Dec. 1767	Unknown	*Alceste*. Score 1769	Score
31 Dec. 1769	Walter Hinrichsen, Lombard, Ill., USA	—	Facsimile IMBA
30 Oct. 1770	Unknown	*Paride ed Elena*. Score 1770	Score
Feb. 1773	Unknown	*Mercure de France* Feb. 1773	*Mercure de France*
1 Aug. 1772	Unknown	*Mercure de France* Oct. 1772	*Mercure de France*
Jan. 1773	Unknown	*Mercure de France* Jan. 1773	*Mercure de France*
14 Aug. 1773	Unknown	Lappenberg: *Briefe von und an Klopstock*. 1867	Lappenberg
26 Oct. 1773	Nationalbibliothek, Vienna	L. Nohl: *Musiker-Briefe*, Leipzig 1867. p. 19	Facsimile IMBA
(after) 10 May 1774	Unknown	*Iphigénie en Aulide*. Score 1774	Score
10 July 1774	Bibliothèque Nationale, Paris	—	Facsimile IMBA
(before) 2 Aug. 1774	Unknown	*Orphée et Eurydice*. Score 1774	Score
11 Aug. 1774	Archiv de l'Opéra, Paris	—	Facsimile IMBA
16 Aug. 1774	Archiv de l'Opéra, Paris	—	Facsimile IMBA
5 Nov. 1774	Steiermärk. Landes-Archiv, Graz	—	Autograph

Letter	*Autograph*	*Printed Source(s)*	*Source used*
1775	Archiv de l'Opéra, Paris	—	Facsimile IMBA
9 March 1775	Formerly Coll. Revel, Paris→ Unknown	—	Copy IMBA
25 March 1775	Formerly Coll. Revel, Paris→ Unknown	—	Copy IMBA
28 March 1775	Formerly Coll. Revel, Paris→ Unknown	—	Copy IMBA
31 March 1775	Bibliothèque Nationale, Paris	—	Facsimile IMBA
15 April 1775 (to Kruthoffer)	Formerly Heyer-Museum, Köln→ Unknown	Kinsky: *Glucks Briefe.* 1927. p. 13	Kinsky
15 April 1775 (to Marchand)	Bibliothèque du Conservatoire, Paris	—	Facsimile IMBA
21 April 1775	Bibliothèque du Conservatoire, Paris	—	Facsimile IMBA
30 April 1775	Unknown→ Copy in Bibliothèque Nationale, Paris)	—	Copy IMBA
12 May 1775	Bibliothèque du Conservatoire, Paris	*La Revue S.I.M.* June 1914, p. 2	Facsimile IMBA
30 May 1775	Bibliothèque du Conservatoire, Paris	*Die Musik*, 1914 vol. 52, p. 10—Kinsky, p. 15	Facsimile IMBA
24 June 1775	Deutsche Staatsbibliothek, Berlin	—	Facsimile IMBA
1 July 1775	Bibliothèque du Conservatoire, Paris	*La Revue S.I.M.* June 1914, p. 3	Facsimile IMBA
19 July 1775	Bibiothèque Nationale, Paris	—	Facsimile IMBA
31 July 1775	Bibliothèque du Conservatoire, Paris	*Die Musik*, 1914 vol. 52, p. 11	Facsimile IMBA
14 Oct. 1775	Bibliothèque du Conservatoire, Paris	*La Revue S.I.M.* June 1914, p. 6	Facsimile IMBA
10 Nov. 1775	Bibliothèque du Conservatoire, Paris	—	Facsimile IMBA
22 Nov. 1775	Bibliothèque du Conservatoire, Paris	*La Revue S.I.M.* June 1914, p. 7	Facsimile IMBA
29 Nov. 1775	Bibliothèque du Conservatoire, Paris	*Die Musik*, 1914 vol. 52, p. 13—Kinsky, *Glucks Briefe* p. 18	Facsimile IMBA
2 Dec. 1775	Bibliothèque du Conservatoire, Paris	—	Facsimile IMBA
13 Dec. 1775	Bibliothèque du Conservatoire, Paris	*La Revue S.I.M.* June 1914, p. 9	Facsimile IMBA
31 Dec. 1775	Formerly Heyer-Museum, Köln→ Unknown	Kinsky: *Glucks Briefe.* 1927. p. 19	Kinsky
31 Jan. 1776	Bibliothèque du Conservatioire, Paris	—	Facsimile IMBA

Letter	*Autograph*	*Printed Source(s)*	*Source used*
10 May 1776	Landesbibliothek, Dresden	—	Facsimile IMBA
30 June 1776	Formerly Heyer-Museum, Köln→ Unknown	Kinsky: *Glucks Briefe.* 1927. p. 20	Kinsky
13 July 1776	Unknown	*Auswahl Denkwürdiger Briefe v. C. M. Wieland* 1815, p. 315	Wieland
July/August 1776	Unknown	*L'Année Littéraire* vol. VII, p. 322 1776	*L'Année Littériare*
7 Aug. 1776	State Archives, Weimar	—	Facsimile IMBA
14 Aug. 1776	Unknown	Metra: *Correspondence Secrète.* vol. III. p. 280	Metra
29 Aug. (1776)	Formerly Heyer-Muse-um, Köln→ Unknown	Kinsky: *Glucks Briefe.* 1927. p. 20	Kinsky
30 Sept. 1776	Coll. K. Geigy-Hagenbach, Basel	Kinsky: *Glucks Briefe.* 1927. p. 23	Autograph
31 Oct. 1776 (to Arnaud)	Bibliothèque Nationale, Paris	—	Facsimile IMBA
31 Oct. 1776 (to Kruthoffer)	Formerly Heyer-Muse-um, Köln→ Unknown	Kinsky: *Glucks Briefe.* 1927. p. 25	Kinsky
Nov. 1776	Unknown	*Mercure de France*, Nov. 1776	*Mercure de France*
Sept. 1776	Unknown	*Mercure de France* Sept. 1776	*Mercure de France*
15 Jan. 1777	Formerly Heyer-Muse-um, Köln→ Unknown	Kinsky: *Glucks Briefe.* 1927. p. 26	Kinsky
31 Jan. 1777	Formerly Heyer-Muse-um, Köln→ Unknown	Kinsky: *Glucks Briefe.* 1927. p. 27	Kinsky
3 March 1777	Formerly Heyer-Muse-um, Köln→ Unknown	Kinsky: *Glucks Briefe.* 1927. p. 28	Kinsky
30 March 1777	Formerly Heyer-Muse-um, Köln→ Unknown	Kinsky: *Glucks Briefe.* 1927. p. 29	Kinsky
Oct. 1777	Unknown	*Journal de Paris*, 12 Oct. 1777	*Journal de Paris*
5 Oct. 1777	Unknown	*Journal de Politique et Littérature*, 5 Oct. 1777	*Journal de Politique*
(before 16th Oct. 1777)	Unknown	*Journal de Paris*, 16 Oct. 1777	*Journal de Paris*
(Oct. 1777)	Unknown	*Journal de Paris*, 21 Oct. 1777	*Journal de Paris*
(before 23 Oct. 1777)	Unknown	*Journal de Paris*, 23 Oct. 1777	*Journal de Paris*
16 Nov. 1777	Formerly Heyer-Muse-um, Köln→ Unknown	I. G. Prod'homme, *Ecrits de Musiciens*, Paris, 1912, p. 419	Facsimile IMBA
(28 Dec. 1777)	Unknown	*Journal de Paris*, 28 Dec. 1777	*Journal de Paris*

Letter	Autograph	Printed Source(s)	Sources used
12 Jan 1778 (to Gluck)	Unknown	*Journal de Paris*, 12 Jan. 1778	*Journal de Paris*
12 Jan. 1778 (to Amateurs)	Unknown	*Journal de Paris*, 12 Jan. 1778	*Journal de Paris*
2 March 1778	Formerly Coll. Westley Manning, London →Unknown	Kinsky: *Glucks Briefe*. 1927. p. 29	Kinsky
16 March 1778	Steiermärkisches Landes-Archiv, Graz	—	Autograph
1 April 1778	Bibliothèque du Conservatoire, Paris	—	Facsimile IMBA
17 June 1778	Bibliothèque, Nantes	Gluck: *Iphigénie en Tauride*, Score. Ed., Pelletan, 1874	Facsimile IMBA
? 1778 (Gossec to Guillard)	Bibliothèque du Conservatoire, Paris	—	Facsimile IMBA
28 June 1778	Coll. R. Ammann, Aarau	Kinsky: *Glucks Briefe*, 1927, p. 30	Facsimile IMBA
15 July 1778	Unknown	*L'Amateur d'autographes* 1864, p. 24	Facsimile IMBA
29 July 1778	Formerly Heyer-Museum, Köln→ Unknown	Kinsky: *Glucks Briefe*, 1927, p. 32	Kinsky
29 Aug. 1778	Bibliothèque du Conservatoire, Paris	*Die Musik*, 1914, vol. 52, p. 14—Kinsky, *Glucks Briefe*, p. 33	Facsimile IMBA
4 Sept. 1778	Bibliothèque Nationale, Paris	—	Facsimile IMBA
15 Sept. 1778	Unknown	*Mercure de France*, 15 Sept. 1778	*Mercure de France*
26 Sept. 1778	Formerly Heyer-Museum, Köln→ Unknown	Kinsky: *Glucks Briefe*, 1927, p. 34	Kinsky
30 Sept. 1778	Formerly Heyer-Museum, Köln→ Unknown	Kinsky: *Glucks Briefe*, 1927, p. 37	Kinsky
5 Oct. 1778	Unknown	*Mercure de France*, 5 Oct. 1778	*Mercure de France*
1 Nov. 1778	Formerly Heyer-Museum, Köln→ Unknown	Kinsky: *Glucks Briefe*, 1927, p. 38	Kinsky
11 Nov. 1778	Formerly Heyer-Museum, Köln→ Unknown	Kinsky: *Glucks Briefe*, 1927, p. 38	Kinsky
22 Feb. 1779	Unknown	—	Facsimile IMBA
5 May 1779	Formerly Heyer-Museum, Köln→ Unknown	—	Copy IMBA
(before 15 May 1779)	Unknown	*Iphigénie en Tauride*, score, 1779	Score
8 June 1779	Bayerische Staatsbibliothek, Munich	L. Nohl: *Musiker-Briefe*, 1867, p. 52	Facsimile IMBA

Letter	*Autograph*	*Printed Source(s)*	*Source used*
6 Oct. 1779	Unknown	*Journal de Paris,* 12 Nov. 1779	*Journal de Paris*
31 Oct. 1779	Formerly Heyer-Museum, Köln→ Unknown	Kinsky: *Glucks Briefe,* 1927, p. 40	Kinsky
30 Nov. 1779 (to Gersin)	Unknown	*Isographie des Hommes Célèbres,* 1837	*Isographie*
30 Nov. 1779 (to Kruthoffer)	Unknown	Kinsky: *Glucks Briefe,* 1927, p. 41	Facsimile IMBA
6 Dec. 1779	Formerly Heyer-Museum, Köln→ Unknown	Kinsky: *Glucks Briefe,* 1927, p. 43	Kinsky
13 Dec. 1779	Formerly Heyer-Museum, Köln→ Unknown	Kinsky: *Glucks Briefe,* 1927, p. 44	Kinsky
31 Dec 1779	Library of Congress, Washington	Kinsky: *Glucks Briefe,* 1927, p. 42	Facsimile IMBA
? 1779	Musée de Mariemont	*L'Amateur d'autographes,* 1864, p. 24	Facsimile IMBA
(1779?) (J. Dorat to Gluck)	Unknown	*Almanach des Muses* 1780	*Almanach des Muses*
29 Dec. 1779	Formerly Heyer-Museum, Köln→ Unknown	Kinsky: *Glucks Briefe,* 1927, p. 45	Kinsky
4 Jan. 1780	Formerly Heyer Museum, Köln→ Unknown	Kinsky: *Glucks Briefe,* 1927, p. 46	Kinsky
19 Jan. 1780	Staatsbibliothek, Munich	—	Facsimile IMBA
31 Jan. 1780	Sibley Musical Society, Eastman School of Music Rochester, New York	Kinsky: *Glucks Briefe,* 1927, p. 45	Facsimile IMBA
10 Feb. 1780	Staatsarchiv, Weimar	*Die Musik,* 1923, p. 652	Facsimile IMBA
2 March 1780	Formerly Heyer-Museum, Köln→ Unknown	Kinsky: *Glucks Briefe,* 1927, p. 48	Kinsky
18 March 1780	Coll. Louis Koch, Aarau	Desnoiresterres: *Gluck et Piccini,* 1872, p. 289	Facsimile IMBA
31 March 1780	Coll. Francois Lang, Royaumont	Kinsky: *Glucks Briefe,* 1927, p. 49	Autograph
29 April 1780	Formerly Coll. K. Geigy-Hagenbach, Basle →Unknown	Kinsky: *Glucks Briefe,* 1927, p. 50	Facsimile IMBA
10 May 1780	Unknown	*Leipziger Neueste Nachrichten,* 11 July 1914	Facsimile IMBA
30 May 1780	Unknown	Kinsky: *Glucks Briefe,* 1927, p. 51	Facsimile IMBA
30 June 1780	Formerly Heyer-Museum, Köln→ Unknown	Kinsky: *Glucks Briefe,* 1927, p. 53	Kinsky
30 July 1780	Formerly Heyer-Museum, Köln→ Unknown	Kinsky: *Glucks Briefe,* 1927, p. 53	Kinsky
4 Aug. 1780	Unknown	Desnoiresterres: *Gluck et Piccinni,* 1872, p. 291	Desnoiresterres

Letter	*Autograph*	*Printed Source(s)*	*Source used*
20 Aug. 1780	Archiv de l'Opéra, Paris	—	Facsimile IMBA
30 Aug. 1780	Formerly Heyer-Museum, Köln→ Unknown	Kinsky: *Glucks Briefe*, 1927, p. 54	Kinsky
30 Sept. 1780	Metropolitan Opera, New York	Kinsky: *Glucks Briefe*, 1927, p. 55	Kinsky
31 Oct. 1780	Stadtbibliothek, Leipzig	Kinsky: *Glucks Briefe*, 1927, p. 56	Facsimile IMBA
29 Nov. 1780	Formerly Heyer-Museum, Köln→ Unknown	Kinsky: *Glucks Briefe*, 1927, p. 57	Kinsky
3 Jan. 1781	Formerly Heyer-Museum, Köln→ Unknown	Kinsky: *Glucks Briefe*, 1927, p. 58	Kinsky
31 Jan. 1781	Formerly Heyer-Museum, Köln→ Unknown	Kinsky: *Glucks Briefe*, 1927, p. 59	Kinsky
28 March 1781	Formerly Heyer-Museum, Köln→ Unknown	Kinsky: *Glucks Briefe*, 1927, p. 60	Facsimile IMBA
1 May 1781	Unknown	Kinsky: *Glucks Briefe*, 1927, p. 61	Facsimile IMBA
11 May 1781	Unknown	Bachaumont: *Mémoires Secrètes*, 30 May 1781	*Mémoires Secrètes*
19 June 1781	Formerly Heyer-Museum, Köln→ Unknown	Kinsky: *Glucks Briefe*, 1927, p. 62	Kinsky
21 Aug. 1781	Staatsarchiv, Weimar	*Die Musik*, 1923, p. 653	Facsimile IMBA
2 Nov. 1781	Formerly Heyer-Museum, Köln→ Unknown	Kinsky: *Glucks Briefe*, 1927, p. 63	Kinsky
30 Nov. 1781	Formerly Westley Manning, London →Unknown	Kinsky: *Glucks Briefe*, 1927, p. 64	Kinsky
30 Dec. 1781	Formerly Heyer-Museum, Köln→ Unknown	Kinsky: *Glucks Briefe*, 1927, p. 67	Kinsky
17 April 1782	Archiv de l'Opéra, Paris	*Revue Musicale*, 1 April 1907	Facsimile IMBA
22 Feb. 1783	Memorial Library of Music at Stanford University, U.S.A.	Kinsky: *Glucks Briefe*, 1927, p. 67	Kinsky
28 March 1783	Formerly Heyer-Museum, Köln→ Unknown	Kinsky: *Glucks Briefe*, 1927, p. 69	Kinsky
9 July 1783	Formerly Heyer-Museum, Köln→ Unknown	Kinsky: *Glucks Briefe*, 1927, p. 70	Kinsky
4 Aug. 1783	Formerly Heyer-Museum, Köln→Unknown	Kinsky: *Glucks Briefe*, 1927, p. 71	Kinsky
11 Nov. 1783	Unknown	*Zeitschrift für Musikwissenschaft*, 1924, vol. VI, p. 351	Copy IMBA
26 April 1784	Unknown	*Journal de Paris*, 16 May 1784	*Journal de Paris*
1 May 1785	Unknown	—	Copy IMBA

Letter	*Autograph*	*Printed Source(s)*	*Source used*
Life Certificate	Unknown	—	Copy IMBA
27 Feb. 1786	Unknown	Hanke: *Robert u. Hannchen*, Klavierauszug, 1786	Hanke
Will	Stadtbibliothek, Vienna	Schmid: *Chr. W. Rr. v. Gluck*, 1854, p. 473	Autograph
9 June 1787	Coll. Louis Koch, Aarau	—	Facsimile IMBA
3 Aug. 1787	Unknown	*Journal de Paris* 3 Oct. 1787	*Journal de Paris*

SUPPLEMENT

17 March 1775	Unknown	Marx: *Gluck und die Oper*. II. p. 143	Marx
1 April 1775	Formerly Heyer-Museum, Köln→ Unknown	Henrici/Liepmannssohn, *Musiker-Autographen aus der Sammlung Wilh. Heyer in Köln*, 1928, Part IV, No. 124	Henrici
18 Sept. 1787	Stadtbibliothek, Vienna	—	Autograph
29 Oct. 1787	Internationales Musiker-Brief-Archiv, Berlin	—	Autograph
20 Nov. 1787	Coll. Louis Koch, Aarau	—	Facsimile IMBA
4 Jan. 1788	Bibliothèque du Conservatoire, Paris	—	Facsimile IMBA
8 March 1789	Bibliothèque du Conservatoire, Paris	—	Facsimile IMBA
25 July 1789	Bibliothèque du Conservatoire, Paris	—	Facsimile IMBA

INDEXES

These indexes do not include material in the Foreword or Source List

Alphabetical Index to the Persons Addressed

Index of Gluck's Works Mentioned in this Book

General Index